THE
PALACE
AND THE
BUNKER

THE PALACE AND THE BUNKER

ROYAL RESISTANCE TO HITLER

FRANK MILLARD

The
History
Press

For Charles

First published 2012

The History Press
The Mill, Brimscombe Port
Stroud, Gloucestershire, GL5 2QG
www.thehistorypress.co.uk

British Library Cataloguing in Publication Data.
A catalogue record for this book is available from the British Library.

ISBN 978 0 7524 6569 2

Typesetting and origination by The History Press
Printed in Great Britain
Manufacturing managed by Jellyfish Print Solutions Ltd

CONTENTS

Foreword   7
Acknowledgements   9
Introduction   11

I The Bunker: the Shadow over Europe
1 The German Tragedy   17
2 The Origins of National Socialism in Germany   30
3 Europe and the West   47
4 The German Resistance Movement   70
   Conclusion   84

II The Palace: Hitler's Royal Enemies
5 Prince Louis Ferdinand of Prussia   91
6 Crown Prince Rupprecht of Bavaria   104
7 Hubertus zu Löwenstein-Wertheim-Freudenberg   121
8 Habsburgs and Hohenbergs   134
9 European Royalty and the Nazis   160
   Conclusion   176

Bibliography   183
Index   187

FOREWORD

The Palace and the Bunker: Royal Resistance to Hitler is actually two books in one, each dependent on the other. *The Bunker: the Shadow Over Europe* relates to how and why Hitler was able to come to power in Germany and threaten the world, whereas *The Palace: Hitler's Royal Enemies* relates, as the title suggests, to certain princes who opposed the Nazis. *The Bunker* section represents a synthesis of information and ideas from many sources distilled into a single volume. It is an exploration of a difficult subject in the context of German history and aspiration. Each section provides context for the other. The first section is vital because without a knowledge of the political and powerful cultural influences on young Germans in the inter-war years, together with an understanding of the effects of war, revolution and the Versailles Treaty upon people, economics and politics, it would be impossible to understand the world in which our protagonists moved.

This book includes four case histories of princely involvement in resistance against the Nazis. They were not the only princes who opposed Hitler; members of the Württemberg and Saxon royal families, for example, suffered for their stand against the National Socialist tyranny. These individuals all represented ancient and distinguished families, many with long histories of rule within Germany or Austria, with their own place within the history of the Germanic peoples going back into the early Middle Ages.

The princes are figures in a frightening landscape, consisting not only of National Socialism and its influences, but also the wider world with its own unsavoury influences on the Nazis that gave them some of their most dangerous ideas. These influences on Hitler, however, affected many others who did not themselves become evil, genocidal maniacs afterwards. So we must look to reception and interpretation as much as transmission in trying to understand how and why Nazism took hold, and why it existed in the first place. Nazism was an alternative to princely rule; they could never exist side by side as Hitler well knew. Where it was attempted in Italy Hitler poured scorn on it as unworkable and proclaimed that he would never have divided 'his' power in that way.

This book is full of heroes; not only royalty but also businessmen, diplomats, soldiers, politicians and ordinary citizens. Furthermore, not all German princes were opposed to Hitler from the start, some saw National Socialism as a possible useful bulwark against Bolshevik influence in Germany and even supported it by joining the SA or SS. These included the Princes of Hesse-Kassel and Prince Augustus Wilhelm of Prussia. Not only was Hitler never going to restore the monarchy as they hoped, but he was fundamentally opposed to the hereditary principle altogether and only courted the monarchists as he courted any group that might help him to power. Similarly his encouragement of 'positive' Christianity was far from Christian. Indeed, Hitler used many stepping stones on his way to power and in doing so crushed each one of them in turn.

I came to the subject of the lead up to the Second World War with little prior knowledge; my research has been a stimulating exploration into a world, which, though past, remains with us in many ways. I hope that this volume conveys something of what has been for me an often dark but always interesting journey with many surprises. There will, no doubt, be errors (all mine), but hopefully none of substance.

I have included an analysis of the Allied perspective of Germany and used a lot of English and American sources because this book is aimed primarily at an English-speaking audience, but also because some of what we find distasteful about Nazi Germany – social Darwinism, white supremacy, eugenics and aggressive secularism – were phenomena of the age and not confined within German borders. On the other hand, some modern virtues such as natural medicine, organic farming, environmentalism, animal welfare, anti-smoking legislation and additive-free foods were actively promoted by Nazi leaders.[1] The common thread in Germany, though, was the genetic health of the Aryan race.[2] Nazi ideology did not exist in isolation from the rest of the world; it just found its most extreme expression in pan-German nationalism, and particularly in racial theory. The Nazis applied sharp measures from blunt logic with ruthless and meticulous efficiency. There was madness both in Nazi ideas and in their obsessive demonic application, but that does not mean the rest of the Western world was sane.

I humbly and respectfully offer this book to the reader and dedicate it to the subjects of my study, for whom I have the greatest respect, to my son Charles, my wife Katrina and to royal families everywhere.

Notes

1 See Proctor, Robert, *Racial Hygiene: Medicine Under the Nazis* (Harvard, 1989) and *Nazi War on Cancer* (Princeton, 1999).

2 Ibid., Professor Proctor's recent research has shown that the Nazis were not anti-science and many scientists worked for the regime with highly successful results.

ACKNOWLEDGEMENTS

Without the help, assistance and encouragement of the following persons this book could not have been written. With due respect I record the help and generosity of:

His (late) Royal & Imperial Majesty Dr Otto von Habsburg of Austria-Hungary
HRH Georg Friedrich Prince of Prussia
HRH Duke Franz of Bavaria
HRH the Duke of Edinburgh
HIH Archduke Franz von Habsburg
HH Georg Duke of Hohenberg
HSH Princess Sophie von Hohenberg de Potesta[1]
HSH Princess Konstanza zu Löwenstein
Fr Rudolf zu Löwenstein OP
Baron Victor Kuchina von Schwanburg
Fr Dr Richard Ounsworth OP
Eva Demmerle (biographer of Dr Otto von Habsburg)
Carmen Schramka
Ulrich Feldhahn MA
Professor Caroline Barron
Quentin Gelder
Kevin Barrett
Peter Wise (author of *A Matter of Doubt: the Life of Claude Bernard*)
Dan Wise
Sue Woolmans
Viktoria Kish
Kevin Wheatland

Bill Baker
Jamie Young
Kenneth Fuller
Barry Smith
Jo Josh

Archivists, librarians and staff at the Royal Archives at Windsor Castle, the German Historical Institute, Churchill Archive, Dachau Archive, The National Archives, the British Library, Institute of Historical Research London, Bodleian Library Oxford and F.D. Roosevelt Library USA.

Notes

1 Her Serene Highness is currently engaged in a legal battle at the Court of Human Rights in Strasbourg for the return of the Hohenberg family home of Konopiště in the Czech Republic, confiscated after the First World War.

INTRODUCTION

Where love stops, power begins, and violence, and terror.

C.G. Jung

In 1933 David Lloyd George confided in Prince Louis Ferdinand of Prussia, the kaiser's grandson, 'We over here never expected nor intended the fall of your dynasty.' He believed as others did that, although public opinion in Britain would have prevented a peace with the kaiser or his eldest son (Louis Ferdinand's father), it would have been acceptable for Louis Ferdinand's elder brother Wilhelm to come to the throne following Regency under his mother. 'If your family had remained in power in Germany,' he went on, 'I am certain that Mr Hitler would not be giving us any headaches right now.'[1] In April 1945, at the conclusion of the Second World War, Winston Churchill declared that:

> This war would never have come unless (sic), under American and modernising pressure, we had driven the Habsburgs out of Austria and the Hohenzollerns out of Germany. By making these vacuums we gave the opening for the Hitlerite monster to crawl out of its sewer on to the vacant thrones.

In the following April he repeated his message:

> I am of the opinion that if the Allies at the peace table at Versailles had not imagined that the sweeping away of long-established dynasties was a form of progress, and if they had allowed a Hohenzollern, a Wittelsbach and a Habsburg to return to their thrones, there would have been no Hitler. To Germany a symbolic point on which the loyalties of the military classes could centre would have been found and a democratic basis of society might have been preserved by a crowned Weimar in contact with the victorious Allies.[2]

This was not a retrospective judgment on the part of the UK's wartime prime minister; in 1934 he had expressed the same view to Germany's ex-chancellor, Heinrich Brüning, adding that he believed that constitutional monarchy in Europe was the best form of government to counter the twin threats of fascism and communism.[3] Brüning himself reflected in November 1949:

> When I think over these years, I come more firmly than I did at the time to the conclusion that only the restoration of the monarchy in some form by a plebiscite could have prevented Hitler from coming to power ... It was my last weapon and to keep it sharp I had to be very cautious, and somewhat vague in talking about it.[4]

Adolf Hitler also believed that he would not have achieved power if German and Austrian royalty had remained in place. 'It would never have been possible for a united German Reich if the princes had not been swept aside,' he remarked.[5] Furthermore, during the war Hitler summoned a former Social Democrat minister in order to inform the confused politician that his researches had shown that the Social Democratic Party (SPD) had 'done Germany the service of deliberately and permanently abolishing the monarchy, and that, in his view, special thanks were due to them on that account'.[6]

Although there were those who believed there was a case for the forced personal abdication of Kaiser Wilhelm because (rightly or wrongly) they blamed him for the outbreak of war, the Emperor Karl von Habsburg of Austria-Hungary had sought peace with the Allies through the mediation of his wife's relatives shortly after his accession, and the heir of Ludwig III of Bavaria, Crown Prince Rupprecht, was similarly a would-be peacemaker. Furthermore, it could be argued that the absence of the German monarchs after 1918 led to an absence of cohesion, direction and national pride, which led in turn to division, disorder, and the surfacing of aggressive nationalism.

Though the monarchies of the central European powers vanished almost overnight, the heirs to the great dynasties continued to work towards their restoration, but preferably as modern constitutional monarchies rather than as absolute rulers, reflecting the new reality. In the political chaos that dominated Germany after the First World War monarchists saw the restoration of the monarchies as a potentially stabilising factor, and later on royalty was seen by many people, including leading Social Democrats, as a foil to a possible takeover by extremist political groups, particularly the National Socialists.

Hitler was as negative towards the old princely order in Germany as he was towards those who had ushered in a republic in November 1918. The heirs to the Hollenzollerns of Prussia and the Wittelsbachs of Bavaria, and those to the Saxon, Hanoverian and other princely houses, retained royal ambitions, and similarly Otto, the Austrian heir to the (blessed) Emperor Karl, expected an eventual return to monarchy, though not absolute and not the old pre-war empire. The fluctuating political situation in Germany between the wars sometimes favoured the monarchists, but more generally turned on the republic's responses to the political extremes of communism and the far Right. Elements of the right-wing of German politics sometimes courted the monarchists in common cause against the communists.

It is true that a few princes allied themselves with, or were ambivalent towards, the Nazis (the National Socialist German Workers' Party, or NSDAP) before 1933, but most were deeply suspicious of Hitler and many openly opposed his politics.[7] Some young princes (like many other young Germans) joined the National Socialist Party as a means of establishing or advancing a career, or out of fear of Bolshevism or dislike of the Weimar Republic. Some of them, however, continued their support into the 1940s and attained positions of rank within the party. Princes who supported Hitler included Prince August Wilhelm, Prince Philipp Landgrave von Hesse-Kassel and Prince Christoph von Hesse-Kassel.[8]

Princely opposition had consequences after Hitler became Chancellor of Germany in 1933. The Führer had stated that the age of princes was over. He despised royalty and particularly regarded the Habsburgs and their German counterparts as weak and politically finished. He himself courted the monarchists in Germany, but only for his own political ends, never at any time ever considering restoring monarchical power, especially not at the expense of his own. He mocked Prince Rupprecht of Bavaria for asking him to step down as Chancellor of Germany and make way for a monarchy as the best way to save Germany. Why should he leave office and forsake power for a dukedom, he asked.[9]

Dachau, Flossenbürg and Sachsenhausen became the residence of several princes, including the children of the Archduke Franz Ferdinand. Other anti-Nazi princes were assassinated, such as Prince Georg of Saxony; some plotted against the regime from within, such as Prince Louis Ferdinand of Prussia; others were exiled, such as Crown Prince Otto von Habsburg, Crown Prince Rupprecht of Bavaria and Prince Hubertus zu Löwenstein-Wertheim-Freudenberg, who as refugees urged the Allies to rid the world of the Nazis.

The anti-Nazi princes were cultured humanitarians of conviction and deep faith. Their role in opposing the Nazis is not easy to assess. Perhaps the results of their opposition were inconsequential as compared with the military activities of the Allies, but their moral authority was immense. Their quiet defiance must have played its part in undermining the pretended authority of the dictator.

Notes

1 Prince Louis Ferdinand of Prussia, *The Rebel Prince: Memoirs of Prince Louis Ferdinand of Prussia* (Chicago, Regnery, 1952), p. 41. Prince Louis Ferdinand wrote that not even the socialists wanted the Hohenzollern dynasty abolished and that the solution mentioned by Lloyd George would have been acceptable to them also.

2 Sir Winston Churchill Archive Trust, The Chartwell Trust, CHAR 20/216, message sent to the British ambassador in Brussels on 26 April 1945. See also Churchill, Winston S., *The Gathering Storm*, p. 10.

3 Patch, William L., *Heinrich Brüning and the Dissolution of the Weimar Republic* (Cambridge, 2006), p. 8.

4 Brüning, H., *Die Brüning Papers*, ed. Peter Lang (Frankfurt, 1993), p. 182.

5 *Hitler's Table Talk*, ed. Hugh Trevor-Roper (New York, Enigma, 2000), p. 186.

6 Wheeler-Bennett, Sir John, *The Nemesis of Power: the German Army in Politics 1918–1945* (London & New York, 1953, rev. 1964), p. 231, footnote. See also: Speer, Albert, *Inside the Third Reich* (London, Sphere, 1970), pp. 95–6.

7 Kaiser Wilhelm II realised what Nazi rule meant after *Kristallnacht* when he declared that he was ashamed to be German. His eldest son, Crown Prince Wilhelm, supported Hitler's candidacy for the presidency, but that was probably more to do with his antipathy towards Hindenburg, who he felt had betrayed the imperial family in 1918, than affiliation with the Führer who deprived the prince of any influence or dignity once he gained power. One of the kaiser's sons, August Wilhelm, became a member of the SA contrary to the wishes of his father and was used by Göbbels for propaganda, but was considered gullible both by his family and those he regarded as his new friends.

8 See especially: Petropoulos, Jonathan, *Royals and the Reich: The Princes von Hessen in Nazi Germany* (Oxford, 2008). The quasi-aristocratic Herman Göring was largely instrumental in wooing potential upper-class supporters. Sally Baranowski writes that upper-class salons and personal contacts between the likes of Göring and August Wilhelm generated financial help and lent respectability to the party, Baranowski, Shelly, *Nazi Empire: German Colonisation and Imperialism from Bismarck to Hitler* (Cambridge, 2010), p. 168. Until, that is, Hitler no longer required his princely followers in whom he had no trust. He then forbade their active military service and imprisoned several of them in concentration camps.

9 *Hitler's Table Talk*, ed. Hugh Trevor-Roper, p. 243.

I

THE BUNKER:
THE SHADOW OVER EUROPE

1

THE GERMAN TRAGEDY

What is this new spirit of German nationalism? The worst of the old Prussian Imperialism, with an added savagery, a racial pride, an exclusiveness which cannot allow to any fellow-subject not of 'pure Nordic birth' equality of rights and citizenship within the nation to which he belongs. Are you going to discuss revision [of the Treaty of Versailles] with a Government like that?

Austen Chamberlain[1]

Historians ascribe motives to actions, yet we are but dimly aware of the multiplicity of influences on our protagonists or the deeper hidden thoughts that have informed their decisions. If we can be better apprised of the truth through interpretation all well and good, but the work of the historian must be more about detection and awareness than interpretation – especially interpretation based on a personal viewpoint obscured by an intervening political chronology. Just as on the eve of the First World War it would have been impossible to predict the circumstances of a second world war, so post-Second World War and post-Cold War it is not easy to reflect on the inter-war period without a hindsight that hinders more than assists our understanding of the people and events of which we speak.

In 1914 the German and Austrian monarchies may not have been as autocratic as has been popularly believed, but they still existed as a real force in national and international affairs. As to whether the German or Austrian emperors were culpable for the outbreak of an internecine war, the scale of which had not been experienced before, is quite another story. The Archduke Franz Ferdinand was trying to revive the *Dreikaiserbund* (understanding between the three emperors in Germany, Austria and Russia) right up until his assassination, which cut off the head (so to speak) of the very means of preventing the war that resulted. His grandson George von Hohenberg said, 'we stumbled into the war,

without knowing what was happening to us. It was the incomprehensible suicide of Europe.'[2]

Nations responded differently to the cultural pessimism of the *fin de siècle* and
the inhumanity of the First World War. Britain, France and Germany were each
affected in different ways. The fundament, however, was a spiritual void as modern
man lost touch with his soul and searched for it everywhere, including the gutter,
and in his despair began to worship the body as if it were immortal. The depression that gripped France in the after-gloom of defeat in the Franco-Prussian war
visited itself on Germany from 1918. However, pessimism in general intruded
into the heart of every nation, eroding former trust in religion, national duty and
an expected eventual golden destiny for the human race. There had been lamen-
tation in Germany that old Germany was disintegrating (after 1871) in spite of its
new unity. It seemed pulled apart by modernity – by liberalism, secularism and
industrialisation – and there appeared to be a decline of the German spirit and
idealism because of politics and materialism. Paul de Lagarde complained of cultural discontent in England as well as Germany: 'Everywhere one gets the sense
that their hope is but a phrase, and that only their despair and resignation are
truth.'[3] The trauma of the First World War added to a movement that questioned
all the values and apparent certainties of the past. The differences between how it
manifested in each state was a response to their particular experiences of war and
its aftermath, informed by pre-existing national aspirations and sentiments.

'Bismark had created a state that had no constitutional theory; its justification,
he thought, was that it worked,' writes Richard Stern Fritz. He continues:

> Power thinly disguised on the one hand, and spirit emptied of all practical-
> ity on the other – these surely were two aspects of imperial Germany. The
> link between the two realms was the idealization of power; the middle classes,
> in Max Webber's phrase, 'ethicized' Bismark's achievement of power. This also
> encouraged a certain idolatry of idealism in politics ... Lagarde, Langbehn, and
> Moeller, outsiders all, appealed as idealists, whether their ideas had a shred of
> practicality or not.[4]

The 'war guilt' that German politicians were forced to accept at the Treaty of
Versailles is still almost a given, but Prince Hubertus zu Löwenstein wrote
that although 'no particular "war guilt" reverted to Germany ... It was Hitler's
unchaining of the Second World War retrospectively, so to speak, made Germany
appear responsible also for the first.'[5] Crown Prince Rupprecht of Bavaria regretted that the idea of Germany's war guilt still had considerable currency in 1922.
He also believed in the kaiser's 'will to peace'. 'During the Moroccan Crisis the
Kaiser at a confidential conference with the commanding generals exclaimed "I
fervently hope peace can be maintained". This never got into the papers, I believe,'
the Crown prince commented to the *New York Times* correspondent .[6] The

Emperor Karl of Austria also rejected German war guilt and believed in the kaiser's 'goodwill'. He further maintained that the kaiser had been too much in the thrall of his generals, Eric Ludendorff in particular.[7] It is hard for anyone brought up in France, Britain or the United States to contemplate that the First World War was not the kaiser's war of course, but that says more about how deeply ingrained are our prejudices than anything about the true origins of the war.

Löwenstein reflected that his father's generation had not experienced war and were not prepared for what followed, its outbreak or its attendant risks. He comments that within days the civilised nations of Europe were engulfed in a wave of mass hysteria: 'Germans, Russians, French, British – depending on which nation you belonged to yourself – changed overnight into veritable beasts, devils in the guise of men. The ties of history, culture, and blood were forgotten as though they had never existed.'[8]

A similar sentiment was expressed in the pages of the *New York Sun* at the outbreak of hostilities:

One day there is civilization, authentic, complex, triumphant; comes war, and in a moment the entire fabric sinks down into a slime of mud and blood. In a day, in an hour, a cycle of civilization is cancelled. What you saw in the morning was suave and ordered life; and the sun sets on howling savagery. In the morning black-coated men lifted their hats to women. Ere nightfall they are slashing them with sabres and burning the houses over their heads.

Modern civilization is the most complex machine imaginable; its infinite cogged wheels turn endlessly upon each other; and perfectly it accomplishes its multifarious purposes; but smash one wheel and it all falls apart into muddle and ruin. The declaration of war was like thrusting a mailed fist into the intricate works of a clock. There was an end of the perfected machine of civilization. Everything stopped. We are savages once more. For science is dead. All the laboratories are shut, save those where poison is brewed and destruction is put up in packages. Education has ceased, save that fierce Nietzschean education which declares: 'The weak and helpless must go to the wall; and we shall help them go.' All that made life humanly fair is hidden in the fetid clouds of war where savages (in terror and hysteria) grope for each other's throats.[9]

It was not the expected quick war promised by the politicians. When the German advance was arrested the two sides dug in. But for the German army, after failing to break through with their 1914 offensive, the war was effectively lost to them. What followed was mutual siege warfare across the trenches. All the Allies really had to do was hold out until their adversary had exhausted himself on their lines and retired out of a lack of will, munitions and rations. However, without the means to sustain a long war themselves the Allies, like the Germans, chose to throw munitions and human beings at the enemy in an attempt to break through and avoid national bankruptcy. The peace moves by the Emperor Karl were the last best hope of saving Europe from catastrophe and prolonged economic decline.

By November 1918 the intricate machinery of German civilisation had been smashed seemingly beyond repair as the country descended into chaos and civil war. When the German High Seas Fleet surrendered at Scapa Flow, Admiral of the British Fleet David Beatty was highly suspicious: 'It seemed too wonderful for an extremely powerful fleet to give themselves up without a blow! One thing I do know – that if we had been in the position of those Hun we would have had a good run for *our* money before we got "put under".'[10] So incredulous was the admiral that he ordered the German battle flags lowered while their ships remained fully armed and ready for action. He could not believe that his powerful and respected adversary could be so beaten in spirit.

In the early 1930s Marshall Hindenburg confided in his chancellor, Heinrich Brüning, that he already knew the war was lost as early as February 1918, but wanted to give General Erich Ludendorff 'one more chance'. Brüning was appalled that a commander-in-chief could ask for 100,000 lives to be sacrificed for an offensive that he did not think could succeed.[11] Commenting on the government of Germany, which had surrendered to the Allies, Eric Ludendorff said in 1919:

> The power of the state failed, as nobody can doubt, because in its external and internal policy, before and during the war, it had not recognized the exigencies of the struggle for existence in which Germany has always been involved. It had demonstrated its inability to understand that politics is war and war is politics … Finally the political leadership disarmed the unconquered army and delivered over Germany to the destructive will of the enemy in order that it might carry through the revolution in Germany unhindered. That was the climax in the betrayal of the German people.[12]

The First World War left Europe in ruins, where even the victors were shattered and entire nations left psychologically – as well as economically and militarily – damaged. If whole peoples can be shell-shocked, the French, British, Belgians and others were almost as damaged as their former enemies, which might somewhat explain their subsequent attitudes and actions.

On 9 November 1918, against a background of naval mutiny, popular uprisings, disorder and the takeover of Munich by the Independent Socialists two days before, Phillip Scheideman, one man acting alone without consultation with his fellow Social Democrats, announced a German republic from the Reichstag building. From this illegal act and the equally illegal grant of power by Prince Maximilian von Baden (who had falsely announced the abdication of the kaiser) to MSPD leader Friedrich Ebert, the Weimar Republic was eventually born.

This had followed the receipt of a note from President Woodrow Wilson of the USA, which suggested that the abdication of the kaiser (voluntary or otherwise) was a pre-condition of peace. Winston Churchill records, 'The prejudice of the Americans ... had made it clear that [Germany] would have better treatment from the Allies as a republic than a monarchy.'[13] It was also a reaction against an intended announcement by the extreme left-wing Sparticist movement of a socialist republic. The Social Democrats did not want the fall of the monarchy, but laboured to convince the kaiser to abdicate so that his line would continue to reign in Germany.

Prince Louis Ferdinand of Prussia doubted that the fall of the monarchy in Germany was the result of any revolutionary fervour on the part of the people:

> The Revolution of November 9, 1918, was neither a social upheaval nor was it directed primarily against our dynasty or against any ruling family in Germany. It was a revolution of hunger, caused by the desperate desire of the people for peace at any price especially after President Wilson had proclaimed his fourteen points. The great majority of the people had no political grudge against the German dynasties.

He added that the German people had a 'lack of talent for revolutions' because of their inherent love of order.[14]

The consequences of this act and the ending of the war were far reaching. At the Versailles Conference that followed the Allies not only demanded territorial concessions and financial reparations, but also an admission of war guilt, before the lifting of a blockade that had caused great hardship in Germany and the official ending of hostilities could take place. The politicians believed that by bowing to the perceived wishes of the Allies in assuming the full government of the Reich and creating a non-militaristic republic that they would be able to negotiate the peace. There was no negotiation; Germany was handed the terms of surrender and, without the means to defend their country, the ministers were forced to accept. As a result of this grossly unequal agreement a myth grew up that the German army, which still occupied large areas of enemy territory in November 1918, was stabbed in the back by the politicians in Berlin who had declared the republic and made peace with the Allies out of their own personal ambition and not in the interests of the Reich.[15] This myth filled many people on the Right in Germany with a loathing for the republic and fed right-wing paramilitary groups the emotional ammunition for counter-revolution. Prince Hubertus zu Löwenstein, however, reminds us that the republic was declared against a background of social and political collapse in Germany and with the knowledge that the left-wing extremist Spartacists, led by Rosa Luxemburg and Karl Liebknecht, were about to declare a socialist republic (*Freie Sozialistische Republik*) in Germany that evening, and fearing it would be the prelude to a communist revolution.[16]

When the republic could not pay its reparations, French and Belgian troops entered the industrial Ruhr region and took over production, which led to a temporary passive resistance by German workers supported by their government. Prince Hubertus zu Löwenstein described the invasion of the Ruhr district in early 1923 as an international tragedy, 'The permanent damage done thereby to the young German republic was never quite repaired. Adolf Hitler had every reason to be grateful for it.'[17] In 1923 Leon Trotsky ordered the German KPD to take advantage of the economic chaos in Germany to launch a full-blown revolution. Communist-inspired insurrection took place in Saxony and Thuringa. Chancellor Gustav Streseman was at heart a monarchist, but he was also a pragmatist. On 26 September he ordered the end of passive resistance in the Ruhr as useless.

Arthur Moeller van den Bruck wrote in his preface to his book, *Das Dritte Reich (The Third Reich)*:

> If the Third Reich is to put an end to strife it will not be born in a pace of philosophic dreaming. The Third Reich will be an empire of organization in the midst of European chaos. The occupation of the Ruhr and its consequences worked a change in the minds of men. It was the first thing that made the nation think. It opened up the possibility of liberation for a betrayed people. It seemed about to put an end to the 'policy of fulfilment' which had been merely party politics disguised as foreign policy. It threw us back on our own power of decision. It restored our will. Parliamentism has become an institution of our public life, whose chief function would appear to be - in the name of the people - to enfeeble all political demands and all national passions.[18]

It was in 1923, with the Reich government in disarray over the occupation of the Ruhr and with Mussolini's 'March on Rome' as inspiration, that Hitler and Ludendorff launched an abortive putsch in Munich, intending to march on Berlin and seize power.[19] Hitler was imprisoned and used the time to write his book *Mein Kampf*. The failure of the rising also led to a change in tactics that added the ballot box to the NSDAP armoury.

During the 1920s the organisation of the party was refined and centralised. Under the Strasser brothers, Gregor and Otto, with their party headquarters in Berlin, the northern and western branches of the NSDAP achieved a large, well-organised membership by presenting a programme that emphasised the socialist aspects of the party.[20] However, the size and strength of the northern group threatened Hitler's personal authority and, when Gregor was offered the vice-chancellorship of Germany, the possibility of his acceptance threatened to split the party. As a result, Hitler asserted his leadership at the Bamberg Conference in 1926, condemning the 'national bolshevist faction' in the party. Otto was forced out of the NSDAP and Gregor was later murdered in the Night of the Long Knives. Although Hitler owed much to the two brothers, he could allow no rivals to overshadow him.

After 1923, the year 'of crises', which featured hyperinflation, the occupation of the Ruhr and civil unrest, conditions improved in Germany due to the receipt of foreign loans, the US Dawes Plan of 1924 and the Young Plan that followed it in 1929, and also due in no small part to the chancellorship of Gustav Stresemann and his tenure as Foreign Secretary. The period between 1923 and 1929 was known as the 'golden era', but was brought to an end with the Wall Street Crash and the economic turmoil that followed, which included the suspending and calling in of loans to Germany.

Economics had severe political consequences throughout the world at this time. For example, the Hawley Smooth Tariff (17 June 1930) raised US import duties to 'stratospheric' levels, preventing foreign nations from easily acquiring dollars to repay war debts, choking international trade and postponing the recovery of many countries across the world.[21] Michael E. Parish points out that less than three months after the first US Neutrality Act became law Mussolini's forces marched into Ethiopia on 3 October 1933. One week after the enactment of the second Neutrality Act (7 March 1936) German troops occupied the Rhineland. Four months later the Spanish Civil War began. In May 1937 the third Neutrality Act was passed, Japanese-Chinese conflict intensified and the road to Munich was wide open.[22]

Carl Jung commented that with the Depression in Germany, 'The whole educated middle-class was utterly ruined, but the state was on top, putting on more and more of the "istic" rouge as war-paint. The country was in a condition of extreme misery and insecurity, and waves of panic swept over the population.'[23] The reasons for a move towards authoritarian government in Germany and elsewhere are not hard to find. Nicholas Lewin points out:

> In those times confusion and anarchy were real threats to society and the rule of law. The fact that later horrors have overshadowed the excesses after World War I should not blind one to the thousands killed by Lenin's consolidation of power after the civil war or the brutality of the revolution in Hungary and the murders on both sides as the communist revolt was put down in Bavaria.[24]

The Weimar Republic was far from universally popular, not even in its glory days in the mid-1920s; too many members of the Reichstag would have favoured its abolition and during the Depression fewer and fewer members were committed to its preservation. Nationalists, communists, Nazis – all wanted to replace outmoded democracy with strong, heroic authoritarian government of the people, but not *by* the people. Gustav Le Bon in his book, *Psychology of the Masses*, referred to crowds as irrational and hysterical. What then was democracy but the irrational and hysterical rule of a heroic nation that deserved proper leadership, not the dictatorship of the mob?

National Socialist government was by no means inevitable, and by the time that Hitler became chancellor the vote for the NSDAP had peaked and was beginning to wane as the economy began to pick up. Extreme politics was shunned again especially as political violence grew. The fallout of the sudden decline in Germany's fortunes led not just to a return to civil unrest, but a rise in the popularity of extremist political parties (such as the NSDAP and communists), reflected in election results at the expense of the traditional parties. In the Reichstag elections of 1928 the National Socialists only achieved twelve seats. However, in the election of 1930, at the height of the economic crisis, they won 107 seats.

By the early 1930s the Weimar Republic ran out of track when the Reichstag became packed with members who didn't believe in it, and many of whom did not even believe in democracy. Democracy was thought outmoded as compared with what appeared to be strong effective dictatorships promoting national interest. It became increasingly difficult for democrats to form a government without negotiating with their natural enemies. German politics had been moving in the direction of more authoritarian government since the collapse of the Grand Coalition in 1930, due to a rejection of a cut in unemployment benefit that could no longer be afforded by the state. A proposal supported by the Social Democrat chancellor was defeated by his own party, prompting his resignation and the fall of the coalition government. Chancellors of ensuing administrations without clear mandates found it increasingly necessary to bypass parliament to get legislation enacted using (or misusing?) emergency powers enshrined in the Weimar Constitution.

Hindenburg appointed Heinrich Brüning of the Centre Party as chancellor of a minority government with the onerous task of making the cuts thought necessary to bring the German economy on track. His first bill of economic reform was passed narrowly by the Reichstag, but the second was rejected, prompting a general election that increased the extremist vote – especially of the Nazis. With Hindenburg's support and the backing of the Social Democrats, who saw the administration preferable to that of the NSDAP, Brüning continued to govern. He despised the Nazis and had the SA and SS banned. Among his other reforms he ordered bankrupt estates to be broken up into small farms, which alienated the Right. It seemed to Hindenburg and his advisor, General Schleicher, that Brüning's government was swinging too far to the Left. Brüning was on the verge of his greatest triumph in getting the Allies to agree in principle to end reparations when he received news that he had been ousted. He had hoped to bring back the Hohenzollerns as constitutional monarchs to prevent extremist parties like the Nazis from being able to introduce dictatorial government to Germany. In spite of authoritarian elements, Brüning's administration was the last hope of preventing a right-wing government of some kind in Germany and the last chance of excluding the Nazis from mainstream politics.

Brüning knew that the office of President of the Republic was up for election again in 1932. It was vital that, even though the octogenarian president was showing signs of the onset of senility, the revered elder statesman Paul von Hindenburg should stand again and win the election – otherwise there was a real risk the post might be filled by a National Socialist, probably Hitler. Furthermore, even if the veteran commander and statesman did stand and win the election convincingly, there was a possibility that he would not survive the term of his office. As a result of the threat posed by a potential National Socialist president, Brüning and his Cabinet agreed that the best course of action would be for a restoration of the monarchy immediately following the election, with Hindenburg being appointed regent for life, after which one of the kaiser's grandsons would succeed to the vacant throne as a constitutional monarch. The plan not only had the support of Social Democrats and trade union leaders, but Brüning shrewdly perceived that representatives of the political Right, such as Alfred Hugenberg for the Nationalists and Steldt of the influential *Stahlhelm* (Steel Helmets political-paramilitary group), would not be able to oppose a restoration. It could also have the benefit of drawing conservatives away from the Nazis and so split the movement. Unfortunately the plan had an irresolvable problem and ran into the sand. The restoration of Wilhelm II was thought impossible for the Allies or the German people to accept, and similarly the candidacy of the Crown prince was also rejected. The obstinate legitimist Hindenburg, however, would never act as regent or hand over power to anyone but his kaiser.[25] Brüning could do nothing because he knew that a restoration by unconstitutional means would destroy the monarchy forever. It had been far easier to abolish a monarchy than it was proving to restore one.

Brüning told British Ambassador Sir Horace Rumbold that only the restoration of what he called a moderate monarchy could save Germany from prolonged unrest and trouble, saying, 'Such a monarchy would make for stability and would be a guarantee against foreign adventures.' Rumbold noted that monarchism had become 'generally accepted among opponents of the Nazis, even Social Democrats'.[26] Brüning, a member of the Catholic Centre Party, became chancellor on 29 March 1930. He decided that it was not necessary to make deals with the NSDAP and banned both the SA and communist paramilitary groups. He also introduced unpopular harsh domestic measures in response to the economic crisis in Germany and contacted Albert of Belgium with a proposal to revise the Versailles Treaty. As a result of his efforts he was able to go to Geneva to negotiate on limited rearmament and an end to reparations to help European recovery, which would have helped Germany's plight considerably. On the verge of success, however, he was required to return to Berlin where he was forced out by Hindenburg at the instigation of fellow Centre Party member General von Schleicher and replaced by Franz von Papen (1 June 1932), who formed a Cabinet friendly to the president. Papen was a facilitator; a trouble-shooter. During the First World War he had developed the dark skills of political intrigue in the USA, from where he was ejected, and supplied arms to Irish dissidents planning an uprising against the British in 1916. He was no bland Weimar politician; he had a past.[27]

Von Papen and Schleicher didn't share Hindenburg's complete distrust and hatred of National Socialism, believing that their worst traits could be curbed and their political support could be directed to upholding conservative government led by them. Hindenburg had wanted a government of gentlemen and preferably ex-army officers. What he got was the opposite.

Franz von Papen's Cabinet was called the 'Barons" or 'Monocle' Cabinet. He repealed the ban of the SA to try to win the Nazi's favour. In the 1932 election, however, the NSDAP had become the largest party, leaving the conservatives without enough tangible support to rule effectively. The communists introduced a vote of censure, supported by Göring and the Nazis. Although the Nazis lost seats in the November 1932 election and their support had obviously peaked, a majority in the Reichstag depended on their support, so von Papen resigned. General Schleicher became chancellor and refused to support a deal that would have made Hitler vice-chancellor. As an alternative he unsuccessfully tried to split the NSDAP by offering the vice-chancellorship to Gregor Strasser. He had previously had secret dealings with Ernst Röhm that would have given the SA a semi-official status even in a threatened takeover by the communists. On 23 January 1933 he told Hindenburg that he could not get a majority and asked for a state of emergency to be declared. Hindenburg would not give him emergency powers, so on 20 January he resigned. Von Papen, supported by some leading industrialists, convinced a reluctant Hindenburg that he could control Hitler and so get a majority, but as Wheeler-Bennett put it, it was only after the politicians had placed the fetters on their own wrists did they realise who was captive and who was captor.[28]

The success of the NSDAP resulted in Hitler being offered the chancellorship by Hindenburg in spite of his party's electoral popularity having already peaked. The president's judgement was entirely trusted by the German people who had elected him. Löwenstein comments:

> The name of Hindenburg, a retired general, suddenly appeared in the limelight of history, never to retreat into the shade again. He and his chief-of-staff, Major-General Eric Ludendorff, who saved East Prussia and maybe Germany, assumed for us a stature not inferior to the heroes of whom we had heard in mythology and ancient history. This myth woven about Hindenburg's name in the minds of even the youngest – the voters of the period of the Weimar Republic – was to elevate him to the presidency in later years and to endow him with an almost magical authority.[29]

The president, however, had acted on the advice of von Papen and others who believed that the Nazis could be tamed by their more politically experienced conservative colleagues. Hindenburg was tricked into granting Hitler more power and, following the president's death, the chancellor assumed the powers of president as well, becoming dictator of Germany in defiance of the constitution.

Prince Louis Ferdinand of Prussia gives some insight into Hitler's dramatic rise to total power:

> I believe it neither just nor reasonable to condemn as criminals all the millions who voted for Hitler after his first pronouncements. Though I am far from comparing Hitler to Roosevelt, many people voted for Hitler in Germany for exactly the same reasons which prompted people in the United States to vote for Roosevelt. The tragedy lies in the fact that Hitler was not a Roosevelt. The German people, in a fit of desperation, fell for a frenzied corporal who began his career in the disguise of a saviour but turned out to be a megalomaniac and satanical tyrant. To my mind it was a gigantic tragedy that this man appeared on the German political horizon at a moment when an aging former war hero, who was highly venerated but unable to restrain Hitler and his cliques, was at the helm.[30]

Once the Nazis had gained power they consolidated it with the Enabling Act, which Brüning thought the 'most monstrous resolution ever demanded of a parliament', and the (racial) Nuremberg Laws. After the burning of the Reichstag and the death of Hindenburg, they implemented their anti-democratic policies and Hitler became the dictator of Germany on a radical centrist programme. Dictatorships were not that uncommon in 1930s Europe and the examples of Mussolini and Ataturk seemed to suggest that Germany too could prosper under a strong leader. 'Middle class liberals also began to turn towards Rome and Ankara without wishing for a totalitarian state,' Löwenstein recalled in his autobiography.[31] Totalitarianism, however, was the food and drink of Nazism, which retained and even gained popularity due to improved economic conditions in Germany that were the result of improving world conditions, but were thought to be due to Hitler's new policies. The dictator, of course, took the credit.[32]

Combining the roles of president and chancellor, Hitler's assumption of the title Reichsführer ended any hopes of a Hohenzollern restoration. 'Monarchists were denounced as "more dangerous than communists!"' *Newsweek* quoted Hitler as warning monarchists 'to keep their hands off the German state. A monarchist restoration was henceforth not even to be discussed.' SA units broke up monarchist meetings and festivals and tore down imperial flags from the front of buildings.[33]

Notes

1 *The Life and Letters of the Rt Hon Sir Austen Chamberlain*, ed. C. Petrie, vol. 2, p. 392, cited in the *Dictionary of National Biography*.
2 From an interview on German television: ARD, *Salzburger Nachrichten*, 22 June 2004.
3 Fritz Richard Stern, *The Politics of Cultural Despair* (California, 1974), p. 10.
4 Ibid., p. 10–12; Arthur van den Moeller, *Das Dritte Reich* (The Third Reich); Paul de Lagarde who originated the idea of a 'positive' Christianity that airbrushed out the

Jewish elements of the Judeo-Christian tradition; and Julius Langbehn who launched a racist attack on the 'degeneracy' of modern art.

5 Löwenstein, Prince Hubertus zu, *Towards the Further Shore* (Victor Gollancz, 1968), p. 33.

6 *New York Times*, 4 January 1922, p. 3. The kaiser visited Tangier in 1905 as a response to the Entente between France, Russia and Britain. The second Moroccan Crisis occurred when Germany accused France of trying to set up a protectorate in Morocco against the former's interests, sending a gunboat when French forces entered Fez to put down a rebellion against the sultan contrary to the Algeciras Agreement of 1906. Although David Lloyd George made a thinly disguised threat of force on France's behalf due to British concerns that Germany may have wanted to establish a naval base at Agadir, Germany declared that it had no territorial ambitions in Morocco and agreed to a compromise that ceded it a corridor of the French Congo and a guarantee of its economic interests in Morocco in exchange for acceptance of a French protectorate there.

7 Demmerle, E., *Mine Vater.* An Interview with Dr Otto von Habsburg. Transcript sent to the author by Eva Demmerle, December 2009. By 1916 the kaiser had lost control to the third supreme council represented by Hindenburg and Ludendorff.

8 Löwenstein, *Towards the Further Shore*, p. 33.

9 Thompson, Vance, *New York Sun*, 13 September 1914.

10 Quoted in Beatty, Charles, *Our Admiral* (London, 1980), p. 114.

11 Patch, William L., *Heinrich Brüning and the Dissolution of the Weimar Republic* (Cambridge, 2006), p. 200.

12 http://www.firstworldwar.com/source/germanassembly_ludendorff.htm.

13 Churchill, Winston S., *The History of the Second World War, vol 1, The Gathering Storm* (Penguin Classics, 2005), p. 10.

14 Prussia, Louis Ferdinand of, *The Rebel Prince*, pp. 42–3.

15 The *Dolchstoßlegende* for which Field Marshal Erich Ludendorff was largely responsible.

16 'In December 1918, Marshal Foch explained to British political leaders the main challenge of the post-war world. Germany would not willingly accept the peace terms imposed upon it, and would constantly agitate to overturn them. But it would not immediately challenge the Western powers. Instead, it would first turn eastwards and seek to dominate the Slavic countries. Then, if allowed to appropriate land and resources in the East, it would turn West with such force as to be practically unstoppable. In strategic terms, therefore, eastern and western Europe were two halves of a single whole, making it unrealistic to pursue the security of western Europe without due regard for the security of eastern Europe as well.'

17 Löwenstein, *Towards the Further Shore*, p. 55. See Chapter 7.

18 Moeller van den Bruck, Arthur, *Germany's Third Empire*, ed. E.O. Lorimer (London, George Allen & Unwin, 1934), p. 15.

19 See Chapter 6.

20 This appealed to many people who were to later turn against National Socialism after learning what Nazism really meant.

21 Parrish, Michael E., *Anxious Decades* (New York, W.W. Norton, 1992), p. 247.

22 Ibid., pp. 446–7.

23 Jung, Carl, *Collected Works*, vol 9, 1986 (1936), p. 41.

24 Lewin, Nicholas Adam, *Jung on War, Politics and Nazi Germany*, p. 48.

25 Wheeler-Bennett, Sir John, *The Nemesis of Power*, p. 230; Churchill, Winston, S., *The Gathering Storm*, p. 56.

26 Patch, William L., *Heinrich Brüning and the Dissolution of the Weimar Republic* (Cambridge, 2006), pp. 301–2. Even Stresemann had suggested Crown Prince Wilhelm as a possible regent to take the place of the aged Hindenburg as president, p. 57.

27 Hitler later appointed Papen ambassador to Austria in 1934 to win friends and undermine the Austrian government. See Chapter 8.

28 Wheeler-Bennett, Sir John, *The Nemesis of Power*, p. 293.

29 Löwenstein, *Towards the Further Shore*, p. 55.

30 Even Prince Louis Ferdinand himself was taken in by the dictator for a short while. In 1939 he wrote to Franklin D. Roosevelt that Germany now had its own 'New Deal'. Franklin D. Roosevelt Library and Archive, letter from Prince Louis Ferdinand of Prussia to F.D.R., 1939.

31 Ibid., p. 20.

32 Oswald Spengler in his *Decline of the West* warned that Western democratic capitalism would be replaced by 'Caeserism': 'By the term "Caesarism" I mean that kind of government which, irrespective of any constitutional formulation that it may have, is in its inward self a return to thorough formlessness. It does not matter that Augustus in Rome, and Huang Ti in China, Amasis in Egypt and Alp Arslan in Baghdad disguised their position under antique forms. The spirit of these forms was dead, and so all institutions, however carefully maintained, were thenceforth destitute of all meaning and weight. Real importance centred in the wholly personal power exercised by the Caesar.'

33 Lee, Stephen, J., *European Dictatorships, 1918–1945* (London, Routledge, 2008), p. 46.

2

THE ORIGINS OF NATIONAL SOCIALISM IN GERMANY

Fascism is based on the grovelling subservience of little bullies to the arch-bully; it is the apotheosis of the cad.

Austin Hopkinson[1]

Nazism was not a single philosophy; it was a union of fascism, extreme pan-German nationalism, socialism and German tribalism. It was the opinion of the Nazis that royalty was decadent, that the middle class had betrayed Germany, and that communism was a foreign plot.[2] It was, therefore, for the *Volk*, the ordinary foot soldiers of the First World War – the tribe itself – to seize (or reclaim) Germany for the Germans.[3] The middle and lower-middle classes would then be left to find their 'inner German' and support or represent the tribe as expressed through its political manifestation of National Socialism. Hitler was the fascist element or twentieth-century expression of nineteenth-century pan-Germanism. What was an aspiration before the First World War, afterwards became an aggressive response to the punitive humiliation of Versailles and those who were blamed.

The German inclination to expand eastwards, *Drang nach Osten*, probably had its roots in the military expeditions of the Teutonic Knights during the Middle Ages into the pagan east, leading to its colonisation (*Ostsiedlung*) and the Christian conversion of its peoples. This move east was unfinished business even (and especially) in the twentieth century, when the high population of the Reich was not reflected by wealth or empire. The Slavic lands were viewed by some as Germany's back-yard – ripe for settlement and economic exploitation, an antidote to the Treaty of Versailles. A revision of the Versailles Treaty and eastern expansion were central to National Socialist policy. The Nazis' policy of *Lebensraum* meant colonisation of eastern European territory. Western political interference (the British and French declaration of war on behalf of Poland) was an impediment that needed to be neutralised as quickly as possible so that the drive east could continue unabated. Hitler regarded Russia as the future equivalent of British India.

Communism, with its internationalist outlook, was at odds with German nationalism and its closely guarded racial identity and beliefs. Communism's threat lay not only in its political stance but also in its cultural implications. Germany was number one target for communist revolution sponsored by the Soviet Union. It was the developed industrial economy where revolution was most likely to take place and be successful. To Germans the eastern hordes represented more than unsavoury politics, they were a potential Slavic deluge swallowing up everything Germanic forever – not just private property, but the very soul of the rightful heirs of the Fatherland. Russia's million-strong army had already crossed its borders into neighbouring Poland and, although repulsed, had indicated its expansionism towards Germany. Communism was believed to have been spread by Jewish activists, as indicated by the Jewish leadership of the communist risings in Berlin and Munich in 1918 and Karl Marx himself. The only solution that seemed to provide sufficient safeguards against the march of communism, internationalism and racial/national oblivion was authoritarian government in a dictatorship, providing indivisible unity of purpose, strength and will against all comers. Democracy was regarded as weak and ineffectual; as a system it appeared to have had its day.

British and French Empires were seen as decadent, whereas Russia's pace of industrialisation and million-strong army was seen as the principle threat; foreign Slavic hordes under Jewish leadership, as indicated by the leadership of communist groups in Germany and Marx himself. Communism was internationalist – a threat to German self-image and racial identification – and authoritarian government seen as national – protective of class interests against communist threat. Socialism was fine as long as it was German socialism. The Nazis tapped into pan-German and *völkisch* sentiments by claiming to revive antique virtues and lifestyle using modern technology and scientific theory. The Nordic race was regarded as the background to Germanism – a thread providing background, provenance and context – defining a people and its perceived destiny in and over territory. Nordic myth and religion was seen as home-grown and therefore valid. A drop in the birth rate in Germany was also seen as a threat – the race required protection from oblivion, defeated and swallowed up by 'inferior' races.

Foreign influences were not tolerated, especially from those within Germany such as its Jewish or Polish residents. Christianity was also considered foreign and could be tolerated only in its German form. The purely Germanic folk roots of the German people were regarded as essential to the establishment and development of the pan-German state. Therefore the German pagan myths, being home-grown and pertaining to the tribe as a palpable identity, were encouraged.

National Socialism did not come from nothing, but seems to have emanated from right-wing interpretations of Hegel towards the end of the nineteenth century, mixed with modernism, social Darwinism, anti-Semitism, imperialism and pan-Germanism.[4] These notions were advanced especially in the writings of Heinrich von Treitschke, a former student of the 'father of German nationality', Friedrich Christoph Dahlmann.[5] Unlike his former mentor, von Treitschke urged the complete dominance of Prussia over the other German states and the extinguishing of the rival German monarchies.

Modernism was condemned by the German poet Stephan George as a 'religion of progress', which would in the end lead to catastrophe.[6] But its obsessive doctrine consumed the Western world with pseudo-science and pseudo-philosophy at the turn of the nineteenth and twentieth centuries, jettisoning the natural and spiritual worlds in favour of a mythical redemption of the flesh through the mysteries of physical fitness, steel and eugenics. Modernism, 'racial hygiene' and social Darwinism were not purely German ideas, far from it, the history of the whole of western Europe and America is stained with this embarrassment. Eugenics, Manifest Destiny and racism were the common currency of the West in the early twentieth century, to our enduring shame.[7] F.G. Bailey explains the warped logic:

> The fusion of eugenics, racial theories and social Darwinism … produced a graphic picture in which racial survival in a world of incessant conflict was predicated upon the maintenance of a healthy population purged of those elements that threatened its integrity. Given the increasing tendency of social Darwinists to present collectivities rather than individuals as the agents of adaptation and survival and thus to assign moral priority to the group, these developments provided a powerful rationale for policies aimed at the elimination of racially undesirable elements.

Treitschke – whose anti-Semitic maxim '*Die Juden sind unser Unglück*' became the motto of the Nazi publication, *Der Stürmer*, has been described as the 'supreme exponent of "power politics"' – can reasonably be seen as 'the forerunner of German militarism and National Socialism in the twentieth century'.[8] One of his students, Heinrich Claß, was president of the *Alldeutscher Verband* (pan-German League) from 1908 until its dissolution in 1939 and steered the organisation towards a radical agenda. In 1912 Claß wrote *Werm ich der Kaiser wär* (*If I were the Emperor*), which reads like an early National Socialist manifesto. He suggested that the activities of socialists should be curbed with stern measures such as banning their newspapers and depriving them of a political voice. Jewish and Polish immigration would be stopped as would Jewish participation in the professions, and their taxes were to be doubled. He also argued for military expansion and the expelling of the indigenous populations of conquered territory if Germany's enemies attacked the Fatherland. He believed that the individual citizen ought to be subordinate to the nation as a whole as expressed through the state, and called for a strong leader to lead Germany:

In the best of our people the need lives on today to follow a strong and virtuous leader. All who have not been seduced by the doctrines of an un-German
democracy long for such a one, not because they are inclined to servility or
weak in character, but because they know that greatness can only exert itself
through the coming together of individual powers — something that can be
achieved only through subordination to a leader.[9]

In 1917 he co-founded the *Vaterlandspartie* with Alfred von Tirpitz and Wolfgang
Kapp as a right-wing response to calls for peace talks, which before dissolved in 1918 had over a million members.[10] Claß and other members of the
Vaterlandspartie supported Luddendorf's assertion that the German army had
been 'stabbed in the back' by the politicians in Berlin (the November Criminals)
who had made peace with the Allies in 1918. One member of the *Vaterlandspartie*,
Anton Drexler, went on to form the German Workers Party, which later became
the National Socialist and Workers Party. In 1918 Claß met Hitler, and supported
his Munich (or Beer Hall) Putsch in 1923. He sat as a National Socialist member
of the Reichstag between 1933 and 1939. It is, therefore, inconceivable that the
development of National Socialism was not directly influenced by his views and
ideas. Another student of von Treitsche, Fredrich von Bernhardi thought of war
in Darwinian terms as a part of the natural selection process and as a struggle for
existence. He commented that war was a 'biological necessity' according with
natural law.

Germany's constituent parts and their separate histories and cultures provide
additional context to the rise of Nazism. Bavaria, for example, had its own powerful political and cultural identity inspired by that of Prussia and by Prussian
advisors at the Bavarian royal court. The sudden overthrow of the Bavarian
monarchy was followed by social and economic chaos, socialist and then communist rule, which was eventually put down by the *Freikorps*. Other regions with
experience of civil strife and communist takeover, including Saxony and Berlin,
narrowly escaped communist rule. The Bavarian experience left many scars and
although extremist nationalist and *völkisch* groups made their home in the former
kingdom, the people as a whole remained moderate and eschewed movements
of the far Right and Left, preferring to support their Crown prince and rightful
monarch. As a consequence the NSDAP had no success in building up its vote in
Bavaria except in the towns. The country in the 1920s and 1930s was of its nature
separatist and was close to seceding from the Reich, whereas Prussia and its sat-
ellites were expansionist and centrist. Northern Germany had a stronger party
membership than the South.

Totalitarianism was imposed by means of a nationalist and socialist seduction
of the people during economic difficulties. They promoted unity of race and the
breaking down of class barriers by means of *Volksgemeinschaft*. In theory it meant
the unity of 'brain and fist', white collar and blue collar in the national (racial)

and mutual self-interest. In reality the workers gained recognition but lost power. With *Gleichschaltung* all social, political and religious groups became Nazi groups or were banned. In this way there was no voice in the state that was not controlled by Nazi ideology. Youth groups were assimilated into the Hitler Youth and its female equivalent. *Gleichschaltung* was complete political and cultural alignment with the Nazi Party. Literally 'put in the same gear', through *Gleichschaltung* Nazism affected and infected every walk of life as a matter of policy. This happened very quickly and before many people were even aware that their clubs, societies, shops and offices had lost their independence Germany became 'one huge dungeon'.[11] Unfortunately for the average German, their gaolers included their next-door neighbours: each a potential informer as to the character, politics and activities of the persons around them.

Völkisch writers such as Julius Langbehn, Paul de Lagarde and Arthur Moeller van den Bruck were influential in the 1920s and '30s. Copies of Lagarde's writings were distributed by the Nazis to their soldiers. He believed in a Germany reborn with the inclusion of the Austrian Empire and liberalism swept away. Langbehn denounced modern art as degenerate and the result of the influence of inferior races in his book *Rembrandt als Erzieher*, in which he suggested that Rembrandt had been a member of a pure German race undefiled by intermarriage with other peoples, and that the quality of his art reflected this. Moeller van den Bruck wrote a book called *Das Dritte Reich*, the title of which was appropriated by the Nazis, though he expressed a personal dislike of Hitler who kept a signed copy. The occupation of the Ruhr, he wrote, made the German nation betrayed by the so-called November Revolutionaries start to think. 'It threw us back on our own power of decision. It restored our will. Parliamentism has become an institution of our public life, whose chief function would appear to be – in the name of the people – to enfeeble all political demands and all national passions.'[12] Evoking theories of *Volk* and race as solutions to the humiliation of Versailles he continued, 'One thing, and one thing only, can save us: a human, spiritual renewal; the evolution of a new race of Germans who shall make good what we have wrecked. The man who already belongs to this new race is the true revolutionary.' Similarly the works of Henri Bergson, Gustave Le Bon, Vilfredo Pareto and movements like the pan-German movement and *Action Française* in France. Moeller van den Bruck helped found the June Club (*Juniklub*, renamed *Deutscher Herren klub*) to oppose the Versailles Treaty. This club was influential in helping Franz von Papen become chancellor in 1932.

This thread running from the mid-nineteenth century to 1933 became more radical as it progressed – stimulated by war, the aftermath of war, revolution, counter-revolution and economic crises. It had several manifestations, but as Prince Hubertus zu Löwenstein writes, 'National Socialism, with its dynamic force related to that of Communism, contained an irrepressible striving for power, for complete power – elements, that is, which are foreign to Conservatism.'[13]

It therefore could not be contained by its conservative opponents or challenged by its radical allies. It had no allies and it tolerated no opponents, for power and power alone was its driving force and its philosophy.[14]

National Socialism was able to gain power, not just because its nationalist agenda appealed to German sensibilities and grievances, or due to the actions and acquiescence of politicians who thought Hitler could be tamed, but also because it reflected (albeit in an extreme form) a secular world view that was then prevalent from Washington to Vladivostok. Catholic priest and former Dachau prisoner Thomas Lenz comments, 'There were many who had no faith in those days, who having once fallen away from the Church were an easy prey to Hitler's substitute for religion. Where there was no living religion the thorns of the Nazi doctrine grew up like the thorns in the parable.'[15] Furthermore, psychologist Carl Jung said he believed that a non-religious society was more vulnerable to fanatical totalitarianism. 'Without an internal religious point of reference the individual was too vulnerable to the external pressures of mass society' and to the dictatorship as religion.

A section of the German people were locked into an Hegelian dialectic, in what was regarded as a Darwinian struggle for the existence of the German identity and state, its evolution stimulated by conflict; an assumption that the race is strengthened through struggle; the physical dominance of the brute portrayed as a positive. Willpower (the 'will to power') rated above subtle intellect and the state, and the (considered superior) race rated above great individuals and everything else.[16]

Without its pan-German movement origins, National Socialism would have had neither substance nor general appeal. However, without the personality cult of the Führer, the Pan-German League would never have achieved its object in the face of its twentieth-century political competitors, democratic and otherwise. Hitler appropriated the ideas and authority of prominent advocates of the pan-German movement like Claß and Ludendorff (and SA leader Ernst Röhm), but, as rival personalities to the one great leader, they had to be seen to be politically marginalised.

Hitler tried to be all things to all men, but only insofar as it was useful to him on the road to power. He was the idol of an atheist counter-religion, but spoke sometimes as if he were Christian and at other times as the leader of a nationalistic pagan religion.[17] A clue as to Hitler's personal 'spiritual' beliefs may be found in the ideas of philosopher Georg Friedrich Hegel (1770–1831) and his seminary room-mates Friedrich Schelling and Friedrich Hölderlin, who proposed a new (unchristian) nature religion derived from the ancient Greeks – a 'synthesis of nature and spirit'. Hegel wrote of 'effusion', whereby cosmic spirit was revealed through all nature throughout history. Following Kant, Hegel and Schelling attempted to establish a system of philosophy into a science. Hegel abandoned Christian philosophy but retained a spiritual (or quasi-spiritual) dimension to

Enlightenment philosophy. This philosophical nature religion was easily grafted onto a linguistic nation of many nations that aspired to believe in itself – that is, its own nature as distinctly German, confident and self-fulfilled. Linguistics became of great importance to a people whose principal uniting factor was a common language rather than a true common heritage. Hitler, however, believed he had outgrown Hegel.

Before his assumption of complete power it was politic to appear to have a faith broadly comparable with most Germans. Hitler spoke of God and Providence in his speeches but that does not mean that be believed in a Judeo-Christian God, and certainly not of the God of Abraham and Moses; nor the tradition of Hillel that immediately preceded Christ's Ministry and arguably provided its ethical context. That is to say that, in his human manifestation, Christ was a radical Jewish reformer who embraced all peoples as God's own. Hitler's world-view appears to have been similar to that of Herder and Hegel, with certain elements of the beliefs of Gustav List and Adolf Josef Lanz to which he was exposed as a young man in Vienna. He may even have been influenced by the teachings of UK-based mystic Madam H.P. Blavatsky and the Theosophical Society, denuded of its universal aspects.

The Nazis tried to neutralise the official German Protestant Church and adapt it for their own purposes. So-called 'positive' Christianity (as promoted by Lagarde) excluded the Old Testament because it was Jewish in origin, and claimed that Christ was not Jewish but Aryan. No longer revered as the Jewish Messiah and Prince of Peace who died on a Roman cross and was the Redeemer of all Mankind, the new German Church remembered a specifically Nordic-German Jesus as having been killed by the Jews.

In 1543 Martin Luther, whom Hitler regarded as a great German reformer, wrote an anti-Semitic book, *Von den Jüden und jren Lügen*. In it he suggests that the Jews should be made to do manual labour to 'earn their bread from the sweat of their brow', their synagogues be burnt down, their money taken from them and their houses destroyed as punishment for their lies and blasphemy, which fuelled extreme xenophobic German nationalism and eventually – and most especially – Nazism. Luther further writes that the Jews have no reason to show hostility to Christians as they live among them and are shown every kindness. Meanwhile, he continues, Christian rulers sleep while Jews steal from them by means of usury and make them 'beggars with their own money'. He suggests that the Jews should be deprived of their privileges, as all they have rightly belongs to the Christians in whose country they reside.

This seems extremist and incendiary, but is an accurate description of *Kristallnacht*. With Luther's translation of the New Testament into the vernacular at Wartburg Castle and the birth of a thoroughly German Church, modern Germany was established and Luther became, thereby, an emblem of its nationalism and independence. The Catholic Church, on the other hand, came to be regarded as a 'Roman', foreign and internationalist intrusion. In October 1817 pan-Germanist students gathered at Wartburg to commemorate the 300th anniversary of the Reformation and four years since Napoleon's defeat at Leipzig. During the 'festival' monarchical, French and Jewish books were burned, which provided the model for the Nazi book burnings of the 1930s.[18]

For Hitler the Church could not be neutral. It was either a potential instrument of Nazi power or propaganda, or an impediment to Nazi ambition: a rival claimant on the German soul. His attempt to transform official German Christian observance into what amounted to an antithesis of Christian morality – its churches festooned with swastikas and racist symbolism, presided over by a tame Nazi Reich bishop – was an example of his complete disregard of the religion and its founder, who was asserted to have been an Aryan and not Jewish at all. Hitler certainly had no respect for the Catholic faith of the Habsburgs. The concordat that was agreed by the Vatican and Germany in 1933 robbed Germany of the political voice that had represented a lot of grass-roots opposition to the political dominion of the National Socialists and their leader. Although it was difficult for individuals to oppose the party line in Nazi Germany, many priests and pastors put their lives at risk by speaking out in the pulpit and elsewhere.

During Hitler's visit to Rome in 1938 the pope gravely pronounced:

> Sad events are taking place, very sad, both at a distance and also near at hand; yes, saddening events indeed, and among them one may well mention the fact that on the feast day of the Holy Cross there is openly borne the badge of another cross, which is not the Cross of Christ. I shall have said enough if I tell you how necessary it is to pray, to pray, very fervently, that God's mercy may not be wanting.[19]

Bishop Galen of Munster said in spring 1939:

> Those who place the race or the Nation or the State ... outside this earthly scale of values, who take these factors as the supreme norm of all things, even of things religious, and deify them with a divine cultus, are distorting the divinely created and divinely ordained order of things ... Only superficial minds can fall into the error of speaking of a national God or of a national religion ... Those who dare to demand obedience to commands and ordinances that are in opposition to the holy will of God misuse their power and forfeit the right to require obedience. In such cases it would be our duty to withstand the authority thus abused, in accordance with the example set by the holy Apostles.

The Catholic Church as an international and internationalist institution that claimed authority over all secular Christian authority was already at odds with the Nazi regime, as here compared with pagan Rome.[20] And on 19 August 1938, a combined pastoral of the bishops at Fulda stated:

Now Christianity is represented as an ancient fossilized remnant from an epoch that has passed, impotent and utterly devoid of present value. Quite apart from that, on the ground of racial and 'blood' theories, it is maintained that the personality and the life of Jesus Christ are alien to the German nature, as are also the main points of the faith he taught – this applies especially to the doctrines of Original Sin, Redemption, reward and punishment after death, which are all superstitions from the Near East forced upon the Germanic tribes when they were perfidiously invaded ... Just as was done to the Holiest One of all, who said, 'I am the Way, the Truth and the Life,' they can take Christian truth prisoner, scourge her, hand her over to the civil power, crown her with thorns of calumny, condemn her to death and crucify her on a German Calvary ... They seek to banish the Christian God, and set up a 'German God' in His place. Is this 'God' a different God from the God of other nations?[21]

For Hitler nationhood, the *Volk*, and its Greater Germany were paramount. He believed that a nation was not as important as its destiny, or the leader by which the national destiny was represented and moved forward. Individualism was suppressed culturally and politically. The nation was a singularity expressed through and in him. The totalitarian state was a termite colony where all were put to work to serve a common aim under a single leader, whether a Hitler or a Stalin. Individuality was sublimated, if not it was extinguished. Hannah Arendt suggests that the camps were the most extreme and demonstrable example of this. The nation was only as good as its unfailing loyalty to its leader, who was at one with the glorious destiny of the Aryan-Nordic race to which every true German belonged.

Hitler made it plain that he did not want National Socialism to be a mystery cult but a people's religion. Robert A. Pois writes:

There was really no need to appeal to an external force. Providence would be revealed in those actions undertaken by the movement; a movement which, embodying within itself laws of life revealed in Nature, was in fact *acting* as Providence. Hence, any acts committed by the National Socialist movement in general or Hitler in particular were justified by their having been committed in the first place.[22]

Naming ceremonies (*namensweihe*) began to replace baptism, and marriages, although often celebrated in churches, were attended by Nazi paraphernalia and the stamp of faith in a secular state rather than the highest authority. For princes who believed that their authority was derived from and by the grace of God and who were deeply aware of the responsibilities of kingship, the National Socialist creed was sacrilege.

Hitler could play the monarchist, socialist, Christian, pagan, urbane citizen, peasant, statesman, revolutionary, soldier or peacemaker as he chose. He used other men's convictions as a way to control them and dispensed with both when they had served their purpose. He courted princes, but only to flatter himself and add a reflected legitimacy to his usurpation of power. He had no affiliation with monarchy which was to him as much a rival in its appeal to the loyalty of the German people as the Church. He mocked Crown Prince Rupprecht of Bavaria, declared himself 'an implacable enemy of the Habsburgs,' and described Kaiser Wilhelm as 'a strutting puppet of no character'.[23] When the kaiser passed away, Hitler wanted to use the occasion to associate himself with the emperor and his residual moral and national authority, but, in a codicil added to his will, Wilhelm II left instructions for his funeral that forbade any intrusion by the Nazis: 'The obsequies are to be simple, unpretentious, quiet, dignified. *No* delegations from home. *No* swastika flags. *No wreaths.*' He wanted no funeral address, just songs and prayer.[24] Hitler had previously made a big show of von Hindenburg's funeral, but in his political will the president had recommended the restoration of the Hohenzollern monarchy, information suppressed by the Führer.[25]

The origins of National Socialism as a potent force depended on the character and oratorical skills of Hitler, which supplanted that of Ludendorff through assertion of personality over authority and experience. Löwenstein wrote that he once attended a Nazi meeting in the *Bürgerbraükeller* beer hall in Munich. Although he could not remember in detail what Hitler said, he recalled:

> His speech, – all his speeches – were like the eruptions of a mud volcano – an outpouring of emotions in a rapid succession of phrases of pompous emptiness. Yet he did possess a certain magnetic power over the masses, from which even foreign listeners who did not understand a word of what he said rarely escaped.

Suddenly, he remembered, his own rapport with the speaker 'snapped', and the words became 'unbearably hollow and meaningless'.[26] For others less immune, the future dictator's words retained their power. Prince Louis Ferdinand of Prussia had one meeting with Hitler, which turned out to be more of a monologue by the dictator than a conversation. The prince recalled:

> His demeanour was courteous, of Austrian ease, and definitely less theatrical than Mussolini [whom he had recently met]. His light blue eyes had a rather forlorn romantic expression directed more into space than at the person he was talking to. I must admit that I sensed a certain magnetic force emanating from him.[27]

Otto von Habsburg received an invitation to meet Hitler, but declined twice because he was quite aware of what the dictator intended for Austria and because he realised that the courting of princes by Hitler was merely an attempt to gain monarchist support for a programme which was never intended to include monarchs. He later reflected that a conversation with Hitler would have been an interesting experience, and that it was the only interesting conversation that he ever avoided in his life.[28] Tatiana Metternich gate-crashed a Nazi function with a friend in 1939 and sat down at table surrounded by the party elite. She recalled:

> A few minutes later the doors were flung open and in marched Hitler, Göring, Goebbels and a few others; they strutted past our table in a tight group. How small they were! They looked like stuffed dolls, unreal, a caricature of the likeness published for the edification of the people, almost as grotesque as targets in a fair, but they exuded importance and frightening power. The fascination they seemed to exercise over the hushed and reverent assembly, frozen into a servile smile, was to the irresistible attraction of might.[29]

The Nazis created a new hierarchy to replace that of nobility, bourgeois and working class with fixed personal relationships. The Nazis hated the old nobility and thought the middle classes had failed, writes George Lachmann Mosse:

> Hitler envisaged the government of the Reich as a hierarchy of leadership: from the local leaders up to himself as the Führer of all the people. In reality the Third Reich was a network of rival leaders, each with his own followers and his own patronage. Hitler kept them competing against one another and in this way was able to control the whole leadership structure.[30]

It was a loose touch, but an iron grip nevertheless.

Richard A. Etlin notes that observers of Nazi Germany in the years before the Second World War were 'faced with a logic that was counter to the humanism of Western civilization grounded in Judeo-Christian values and sustained by the Enlightenment ideals of freedom, brotherhood, and humanity'. Aurel Kolnai Wrote in 1938 that in Nazi Germany, 'Individual rights are not encroached upon, they are deprived of meaning: the access to humanity is not obstructed, it is entirely cut off; humanitarian standards are not violated or disregarded, they are denied outright.'[31] For the Nazis, race was politics and politics was race.

The Nazis were nationalists fighting a race war; the communists were internationalists fighting a class war. The Nazis were race elitists; class was immaterial. The whole of their classless society was already at the top of the pile internationally. The word 'racial' can be substituted for 'Nazi' almost in every case that it is used as a prefix. Race was the politics of the NSDAP – the master race had enemies who were racial enemies or their allies. For example, as far as the Nazis were concerned, the November Criminals were Jewish and so were the leaders of the communists and Spartacists.

When a country becomes ruled by a faction it becomes dangerous. Political parties, if they are not representative of something beyond themselves – of the nation, the land, the wider international interest – cannot be regarded as civilised.

Democracy is not automatically representative and what is representative is not always democratic, but sensibly there was general agreement among the princes featured in this book, and there is agreement among their heirs, that democracy should be the principal element of government guided, assisted and defended by other constitutional elements such as the hereditary principle and the rule of law as enshrined constitutionally. Some might say that better a conscientious and dutiful king who loves his country, than a personally ambitious politician. Oswald Spengler commented:

> Through money, democracy becomes its own destroyer, after money has destroyed intellect. But, just because the illusion that actuality can allow itself to be improved by the ideas of any Zeno or Marx has fled away; because men have learned that in the realm of reality one power-will can be overthrown only by another (for that is the great human experience of Contending States periods); there wakes at last a deep yearning for all old and worthy tradition that still lingers alive... And now dawns the time when the form-filled powers of the blood, which the rationalism of the Megolopolis has suppressed, reawaken in the depth. Everything in the order of dynastic tradition and old nobility that has saved itself up for the future, everything that there is of high money-disdaining ethic, everything that is intrinsically sound enough to be, in Frederick the Great's words, the servant − the hard-working, self-sacrificing, caring servant − of the State − all this becomes suddenly the focus of immense life-forces ...

Hitler used several stepping stones to power and crushed every one of them in the process. Friedrich Meinecke puts the case in his book, *The German Catastrophe*, that Hitler was not consistent in his ideology, and that power was his principal overriding ambition.[32] However, the triumph of the Nordic race in its perceived heroic Darwinian struggle for existence and dominance was central to his personal struggle for exclusive power. In an early speech by Hitler to his generals he said − as recalled by Colonel General Heinrici in a conversation with Albert Speer − that he was the first man since Charlemagne to hold unlimited power in his own hand and that he would know how to use it in a struggle for Germany, 'If the war were not won, that would mean that Germany had not stood the test of strength; in that case she would deserve to be and would be doomed.'[33]

Hitler appealed to the depths of humanity, entering people though their moral fault lines. Ambition, avarice and sadism were the building blocks of National Socialism. On the other side was fear, deep terror, not only for oneself, but for one's entire family, this and the hopelessness of having no means of public expression left through which to maintain one's humanity. Victory in the racial and political and personal struggle was offered to any pure German (or anyone not belonging to the most 'inferior' races) who was prepared to follow the Führer and have their individuality and higher nature dissolved by the state for the greater good of the race – so perverting the internationalism and potential benefits of real socialism or, for that matter, real conservatism. 'None are so hopelessly enslaved as those who falsely believe they are free,' said Johann Wolfgang von Goethe.

The Esoteric Politics and Political Esotericism of National Socialism

The princes who opposed Hitler were all devoted Christians with all the high moral values associated with the Christian faith. Although both Catholic and Protestant, and sometimes politically at odds with one another, their Christianity united them. There is more debate as to Hitler's personal faith, if any. Leading National Socialists like Himmler were demonstrably pagan in their beliefs, but the Führer remained aloof and enigmatic about his spiritual beliefs as with much else.

Among the occult influences on pan-Germanism and the Nazis, Guido von List was a follower of Madame Blavatsky founder of the British Theosophical Society.[34] One of List's followers was Adolf Josef Lanz von Liebenfels (1874–1954) who in 1917 founded the *Ordo Novi Templi* (Order of the New Temple) at Castle Werfenstein. It promoted an occult Aryan philosophy called Ariosophy, which entailed an obsession with medieval knighthood, especially the Knights Templar, and published a magazine, *Ostara*, from 1905, that promoted Aryanism and racism and used the swastika as a symbol. Favouring social Darwinist 'survival of the fittest' philosophy he suggested an ancient extraterrestrial origin of the Aryan race as compared with inferior races. Lanz claimed that other creatures were created after Adam and Eve and that it was through interbreeding with these creatures that the darker races came into being. For Lanz the Aryan race was indisputably a 'master' race over the others, as it was the only pure strong expression of humanity unadulterated by interbreeding.

Guido von List's writings were promoted by pan-Germanists. He believed in a pure Aryan master race as the supreme exemplar of humanity, whereas other races were the result of intermixing and were thus best suited to serve representatives of the unpolluted race. List thought that the Aryans' worst enemies were the Catholic Church, Jews and Freemasons, who were intent on the elimination of their race. 'The clerics in Rome and the aristocracy they rule,' he declared, alluding, no doubt, to the Habsburgs and the Austrian nobility, 'Have suppressed and destroyed German customs, the German way of thinking, and German law.' He predicted a world war through which the Aryan Germans would restore order and regain their privileges.[35] Among Hitler's books was one on nationalism by Tagore that included the dedication in 1921, for his birthday, 'To Mr Adolf Hitler, my dear *Arman* brother,' which could well indicate Hitler's early membership of a secret society.[36] For Brigitte Hamann the influence of List was unmistakable and present in Hitler's speeches.[37] List prophesied a Germanic leader, a 'strong one from above', who was infallible and in harmony with natural forces. This 'saviour' could never be wrong and his final victory was inevitable.[38]

Also influenced by Blavatsky, Adam Alfred Rudolf Glauer (AKA Rudolf von Sebottendorf), helped found the Thule Society in Munich at the conclusion of the First World War, which included a number of Nazis as members and promoted race mysticism, anti-Semitism, extreme ethnic nationalism and occult practices. Anton Drexler was asked to establish links with nationalist workers' organisations such as the workers' party he had helped found, the result was a merged party, the DAP.

Founder members of the DAP Anton Drexler, Alfred Rosenberg, Karl Harrer, Dietrich Eckart and Gottfried Feder were also members of the Thule Society, of which the DAP could be described as its public and political wing. If the DAP (later the NSDAP) was its political face, was Hitler its front man, and regarded as *just* its front man, the means whereby its policies would be realised and its world-view become German orthodoxy? The word 'just' does not give the party's leader justice. He was given unlimited power of command, but when the secular wing of the party – the militants and revolutionaries represented by Röhm and the SA – became an impediment to the party's core objectives, it was decapitated. The main reason why there has been so much debate as to what extent the 'final solution' (for example) was Hitler's brainchild or originated in the imaginations of his supporters who interpreted Nazi doctrine in ever-more extreme forms, is that there really was a division between the man and the party. He intentionally remained aloof, but Nazi policy rolled on with him on board, not directing it by orders as an individual tyrant would, but as representative of an entire ideology to which he subscribed and was best placed to manifest. In other words, it would be wrong to place to much emphasis on Hitler the man who, for all his wickedness, should not divert us from seeing the wickedness of those who were called his followers as if he were their leader in everything, so assuaging their guilt in some way. At the time there were people who thought that much was being done in his name that if he had known about it he would stop. His aloofness was convenient but his culpability was complete and undeniable. He was the personal embodiment and expression of that warped ideology that turned Germany into a butcher's yard.

Wewelsburg Castle, so Heinrich Himmler believed, had a deep mystical or magical significance that placed it at the centre of the world. It became a 'Nazi Camelot' where he could found an elite order of twelve pagan SS 'knights' who would meet in full ceremonial regalia in a specially designed chamber in the castle. The knights would wear coat armour at important ceremonies and their shields would decorate the walls. It was Himmler's intention to establish a new unchristian (or rather anti-Christian) counter-aristocracy to rule the world according to pagan and racist principles. Himmler had been guided there by his 'spiritual' advisor, the Nazi occultist SS Brigadeführer Karl Maria Wiligut who had been a follower of Guido von List, a founder of Ariosophy and a devotee of the Nordic god Wotan, but Wiligut later promoted *Irminenschaft*. In 1940 Himmler got Hitler's permission to demolish a local church in order to enlarge the castle. Himmler claimed to have had conversations with the ghost of Heinrich I (Heinrich der Volger, Duke of Saxony and King of Germany) and may have believed that he was a reincarnation of the king.[39]

The SS and Hitler Youth were encouraged to celebrate the Winter and Summer Solstice and pagan festivals rather than Christian ones. Wewelsburg Castle was thought to be on the crossing of a pattern of ley lines, suggesting enormous geographic and 'spiritual' significance. Home-grown pre-Christian beliefs and practices were promoted at the expense of the Judeo-Christian tradition, which was further undermined by questioning of Scripture and introduction of questionable theories, a belief in the coming of a super-race of humanity with whom each new generation can identify as superior to the old.

Alfred Rosenberg was an early member of the National Socialist Party and a member of the Thule Society. He was one of the principal Nazi ideologues and wrote a book, *The Myth of the Twentieth Century*, which contrasted the Aryan and Jewish races and was highly influential. He rejected international Christianity and argued instead for a German 'religion of the blood'.

Hitler confided in both Himmler and Albert Speer his antipathy to Christianity, which he considered had corrupted the world of antiquity of which he approved and was 'meek' and 'flabby'.[40] But what he personally believed is less certain. Like any master criminal he covered his tracks well. Theosophists, Freemasons and other Ariosophists were arrested along with members of rival fascist groups and any firm links with the Führer eradicated. Himmler's SS hierarchy was intended to have facilitated an SS state within the state, which would have become the basis of a command structure of a continent; possibly the world.

Notes

1 Hopkinson, Austin, 'Reflections on Fascism' in *The Nineteenth Century*, April 1934.

2 Hannah Arendt asserts that Italian Fascism was indeed fascist, but Nazism was not, it was totalitarian with fascist elements. Similarly Stalinism was totalitarian, not communist.

3 Germany, of course, was not the Germany of the early 1930s, but that territory annexed under the Treaty of Versailles and any territory adjoining Germany that was occupied by Germanic peoples. Furthermore, Hitler argued that the Germans should take up the 'soil policy' left off 600 years before and make territorial acquisitions in the east for *Lebensraum* (living space), specifically in the Ukraine as a matter of policy. Crozier, Andrew J., *The Causes of the Second World War* (Blackwell, 1997), p. 84.

4 Hitler admired Kant and Schopenhauer, whom he said had destroyed Hegel's pragmatism and whose work, *The World as Will and Idea*, he claimed to have carried with him throughout the First World War. He also read and admired Nietzsche. Being self-taught and unguided by appropriate scholarship, however, he misunderstood what he was reading and seems to have interpreted it according to his politically motivated preconceptions. *Hitler's Table Talk*, pp. 89, 358. There were many early influences upon which extreme German nationalism were built: German nationalist Friedrich Ludwig Jahn advocated

a union of the German states under the Hohenzollerns following the withdrawal of Napoleon's troops. In 1810 he wrote, summing up the worst prejudices of his nation and his age, 'Poles, French, priests, aristocrats and Jews are Germany's misfortune.'

5 Hitler quoted Treitschke and mentioned his name in a way that suggested that he expected his listeners to know exactly to whom he was referring, as fellow admirers would. *Hitler's Table Talk*, ed. Hugh Trevor-Roper, p. 711.

6 Löwenstein, Prince Hubertus, *Towards the Further Shore*, p. 15.

7 Social Darwinism was exemplified by US Manifest Destiny, by which racial superiority was thought demonstrated by the evident dominance of the white race over the indigenous American peoples, implying a right of conquest based on the struggle of natural selection.

8 *International Relations in Political Thought*, ed. by Chris Braun; Terry Nardin; Nicholas Rengger (Cambridge) p. 494.

9 Online translation of *Wenn ich der Kaiser wär.* http://h-net.org/~german/gtext/ kaiserreich/class.html (accessed December 2009).

10 Tirpitz was another student of Treitschke's.

11 Quote from Prince Louis Ferdinand of Prussia, *The Rebel Prince*, p. 49.

12 From the preface to *The Third Reich*, Arthur Moeller van den Bruck. English trans.: Moeller van den Bruck, Arthur, *Germany's Third Empire*, ed. E.O. Lorimer (London, George Allen & Unwin, 1934).

13 Löwenstein, *What was the German Resistance Movement?* (Bad Godesberg Grafes, 1965), p. 27–8.

14 'The moral code of National Socialism could be expressed in the one fundamental maxim: "The interests of the community override those of the individual." Whoever has understood this fact, whoever has understood that he is a German and thus part of a trendous (sic) current of Life and Blood, has acquired an unassailable standard of action. For such a man the problem of moral freedom is no longer bound up with preliminary questions about moral responsibility.' N.S. Monatshefte, cited in *The Persecution of the Catholic Church in the Third Reich* (Pelican, 2008), pp. 460–1. In a speech to a meeting of the National Socialist University Professors' Union, Professor Wetzel von Tubingen was reported in the *Frankfurter Zeitung* as saying: 'There was a hierarchy of living beings, starting from the cell and ending in the nation, each of them endowed with the instinct of self-preservation and service – i.e. carrying out orders: thus the cell carries out the orders of its organism, the individual those of his nation and his Führer. The cell and the individual are mortal. The nation is immortal. It is not a part, but a unity and a whole; properly speaking only the nation can be called God's creature.' *The Persecution of the Catholic Church in the Third Reich*, p. 158.

15 'Those who chose to leave God out of their dealings and encourage others to follow them are certainly only undermining their country's fortune.' Lenz, John M., *Christ in Dachau* (Roman Catholic Books, 1960), pp. 6–7.

16 'Struggle set the course of National Socialism throughout, and it supplied the most effective patterns for all its excursions into civil war, psychological and terrorist warfare, social imperialism, and finally total war followed by total collapse. Preference for violent methods is not to be explained by the impatient radicalism of a group of revolutionaries eager to implement an idea; violent struggle was itself an ideology, and if it had a goal above and beyond mere self-assertion it was the power that beckoned at its end.' Fest, Joachim C., *The Face Of The Third Reich*, pub. online at http://ourcivilisation.com/ smartboard/shop/festjc/index.htm.

17 In 1941 Martin Bormann declared Christianity and National Socialism to be irreconcilable. He poured scorn on Christian belief and doctrines that he described as unscientific, proclaiming that any reference made by National Socialists to the divine

or Almighty referred to a 'world force' of the universe to which they were biologically committed, and not to the Christian God. *Documents on Nazism 1919–1945*, ed. Jeremy Noakes; Geoffrey Pridham (London, Cape, 1974) p. 374.

18 The black, red and gold colour scheme of the Lützow Free Corps (the original Free Corps), which had been raised to fight Napoleon from all over Germany, was adopted as the flag of the student fraternities at Wartburg. A secret society, the Wehrschaft, which had been founded at Jena in 1814, adopted those same colours. They were later adopted by the revolutionaries of 1848 and eventually by the Weimar Republic.

19 Anonymous, *Persecution of the Catholic Church in the Third Reich*, (Pelican, 2008), p. 11.

20 Ibid., p. 34.

21 Ibid., p. 30–3.

22 Pois, Robert A., *National Socialism and the Religion of Nature* (Croom Helm Beckenham, 1986) p. 50.

23 *Hitler's Table Talk*, ed. Hugh Trevor-Roper, p. 679.

24 Prussia, Prince Louis Ferdinand of, *The Rebel Prince*, p. 300.

25 Ibid., p. 222.

26 Löwenstein, Prince Hurbertus, *Towards the Further Shore*, p. 54.

27 Prussia, Prince Louis Ferdinand of, *The Rebel Prince*, p. 240.

28 Dr von Habsburg quoted in Brook-Shepherd, Gordon, *Uncrowned Emperor: The Life and Times of Otto von Habsburg* (London, 2003), p. 80.

29 Metternich, Tatiana, *Tatiana* (London, 2004; first pub. 1976), p. 82.

30 Mosse, George Lachmann, *Nazi Culture, Intellectual, Cultural and Social Life in the Third Reich* (Wisconsin, 2003) p. 36.

31 Etlin, Richard A., *Art, Culture and Media under the Third Reich* (Chicago, 2002), pp. 1–5.

32 Meinecke, Friedrich, *The German Catastrophe*, trans. by Sydney B. Faye (Harvard, 1950), pp. 58–61.

33 Speer, Albert, *Inside the Third Reich* (London, 1995, first pub. 1970), p. 240.

34 See her *Secret Doctrine* for her views on race and spirituality.

35 Hamann, Brigitte; Hans Mommsen, *Hitler's Vienna: A Portrait of the Tyrant as a Young Man*, pp. 206–8.

36 Ibid., pp. 211.

37 Ibid., pp. 211–2.

38 Ibid., pp. 214.

39 Klimczuk, Stephen; Gerald Warner, *Secret Places, Hidden Sanctuaries: Uncovering Mysterious Sights, Symbols* (Stirling, 2010), pp. 66–7.

40 Speer, Albert, *Inside the Third Reich: Memoirs*, trans. by Richard Winston, Clara Winston (New York, Simon and Schuster, 1997), p. 96.

3

EUROPE AND THE WEST

While treated retrospectively as positive, the break-up of empires and the re-drawing of national boundaries following the First World War resulted in a fracturing of European unity into a multiplicity of self-serving states of dubious leadership and belligerent attitude towards their neighbours. Baron Viktor Kuchina von Schwanburg refers to the Austro-Hungarian Empire as a 'very strong economic unit', which came to an end in 1918. He goes on:

Instead of the '*Viribus unitis*' (with combined efforts) new, small, weak successor states, hostile to one another, were brought into being. These small countries soon became the prey of their powerful neighbours and with their position virtually prepared, the advancement of first the German and later Russian expansions. The dismemberment of the Habsburg Empire meant a catastrophe, primarily from the economical point of view. The railways of the successor states led to nowhere or into cul-de-sacs. At the time those were built the traffic led from Yugoslavia, Poland, Czechoslovakia, Hungary, etc, towards Vienna. The new situation, however, deprived these territories of produce for their markets. The sea ports and the Danube ports were cut off from the hinterland, which meant that everywhere the standard of living dropped. From the political point of view, also, it meant a considerable relapse: those important lands like the Carpathan basin, the valley of the Danube, etc., which were part of a great power with great ideas, belonged now to small nations with little foresight. These small nations introduced strange new ideas, alien morals, ideologies and theories which could not match the old experienced, refined and politic basis (sic) principle of the Monarchy. No doubt the Monarchy also had its faults, but while Franz Joseph was alive the empire enjoyed a great deal of prestige and authority, which was mainly due to him. The successor states on the other hand were only caricatures of the greatness of the past.[1]

The states of central and eastern Europe were dominated by territorial disputes and the politics of dictatorship. This absence of cohesion or mutual recognition of borders was an invitation to German political interference and its inevitable hegemony. Divested of royal or imperial guidance and protection, the new or reborn little nations did not become beacons of democracy but the prey of dictators. During the 1930s dictatorship rather than democracy was the norm among the states of central and eastern Europe, including the successor states to the Austro-Hungarian Empire. It is ironic that at the Munich Agreement in 1938 Britain and France left the only parliamentary democracy in central and eastern Europe to its fate, whereas a year later they went to war in support of a Polish dictatorship against invasion by a German.

In Europe democracy was the exception rather than the rule. By 1938 eighteen of the twenty-eight European states were dictatorships: Germany, Italy, Austria, Yugoslavia, Albania, Greece, Turkey, Spain, Portugal, Hungary, Switzerland, Bulgaria, Romania, Poland, Lithuania, Latvia, Estonia and the USSR (a left-wing dictatorship under Stalin). Democracies such as France, Belgium, the Netherlands, Denmark and Norway ceased to be democracies following invasion in 1940. Only the UK, Eire, Sweden and Finland remained as parliamentary democracies in Europe and only the UK remained in the war against Germany.[2] One reason for the rise of dictatorships in Europe was economic. Strong government was seen as the only way to regain prosperity and withstand the threat of international communism. Stephen Lee writes:

> By 1925 Europe's industrial production was the same as that of 1913, but her share of world trade was down from 63 per cent to 52 per cent. It was clear, therefore, that Europe had not succeeded in fully replacing the markets lost during the First World War. The United States, in fact, hoped to prevent Europe from doing so.[3]

The Road to Appeasement

Winston Churchill said, 'An appeaser is someone who feeds a crocodile and hopes it will eat him last.' It should be noted, however, that most of those who argued against appeasement and for rearmament in the 1930s were not always of that opinion, even Churchill; they just awoke to the dangers of Hitlerism and the futility of appeasing him at different times. Furthermore, there were several motives for supporting the policy of appeasement.

A number of British MPs had first-hand experience of trench warfare during the First World War and wanted to avoid a repeat of the carnage at almost all costs. A large proportion of the young men who would have become the domestic and colonial administrators of a great empire had been killed in action due to the disproportionate attrition rate of young officers. In the country at large the memory of the 'war to end all wars' was still fresh (and raw) in the minds of the people. There were painful visual reminders of it everywhere in disabled veterans and village memorials, in the numbers of widows and maiden aunts, imperial decline and a deep-pervading pessimism and scepticism in society. The view in Germany was that they hadn't lost the war, while the view in Britain and France was that they hadn't won. Militarism, imperialism and a generation blamed for the war and its bitter consequences were treated with disdain by many young men and women, whose values were intentionally different from their parents. The mood of the public was not just for peace but vehemently anti-militarism and against military spending.

This was the background of the ten-year rule that reduced defence spending based on an assumption that a new war would not occur for the next ten years and the disarmament peace conferences that dominated the inter-war years. Another factor was that application of the harsher terms of the Versailles Treaty was considered by many as unfair so long after hostilities had ceased, especially given that the Left was considered a far greater threat to world peace and national security than a prosperous Germany. Furthermore, Hitler was an unknown quantity when he first gained prominence in German politics and appeared to have adopted constitutional rather than revolutionary tactics. If many German politicians were taken in, what hope the British and French? British ambassador in Germany, Sir Neville Henderson, believed that a happy and prosperous Germany was a 'vital British interest'.[4] If a strong government didn't come to power in Germany, it was thought, there was a real possibility that it would fall prey to Russian communism, its neighbours then following. Far better, it was thought, that Germany became a bulwark against the spread of Russian communism than weak and prey to Bolshivik revolution within. Another reason for the policy of appeasement continuing into the late 1930s was the weakness of the military position of Britain, and even France, as compared with a swiftly rearming Germany. By 1938 Henderson had woken up and realised that military efficiency was now the god to which all Germans must offer sacrifice, 'It is not the army, but the whole German nation which is being prepared for war'.[5] Germany, he said, could be neither prosperous nor happy till she recovered her individual and personal freedom of life and thought, 'and has learnt that the true responsibility of strength is to protect and not oppress the weak'.[6]

Appeasement and the Milner Group

When Hitler first came to power in 1933 politicians (of the real and the armchair variety) in Britain and France were not too sure what to make of him. Some continued to regard the new regime as if it were composed of patriots and democrats like themselves, but with understandable grievances about how Germany had been treated – and was continuing to be treated – by the terms of the Treaty of Versailles following the First World War. Like many Germans, the spectre of a Bolshevik takeover of central Europe was a very real and terrifying prospect, so a strong and united Germany was actually highly desirable as a first line of defence against the red threat. This does not mean that all politicians were blinded to the real nature of Hitler and his government, however, or all seduced by their pacific language and promises. Conservative MP John Davidson wrote that although British Prime Minister Stanley Baldwin wanted peace, it was not to be at any price and the UK would not make sacrifices to Germany in order to have peace. Baldwin regarded the Anglo-German Naval Agreement from 1935 not as an expression of friendship or trust, but as a test of German intentions.[7] 'SB [Stanley Baldwin] realised very early that Hitler was an evil man,' Davidson recalled, 'I don't think that at any time he believed in Hitler as an honest man, but we all thought that there was a possibility of his being deposed by a military coup … B's attitude was one of retaining our strength, but he also had a really profound hope of peace.'[8]

A White Paper on Defence was presented to the UK Parliament in March 1935 inspiring a vote of censure by the Labour Party, which argued against a build-up of armaments and increased air power.[9] British policy was not uniform, however, or consistent. It evolved piecemeal with some rearmament strictly for the coast-line defence of the UK, but with conciliatory language to placate a vocal peace movement and no enthusiasm whatsoever to risk any military involvement in European politics. It was not until 1939 that it became clear that Britain needed to pay for a possible expeditionary force as a deterrent against German aggression. The reluctance of any nation that had suffered during the First World War ('to end all wars') to risk going through it all again should not be underestimated.

During the 1930s a small group of middle and upper-middle-class Englishmen were accused of being Nazi sympathisers and having considerable influence within the British Establishment. Known as the 'Cliveden Set' from a reference to their activities in the left-wing journal *The Week*, by Claud Cockburn, who wanted to depict this group in class terms, the Cliveden Set contained members of 'Milner's Kindergarten' – a group of young men who had worked for Alfred Lord Milner in South Africa as followers of the Cecil Rhodes dream of a British Imperial Federation of the Commonwealth allied with the USA and Germany.[10] The Milner Group concerned itself with the English-speaking world, together with the rest of the empire, as a distinct group that ultimately intended universal dominion through federal world government. They were not traditional impe-rialists as such, they were world federalists; a world that would they hoped be governed by a dominant Anglo-Saxon elite and based on the English-speaking nations and British colonial Africa. They were influenced by theories of social Darwinism and eugenics that fed into their political and imperialist aspirations and elitism. The group consisted mainly of young career diplomats and journalists.

One of its leading members and chief exponents of world federalism was Lord Lothian. He had helped draft the Versailles Treaty and was keen on the revision of its 'unfair' restrictions. The set, such as it was, revolved around American-born Viscount Waldorf Astor and his wife Nancy, after whose country house the 'set' were named and in which they often met. The biggest impediment to their plans during the 1920s and '30s was conceived to be communism. National Socialism was also regarded as loathsome but useful if it could be pitted against their principle enemy in the East.

To this end it was believed that the 1919 Treaty of Versailles should be revised to allow Germany to be strong enough to be a bulwark to their Russian rival. Versailles was regarded as having been wrong and unfair. At Versailles, it was thought, the Americans had been naïve, the French acquisitive and the British weak. For the Milner Group, in their Cliveden incarnation, appeasement was the tool. Although their influence extended right into the heart of government, they were not the cohesive group with a common agenda of their portrayal in the press; they were just as unlikely to have had any great influence on policy. Lord Halifax was associated with the group and Neville Chamberlain dined at Cliveden, Astor's house, several times, but Chamberlain needed no encouragement to follow a policy of appeasement that had broad support in the country. In any case, not even Viscount Astor can be described as anything like a fascist sympathiser; on the single occasion that he met Hitler he told the dictator that it was imperative that he stop persecuting the Jews if he hoped for any improvement in Anglo-German relations. This sent the Führer into a white rage. Garvin was a vocal supporter of rearmament from 1933 and Lord Lothian rejected appeasement when the Nazi's barbarism and aggressive anti-Semitism became obvious.[11] Other members of the circle believed that they could control Hitler and use his declared agenda, occupying territory (living space) in the communist East, to benefit their own cause. They thought they could prevent German military takeovers of his non-communist neighbours. In 1938, however, it became obvious to them that they had been misled. They were deluded into underestimating Hitler very much as von Papen and his supporters had been. They were also deluded into thinking that they could negotiate with the dictator and prevent him from using force to 'revise' and reverse Versailles by 'reuniting' Germans with the Reich, without doing so from a position of British military might and the threat of its imminent use.

But Britain was militarily weak, not only from formal disarmament, but also from its response to the Great Depression, its aftermath, and the politicians' reluctance to build up national defence at the expense of ongoing economic recovery and public (feel-good) popularity. Military expenditure was not popular; people who had survived the 'war to end all wars' were not about to think about the possibility of another – they weren't playing that game any more. As a consequence, when Chamberlain and his team sat down with Hitler to discuss the Sudeten Germans and Czechoslovakia they could only play the hand they had been dealt.

Let's be clear, there was very little, if any, sympathy with the Nazis by anyone in the British ruling caste, but there was a lot of sympathy for Germany. The unfair clauses of Versailles needed revision it was thought, reparations ended and German national identity and pride restored. Unfortunately however, whether or not Hitler's rise to power was a consequence of Germany's unfair treatment, he was not about to reveal a virtuous nature and temper his policies as a result of sympathy and reasonable treatment by British diplomats and politicians.

Unfortunately, much of Western diplomacy in the 1930s was based on the politics of disarmament as a way of achieving lasting peace. If nations could be confined to purely defensive forces without the ability to threaten their neighbours, it was thought the world would be a safe place in which to live. Under the Versailles restrictions Germany was hardly likely to be able to be in a position to threaten the vast land forces of France even if it did rearm. However, in 1932, Englishman Cecil F. Melville had written a book, *The Russian Face of Germany*, exposing an illegal German rearmament programme, which revealed that factories had been established in Russia and that from 1921 till the time of writing: 'Russia has been able, thanks to Germany, to equip herself with all kinds of arms and munitions.' Meanwhile, thanks to her factories in Russia built by companies such as Krupp's of Essen, Melville continues, 'Germany has been able to assure herself not only of secret supplies of war material and the training of officers and other ranks in the use of this material, but also, in the event of war, the possession of the best stocked arsenals in Russia.' Melville believed that should Hitler assume power Stalin would, as a realist, continue to do business with Germany. Additionally, considering that the German-Soviet programme had continued unchanged whomever was in power in Germany irrespective of their political orientation, even Hitler would continue the arrangement – especially as his external aims were similar to the nationalists and military leaders in Germany who had initiated the arrangement.[12]

A major problem for the Allies addressing the crisis over Czechoslovakia and the Sudeten Germans was a lack of trust and common purpose among them. Chamberlain wrote:

> With Franco winning in Spain by the aid of German guns and Italian planes, with a French government in which one cannot have the slightest confidence, and which I suspect to be in closish touch with our Opposition, with the Russians stealthily and cunningly pulling all the strings behind the scenes to get us involved in a war with Germany (our secret service doesn't spend all its time looking out of the window), and finally with a Germany flushed with triumph, and all too conscious of her power, the prospect looked black indeed.

He dismissed the idea of a 'grand alliance' because logistically Britain could not prevent Germany from taking over Czechoslovakia. It would simply be a pretext for going to war with Germany. 'That we could not think of unless we had a reasonable prospect of being able to beat her to her knees in a reasonable time, and of that I see no sign.' Therefore he felt that Britain could give no guarantees to Czechoslovakia.[13]

British attitudes were further influenced by the scary possibility of a military alliance between Germany, Italy and Japan, which was not lost on the British chiefs of staff who warned Chamberlain in May 1937:

> We cannot foresee the time when our defence forces will be strong enough to safeguard our trade, territory and vital interests against Germany, Italy and Japan at the same time … We cannot exaggerate the importance from the point of view of Imperial Defence of any political or international action which could be taken to reduce the number of our potential enemies and to gain the support of potential allies.[14]

Had Britain and France taken a stand on the Italian annexation of Abyssinia (Ethiopia) and/or over German and Italian interference in the Spanish Civil War, such a show of strength may have averted a general European war later. However, for politicians at the time whose vision was confined to ground level (without the benefit of retrospect) and whose judgement was based on mis-placed assumptions and what was perceived to be the limits of public acceptance, the doubtful benefits of intervention with limited and stretched resources didn't seem worth the risk.

The French government, however, did at least seriously contemplate an alter-native to leaving Czechoslovakia to its fate. The French Permanent Committee of National Defence met on 15 March 1938 under presidency of Édouard Daladier, Minister of National Defence and War, to discuss aid for Czechoslovakia in the event of German aggression and possible French intervention in Spain. It was reported that the British had asked them, 'You say you will help Czechoslovakia, but in practical terms what will you do?' It was agreed that no direct help was possible, but mobilising troops and deploying them on the border, Germany it was thought, would have to move troops towards its frontier with France so depleting such forces that were intended to annex Czechoslovakia. The chief of the defence staff said that this could be reinforced by an attack across the border, but would probably result in lengthy operations. The prime minister, Leon Blum, declared that Russia would also intervene in support of the Czechs, but the chief of the defence staff questioned what effective help the Russians could give, espe-cially as it would be conditional on the attitude of Poland and Romania whose territories lay in between.[15]

On 22 February 1938 Winston Churchill warned against continued appease-ment, recalling in the House of Commons a grave and largely irreparable injury to the world security that had taken place in the years 1932–35:

In those days I ventured repeatedly to submit to the House the maxim that the grievances of the vanquished should be redressed before the disarmament of the victors was begun. But the reverse was done. Then was the time to make concessions to the German people and to the German ruler. Then was the time when they would have had their real value. But no attempt was made. All that was done was to neglect our own defences and endeavour to encourage the French to follow a course equally imprudent. The next opportunity when these Sybilline Books were presented to us was when the reoccupation of the Rhineland took place at the beginning of 1936. Now we know that a firm stand by France and Britain with the other Powers associated with them at that time, and with the authority of the League of Nations, would have been followed by the immediate evacuation of the Rhineland without the shedding of a drop of blood, and the effects of that might have been blessed beyond all compare, because it would have enabled the more prudent elements in the German Army to regain their proper position and would not have given to the political head of Germany that enormous ascendancy which has enabled him to move forward. On the morrow of such a success we could have made a great and generous settlement.

Now we are in a moment when a third move is made; but when that opportunity does not present itself in the same favourable manner. Austria has been laid in thrall, and we do not know whether Czechoslovakia will not suffer a similar attack. Let me remind honourable Members when they talk about Germany's desire for peace, that this small country has declared that it will resist, and if it resists that may well light up the flames of war, the limits of which no man can predict. It is because we have lost these opportunities of standing firm, of having strong united forces and a good heart, and a resolute desire to defend the right and afterwards to do generously as the result of strength; it is because we have lost these successive opportunities which have presented themselves, that, when our resources are less and the dangers greater, we have been brought to this pass. I predict that the day will come when at some point or other on some issue or other you will have to make a stand, and I pray God that when that day comes we may not find that through an unwise policy we are left to make that stand alone.[16]

On 24 March Churchill continued to warn:

A country like ours, possessed of immense territory and wealth, whose defences have been neglected, cannot avoid war by dilating upon its horrors, or even by a continuous display of pacific qualities, or by ignoring the fate of the victims of aggression elsewhere. War will be avoided, in present circumstances, only by the accumulation of deterrents against the aggressor.[17]

Austen Chamberlain, Neville's half-brother, had predicted with unnerving accuracy and insight:

> If Austria perishes Czechoslovakia becomes indefensible, the whole of the Balkans becomes submitted to a gigantic new influence. Then the old German dream of a Central Europe ruled by and subject to Berlin becomes a reality ... with incalculable consequences not only for our country but for the whole empire.[18]

Although he has been regarded as a supporter of appeasement, it has been revealed that Lord Halifax, influenced by his permanent under-secretary, Sir Alexander Cadogan, persuaded the Cabinet to reject the terms, which Chamberlain brought back from his second meeting with Hitler at Godesberg. This brought about a crisis that led to the prime minister's (in)famous flight to Munich. Furthermore, after Chamberlain's *triumphant* return, Halifax urged him not to call a general election to take advantage of public relief but to include critics such as Churchill and Eden in government and, if possible, some Labour and Liberal members. Chamberlain did not call an election but neither did he broaden his government. Halifax became increasingly distressed by reports of Nazi atrocities, especially against the Jews, and concluded that German expansion eastwards would not bring peace but would merely bring those countries into the German economic orbit. In January 1939 Halifax proposed talks with the French to prepare for a possible war with Germany and Italy. He was also behind Chamberlain's guarantee of Polish independence in a speech in Birmingham on 17 March 1939, and argued for an alliance with the Soviet Union to underwrite it and give it military realism.

Neville Chamberlain was painted retrospectively as an appeaser, but in the late 1930s his additional spending on defence was regarded as unduly provocative towards Germany by some on the Labour benches of the House of Commons, who cast him in the role of warmonger. Appeasement had not been so much of a choice for many in the UK government, but an admission that in 1938 Britain was woefully unprepared for a European war. During the Munich Crisis Göring warned the British ambassador in Berlin, Sir Neville Henderson, that if Britain were to go to war with Germany over Czechoslovakia, 'there would be very few Czechs left alive and very little of London left standing' afterwards. He then gave a scarily accurate assessment of Britain's inadequate air defences including a paucity of anti-aircraft guns. Germany's Luftwaffe, he revealed, had a numerical superiority over the air forces of Britain, France, Belgium and Czechoslovakia combined.[19] It is highly unlikely than any British prime minister, not even Churchill, would have felt comfortable calling, or indeed would have been able to call, Hitler's bluff at that time, lest the dictator called his with predictably dire consequences.[20] The Cliveden Set may have been influential, but even without their alleged influence Britain's ability and inclination to act decisively to prevent or punish Nazi expansionism in the 1930s would have been limited. Scott

Kelly points out that the Labour landslide election victory of 1945 was not due to almost universal acclaim of Labour policy or an unpopular prime minister. Churchill remained extremely popular, but the Conservatives as a party were tarred with an appeasement brush encouraged by the Leftist press and books such as *The Guilty Men*, and suffered due to the continued inclusion of some of the *guilty* on the front benches.[21]

On 6 February 1939 Daladier told American official William C. Bullitt that he fully expected to be betrayed by the British and added that it was the customary fate of their allies. He felt that England had become so feeble and senile that the British would give away every possession of their friends rather than stand up to Germany and Italy. Göring, he said, had told Daladier, 'Why should France continue to tie herself to a decayed old nation like England – a rouged old maid trying to pretend that she is still young and vigorous and capable of being a satisfactory partner to anyone.' He proposed that France join with Germany in 'finishing off England', and that the British Empire should then be divided between France and Germany. Daladier said he replied that this 'sounded very pleasant but the moment the British Empire was finished France would be the next morsel for Germany'. Besides which Daladier thought that Göring's friendliness was based on a recognition that the French army was the only real land fighting force in Europe then opposed to Germany.[22]

The terms that Hitler offered Britain in 1940 can be seen to have been based on discussions that Ribbentrop and others had with the Milner/Cliveden Group, recognising their separate agenda as well as their mutual interests. Even the approaches of the embryonic resistance movement made suggestions that they believed the British wanted to hear regarding a Hitler-less Germany that would was still prepared to take on the Russian communists. The recipient of these (both Nazi and anti-Nazi) overtures, however, was a completely different administration with a radically revised agenda. The Milner Group thought that Germany would save Britain and the West from the USSR, whereas in fact the USSR can be said to have saved Britain and the West from Nazi Germany, diverting enough of its troops to allow the Allies to land invasion forces in Europe in 1944.

There were men of high moral principles in England who believed that Germany had been badly mistreated by the Versailles Treaty and that their territorial claims were legitimate. Recognition of this old sin, however, obscured the current sins of the Nazi regime, and retrospective atonement could not transform nor tame the beast in Berlin. This misplaced moral attitude disarmed Great Britain more effectively than the conferences of Washington, Geneva or Locarno ever could or did.

Peter Viereck, in his book of 1942, wrote that he did not believe the principle behind the Munich Agreement was in itself bad, but, 'What was scandalously bad was that the British and French governments applied it to Hitler, with whom peace was pragmatically improbable, instead of the earlier Social Democrat and Centrist regime.' Brüning and Schleicher had wanted to establish a Liberal-Conservative monarchy in Germany to replace an 'insufficiently anchored Republic', which they had established in part only to please President Woodrow Wilson. 'Their liberal Western solution for revising the Versailles Republic was,' wrote Viereck, 'racing neck and neck with Hitler's dictatorial anti-Western solution. In 1933, by only a slim margin and perhaps not inevitably, Hitler won the race.'[23]

As in every age including our own, persons of influence are subject to their own influences and ideologies that have become attached to them. Not just left or right-wing ideas, but all sorts of national, supra-national, and scientific prejudice. In the 1930s writers and politicians bore the emotional and psychological scars of the First World War and at the same time wore the dreams and aspirations of peace, reconciliation, federalism, socialism, and national or racial dominance or preservation. Democracy for all its undoubted benefits and strengths was a huge lumbering ship to turn around in a storm in comparison with more authoritarian forms of government in the 1930s. Consequently disarmament and appeasement remained the policies of preference, whereas supporters of rearmament and a tough line with the dictatorships, although they slowly gained in number, were exceptions. Even Churchill had been a poacher-turned-gamekeeper when it came to rearmament; he was a disarmer in the 1920s. There was no one in Europe who did not see the maimed, blinded and scarred on a daily basis, or who could fail to notice the women in black and the maiden aunts in every family. Nations were in shock from a world war, economic collapse and Great Depression. Diplomacy, it seemed, had achieved great things after the First World War: the Kellogg-Briand Pact, the Washington Conference, Geneva and Locarno. The world appeared to be moving away from war, military alliances, and the expectation and preparation for war, towards peace, civilisation, Christian morality, and a bright new modern era without fear. Those who warned of the possibility of war were treated in the same way as those who prepared for or glorified it. Unfortunately, it was also the age of immerging dictatorships when democracy started to look old-fashioned and against the national interest. It is easy, in retrospect, to point a finger at those most identifiable appeasers (an insult that was once a compliment), but they were of their generation and far from rare – they responded to public opinion, which continued to move away from military might and nationalism until the failure of the policy. The electorate, having been convinced by post-war promises of peace, prosperity and improved living conditions were unlikely to support an expensive rearmament programme that threatened their economic security and well-being so soon after the Depression for reasons by which they were unconvinced. They had peace; it was the job of the politicians to ensure that peace continued. Once war became inevitable, however, the culpability of the general public was covered by the blame they placed on their former political servants.

Pitted against appeasement in Parliament were two Conservative groups, the 'old guard' around Churchill and 'the glory boys' around Anthony Eden. Less formally, the redoubtable Duchess of Athol stood fully against fascism in all its forms and not only argued for British military involvement in the Spanish Civil War on the side of the republicans, but resigned the whip and took the stewardship of the Chiltern Hundreds in protest at the Munich Agreement between Chamberlain and Hitler in 1938. Duff Cooper also resigned from the government over Munich. Cooper turned social Darwinism on its head, in 1939 he wrote:

> The doctrine of the survival of the fittest may be sound when applied to the animal world in general and it may even be sound when applied to human beings if by 'the fittest' we mean the most brutal and the most pitiless, but the study of the greatness and decay of culture must lead to the conclusion that the higher civilisation inevitably perishes at the hands of the lower.
>
> The pseudo-philosophy of the barbarian leads him to consider war one of the stern necessities of existence and an agreeable alternative to his usual existence. Civilisation means individuality and healthy scepticism and dissention. It is indeed melancholy to feel bound to bring such an indictment against a great people, who in the past have made numberless contributions to the literature, art and science of the world, but I hold it just and necessary to state plainly that a regime which begins by the public burning of books, which continues by abolishing freedom of thought and of speech, which persecutes religion and which seeks by cruelty to exterminate an ancient race that gave Christianity to the world amongst other benefits, is barbarous in the worst meaning of the word and is the enemy of true civilisation.[24]

He reminded his readers that a hatred of war had been inculcated on the people of France and Britain since 1918 as opposed to Germany where military strength was coveted.[25] Anthony Eden summed up in the British House of Commons the argument against appeasement of Nazi Germany: 'Surely the House will be agreed that foreign affairs cannot indefinitely be continued on the basis of "stand and deliver!" Successive surrenders bring only successive humiliation, and they, in their turn, more humiliating demands.'[26] Almost everyone knew that sooner or later Britain would have to fight. When and how it would fight remained in debate.

Leo Amery was a vocal opponent of appeasement and it was his words in the House of Commons that marked the end of Chamberlain's tenure as Prime Minister of Great Britain. On 24 August 1939 he said in the House of Commons:

> We have never stood in graver danger than we stand to-day. It may be that a show of firmness, of action, might yet influence, if not Herr Hitler, possibly Italy. I doubt it. I believe the mind of the dictators to-day is that they have more than a good chance of crushing us, that all the odds are in their favour and that they are prepared to risk it. Therefore, the only thing we can do is to face up to

that situation frankly and whole heartedly and take now, without a moment's delay, the action which is necessary.

In 1939, as Britain stared into the jaws of imminent war, Halifax spoke to his peers in the House of Lords:

> There are some who say that the fate of European nations is no concern of ours, and that we should not look far beyond our own frontiers. But those who thus argue forget, I think, that in failing to uphold the liberties of others we run great risk of betraying the principle of liberty itself, and with it our own freedom and independence. We have built up a society with values which are accepted not only in this country but over vast areas of the world. If we stand by and see these values set at nought the security of all those things on which life itself depends seems, to my judgment, to be undermined, and that is a fundamental matter on which I scarcely think that there will be any difference of opinion.

When war broke out, Chamberlain spelled out his core beliefs in a message to the German nation, 'In this war we are not fighting against you, the German people, for whom we have no bitter feeling, but against a tyrannous and forsworn regime which has betrayed not only its own people but the whole of Western civilisation and all that you and we hold dear.' The prime minister concluded solemnly, 'May God defend the right!'[27]

Eugenics programmes in the USA led the way for the rest and were copied in Germany.[28] Social Darwinism was widespread in Europe and the English-speaking world. The Milner Group could be said to have been typical of a type: the modern, materialist middle-class administrator, banker or industrialist of European descent. Middle-ranking administrators whose responsibility it was to administer first-world nations and their empires were an elite group in themselves. They wanted to construct nations and their governing elites in their own image, which they were deluded into thinking was at the vanguard of evolutionary perfection and the apotheosis of civilisation and culture. The pseudo-anthropological position of the social Darwinists was a materialist counter-religion, where the dominant creatures of the dominant tribes of the dominant races of the earth thought of themselves as gods – with rights of governance over all the species they regarded as being beneath their evolutionary attainment. Such blasphemy was perpetrated in the name of science and/or the Enlightenment.

The two men who were the grandfathers of appeasement with Germany were Cecil Rhodes, Liberal Prime Minister of Cape Town, and South African Foreign Minister Alfred Viscount Milner. Rhodes argued for a continuous expansion of the British Empire as he believed the Anglo-Saxon race was destined for greatness. He believed that the more of the world that the Anglo-Saxons inhabited the better for the human race as a whole, and wanted Canada, Australia, New

Zealand and Cape Colony to be represented in the British Parliament. He also wanted the USA to rejoin the empire. The Rhodes Scholarship that he founded was open to Americans and Germans as he believed that Great Britain, the USA and Germany together could dominate the world and so ensure peace. He had great admiration for Germany and the kaiser personally too.

Tatiana Metternich believed that a British 'romantic streak' accounted for their unrealistic attitude whenever political theories were discussed. She remembered that at Oxford, where she often visited cousins or friends, their views on communism, 'Russia or anything concerning the evil side of Soviet reality such as the purges, the camps and so on were brushed aside with supercilious contempt. "You're obviously prejudiced," we would hear.' She later reflected whether this did not explain the careers of Philby, Burgess, Maclean and others.[29]

Malthus, Darwin and the Influence of Nineteenth-Century Materialism and Socio-Biological Theory

The Revd Thomas Robert Malthus was son of Daniel Malthus of the Rookery, Dorking, Surrey, UK, a friend of David Hume and of Jean Jaques Rousseau, and executor of the latter's will. Malthus put forward the proposition that unrestrained population growth would outgrow the agricultural means to sustain it, and therefore a perfect society would be impossible without a limit on population. The writings of Malthus had an unfortunate effect on social welfare in England. Tory paternalism came to be seen as encouraging population increase, so as a result the new Poor Law came into being. Although Malthus himself opposed the Poor Laws, workhouses replaced other forms of relief by law with few exceptions. Malthus believed that inculcating middle-class values on the poorer classes and improving their standard of living in an economic levelling up would encourage smaller families and fewer children born out of wedlock. Charles Darwin was greatly influenced by reading Malthus' works.

Erasmus Darwin, the grandfather of Charles and of Francis Galton, the originator of eugenics, wrote anticipating and providing the basis for the work of his grandson:

> Would it be too bold to imagine that, in the great length of time since the earth began to exist, perhaps millions of ages before the commencement of the history of mankind would it be too bold to imagine that all warm-blooded animals have arisen from one living filament, which the great First Cause endued with animality, with the power of acquiring new parts, attended with new propensities, directed by irritations, sensations, volitions and associations, and thus possessing the faculty of continuing to improve by its own inherent activity, and

of delivering down these improvements by generation to its posterity, world without end!³⁰

Charles Darwin's cousin, Francis Galton, not only invented eugenics but was also the father of psychometrics. Galton described eugenics as 'the science which deals with all influences that improve the inborn qualities of a race; also with those that develop them to the utmost advantage'. His views tended towards a genetic aristocracy based on selective breeding, an idea pursued with vigour by Nazi eugenicists. It is particularly unfortunate that Galton continually used the word 'race' in relation to eugenics rather than 'national stock' or 'individual characteristics within family groups', or similar.

Galton had no professional admiration of the hereditary aristocracy, which he thought a 'disastrous institution' for 'our valuable races'. He observed that younger sons of peers either did not marry or married heiresses whose families were demonstrably not over fertile having only produced them. As a result offspring was not likely to be numerous.³¹

Although Darwin's own ideas steered away from social forms of his theories, he nevertheless endorsed the work of his cousin, 'We now know, through the admirable work of Mr Galton, that genius … tends to be inherited.'³² Citing Galton, Darwin stated that because the 'poor and reckless' tended to marry and have children earlier than men of 'a superior class' the women they married tended to have been younger and in their prime, bearing a larger number of stronger and more vigorous babies than the middle classes:

> Thus the reckless, degraded, and often vicious members of society, tend to increase at a quicker rate than the provident and generally virtuous members. Or as Mr Greg puts the case: 'The careless, squalid, unaspiring Irishman multiplies like rabbits: the frugal, foreseeing, self-respecting, ambitious Scot, stern in his faith, sagacious and disciplined in his intelligence, passes his best years in struggle and in celibacy, marries late and leaves few behind him. Given a land peopled by a thousand Saxons and a thousand Celts – and in a dozen generations five-sixths of the population would be Celts, but five-sixths of the property, of the power, of the intellect, would belong to the one-sixth of Saxons that remained. In the eternal "struggle for existence", it would be the inferior and LESS favoured race that had prevailed – and prevailed by virtue not of its good qualities but of its faults'.

Darwin had a particular regard for the pioneering spirit as a source of good breeding stock for future generations:

> There is apparently much truth in the belief that the wonderful progress of the United States, as well as the character of the people, are the results of natural

selection; for the more energetic, restless, and courageous men from all parts of Europe have emigrated during the last ten or twelve generations to that great country, and have there succeeded best.[33]

Herbert Spencer, the philosopher and biologist who first coined the phrase 'survival of the fittest' was secretary of the (scientific) Derby Philosophical Society, which had been founded by Erasmus Darwin. He was a follower of the teachings of (Erasmus) Darwin and Jean-Baptiste Lamarck's early evolutionary theory and coined his (in)famous phrase after reading Charles Darwin's evolutionary theory. He attempted to merge John Stuart Mill's theories about thought with those of phrenology and so explain the workings of the human mind in physiological terms. Another Darwin associate and close friend was John Lubbock, an archaeologist (as well as banker, philosopher and biologist), who invented the terms Paleolithic and Neolithic. He was a member of the X Club with William Henry Huxley and other scientific followers of Darwin. Lubbock believed that, 'As a result of natural selection, human groups had become different from each other, not only culturally, but also in their biological capacities to utilise culture.'

Malthus, Erasmus Darwin and Charles Darwin surely had the highest motives and positive expectations as regards their theorising. However, Darwin's relatives and friends were not so constrained by Christian morality when it came to the promotion of eugenics and social Darwinism.[34] Darwin's cousin, Francis Galton, referred to race in discussing the inheritance of intelligence and eugenics. His friend and biographer Karl Pearson studied in Berlin and Heidelberg and promoted the idea of war to eliminate 'inferior' races. He wrote:

> History shows me one way, and one way only, in which a high state of civilization has been produced, namely, the struggle of race with race, and the survival of the physically and mentally fitter race. If you want to know whether the lower races of man can evolve a higher type, I fear the only course is to leave them to fight it out among themselves, and even then the struggle for existence between individual and individual, between tribe and tribe, may not be supported by that physical selection due to a particular climate on which probably so much of the Aryan's success depended ...

He was a well-known figure in Germany. He believed that acquired characteristics could not be inherited and therefore it was pointless in trying to improve the vulgar and unintelligent. Pearson saw the triumphs of European empire in terms of social Darwinism:

> The path of progress is strewn with the wrecks of nations; traces are everywhere to be seen of the hecatombs of inferior races, and of victims who found not the narrow way to perfection. Yet these dead people are, in very truth, the

stepping stones on which mankind has arisen to the higher intellectual and deeper emotional life of today.[35]

His attitude towards the peoples of Africa, whom he claimed had not produced a civilisation 'in the least comparable with the Aryan', was supportive of expansion and dominion rather than global duty and the benefits of trade and interaction. He said, 'Educate and nurture them as you will, I do not believe that you will succeed in modifying the stock. These sentiments had the approval of well-placed commentators, scientists and politicians in Britain, the USA and all of the future allies against Hitler's Germany in the years before he plunged the world into war. One cannot blame the far Right in these countries, for socialists and liberals were similarly affected.

Karl Pearson subscribed to a version of socialism based on Fitch's imperative of subordinating the mass of citizens to the welfare of the nation state. Daniel Kelves explains, 'Pearson began to equate morality with the advancement of social evolution, the outcome of the Darwinian struggle with the ascendancy of the fittest nation, and the achievement of fitness with a nationalist socialism.'[36] Pearson did not believe that intelligence could be created by education, but must be bred. Therefore, he saw little point in expanding education. Natural selection had, he believed, been replaced by reproductive selection favouring the most fertile rather than the most fit. He believed that reductions in infant mortality, free medical treatment, restrictions of the working week and higher wages merely encouraged the reproduction of the unfit.[37] Pearson was a statistical mathematician whose book *The Grammar of Science*, which dealt with the relativity of time and space, had a profound influence on the young Albert Einstein.

In 1904 Galton committed £500 a year to University College London for a Research Fellowship in National Eugenics, and in 1911 UCL received £45,000 in Galton's will to establish a Galton Eugenics Professorship. Karl Pearson was awarded the chair. One cannot blame Darwin for all of the ills of the twentieth century, but the materialist mindset misapplied his theories in a social and racial context. Furthermore, the apparent certainty of science removed the certainty of life's meaning in a higher context in the minds of many people and replaced it with an apparently meaningless struggle for existence before, during and after the First World War of 1914–18. Whole worlds had collided in internecine brutality, followed by cultural pessimism, emptiness and a meaningless search for a materialist Valhalla.

Francis Galton believed that artificial selection and selective breeding could be applied to humans as well as animals as a way of reversing a perceived tendency for intelligence to be bred out of a civilization. This was because the advantage that civilization and philanthropy afforded the poorer classes led to a higher birth rate among the group compared with the (assumed) more intelligent upper and middle classes. These assumptions somewhat echoed Malthus.

Social Darwinism and racism drip-fed National Socialism from a number of different sources. For example, the writings of Joseph-Arthur comte de Gobineau (1816–82) were a considerable influence on race theory. Gobineau was not a real count, but nevertheless belonged to an aristocratic French family. A diplomat, literary critic and writer, he developed a theory of race that earned him, however inaccurately, the title 'father of racism'. In 1855 he published *Essai sur l'inégalité des races humaines*, which claimed a superiority of the white races above the others and, in particular, celebrated the Aryan race as the most civilised. It cautioned that Aryans should not intermarry with members of other races and that miscegenation would dilute the strain and lead to a loss in its creative vitality and subsequently its corruption and destruction. His theories influenced Wagner (whom he knew), Nietzsche and Hitler, who paraphrased the Frenchman in one or two of his speeches.

Another influence on Nazism was Houston Stewart Chamberlain (1855–1927), a Germanophile Englishman who was an admirer of Wagner and deeply influenced and inspired by Gobineau. Although he did not meet the composer he married Wagner's daughter Eva. In his writings Chamberlain ascribed the moral, scientific and technological superiority of Western civilisation to the influence of the Germanic (Aryan) races: the most 'highly gifted group'. He claimed that opponents of the Germanic race included both Jews and the Roman Catholic Church who were fighting a racial war against it.

A supporter of Wilhelm II, Chamberlain sided with Germany during the First World War, regarding his home country as having betrayed the Germanic race. He met Hitler afterwards and sent him a letter of support. Chamberlain is mentioned in *Mein Kampf*, but Hitler's letters to the English-born writer are lost. There seems little doubt that Hitler was influenced by both Gobineau and Chamberlain, as were the top tier of the Third Reich to some extent. Chamberlain repeatedly claimed that Jesus was not a Jew and believed that the Old Testament should be removed from the Bible. According to his world-view, the Church of Luther was the true Church reflecting what the Aryan Jesus had preached.

In 1930s Germany natural medicine and diet were encouraged in the interests of maintaining the genetic health of the stock. Wholemeal bread and organic produce free of genetic poisons such as artificial flavourings and preservatives and heavy metal traces, became the foods of choice and other environmental poisons were excluded as much as possible for the sake of racial health. Environmental science was encouraged as a way of preserving the genetic health of the German breeding stock. Hitler was warned that DDT was useless and potentially dangerous to health.[38] Robert Proctor points out that at the end of the war thousands of American and Swiss cigarettes were smuggled into Germany, so ending a Nazi anti-smoking experiment that had a subsequent, though short-lived, positive effect on incidents of lung cancer – especially among former members of the armed services.[39]

The word 'ecology' was first coined by Ernst Haeckel, who believed that the human races originated independently and are at different stages of evolution. Haeckel also stated that 'politics is applied biology', a quote used by Nazi propagandists. The Nazi party used not only Haeckel's quotes, but also Haeckel's apparent justifications for racism, nationalism and social Darwinism. Environmental science, nature reserves and animal welfare were encouraged by the Nazi hierarchy. The Nazis promoted natural complimentary medicine to support rather than replace conventional medicine. They sustained an aggressive anti-smoking campaign right up until the end of the war, having discovered the link between smoking and lung cancer and looked at a number of potential cures. They introduced restrictions on tobacco advertising and smoking in public places, including smoking bans on city trains, trams and buses. Dietary causes and potential cures for cancer were explored. Raw food was considered beneficial as was fasting, fruit, milk, bismuth, gold, iodine, magnesium, potassium and selenium. German scientists also looked at vitamin therapies, acid-alkaline balance in the diet and the influence of oxygen, as well as the adverse effects of life-threatening contaminants.[40]

The Nazis also introduced bans on asbestos, pesticides and food dyes. Nazi nutritionists favoured healthy workplaces with a diet free of petrochemical dyes and preservatives; Nazi doctors cautioned against x-rays and over-medication. Many Nazis were environmentalists and/or vegetarians. Soya beans were called Nazi beans and bakeries were ordered to produce wholemeal bread, which was considered to be healthier than the popular white varieties as it was full of vitamins and fibre, and free of artificial ingredients.[41] The SS took over most of Germany's mineral springs and medicinal herb gardens were planted in concentration camps. The prisoners at Dachau were ordered to produce organic honey.[42]

Robert Proctor asserts that their motivation, however, was racial: the 'sanitising' and de-toxification of the German race. The Waffen SS were encouraged to be non-drinking, non-smoking vegetarians. Rudolf Hess was an advocate of herbalism and homeopathy. Himmler opposed artificial foods and additives. He complained that Germans were in the hands of food companies whose economic clout and advertising enabled them to determine what the German people could and could not eat. He complained about canned food, refined flour and sugar and white bread. He said that after the war 'energetic' steps would be taken to prevent the 'ruin' of the people by the food industries.[43]

Nazi science cannot all be disregarded as anti-science or pseudo-science; much of it included the cutting-edge scientific research of its day. Science, however, goes to the money. Political and economic priorities dictate research, not some nebulous quest for scientific truth. Those who pay the piper today are government departments with agendas on climate change and food and energy supplies, pharmaceutical companies and oil companies. In 1930s Germany it was race theory, eugenics and social Darwinist research that got government support and funding.

Science is not a moral code, and as a practice does not contain an implicit morality. Fire is something that can warm, cook, burn and destroy depending on its use.

Royalty and Selective Breeding

Were not the royal and noble families of Europe themselves indulging in selective breeding in their marriage arrangements? If not, marriages like that of the Archduke Franz Ferdinand of Austria-Hungary and Prince Wilhelm, son of the Crown Prince of Prussia, would not have been declared morganatic, with their descendants barred from a claim to their respective Crowns. Royalty was not, however, breeding a race or ensuring that its class was fittest for survival and dominance over the tribe; if so, it was going about it in the wrong way. The royal families of Europe were ring-fencing an idea, a noble separateness. They comprised an elite of blood, but not of biology. Although the royal families of Europe comprised a gene pool that was very much larger than the average village or even small town, it was limited, so genetic problems like haemophilia could spread through it with ease. Even in 1816 there were concerns about the effects of interbreeding on the British royal family. *The Political Examiner* commented on the marriage of Princess Mary to her first cousin:

> The most objectionable thing in these royal connexions – and of late years it has been lamentably obvious – is that they have too great a tendency to deteriorate the stock. It is well understood, we believe, in natural history, that this is the case with regard to less lordly animals than man; and at whatever distance we may be, or effect to be, from those animals, yet it cannot be denied that we have many things with them in common – such as teeth, eyes and senses – that we are animals, as they are – that ladies catch cold as well as their horses and the kind and vivacious among us owe their delightfulness to pretty much the same things as the birds and the greyhounds.[44]

Darwin himself comments on primogeniture, 'Most elder sons, though they may be weak in body or mind, marry, whilst the younger sons, however superior in these respects, do not so generally marry.' Although rich elder sons can choose beautiful and charming wives who must be generally healthy in body and mentally active, men of rank wanting to increase their wealth and power, tend to marry heiresses. He continued:

> But the daughters of children who have produced single children, are themselves, as Mr Galton has shewn, apt to be sterile; and thus noble families are continually cut off in the direct line, and their wealth flows into some side channel; but unfortunately this channel is not determined by superiority of any kind.[45]

However, such considerations did not determine the lines of descent of the European monarchies. Marriage suitors were not chosen for their fertility, their physical strength or any other characteristic that could (theoretically) have ensured the success and continuation of their line. The determinant factors were family alliance, peaceful relations between rival kingdoms and a comparable bloodline, demonstrating a right to title that stretched back into antiquity.

Monarchy and aristocracy were fundamentally at odds with social Darwinist, nationalist and racial theories. The aristocracy were thoroughbreds but not bred for strength or fecundity. They represented national interests but frequently married persons from outside the nation's borders. They married by class or caste not by ethnic origin. Imperialism, as in Austro-Hungarian Vienna, made for polyglot internationalist communities where intermarriage was commonplace.

For sovereigns the care of their subjects was a duty above price. They were 'above the parties', representative of those who had no other representation and servants of the whole nation. They were above all servants of God and therefore at odds with any materialist biological racial agenda. Representation can be said to be the key to good government. Democracy goes a long way towards achieving it, but is not necessarily the whole answer.

Notes

1 Schwanburg, Baron Viktor Kuchina de, from an unpublished book about the de Schwanburg family, contains some autobiographical material.

2 Lee, Stephen, J., *European Dictatorships, 1918–1945*, p. 1.

3 Ibid., p. 19.

4 Henderson, Sir Neville, *Failure of a Mission* (London, 1940), p. vii, see also below.

5 Ibid., pp. 101–2.

6 Ibid., p. vii.

7 James, Robert Rhodes, *Memoirs of a Conservative 1910–1937* (London, Weidenfeld and Nicholson, 1969), p. 399.

8 Ibid., pp. 399–400.

9 Ibid., pp. 402–3.

10 Alfred Viscount Milner was of mixed British and German ancestry. He mentored the young members of the South African civil service, known as Milner's Kindergarten, many of whom later gained prominent administrative positions in Britain and the empire. Milner also believed in a global imperial parliament in London with delegates from Canada, Australia, New Zealand and South Africa. He referred to himself as a British race patriot. 'I am a British (indeed primarily an English) Nationalist,' he wrote, 'If I am also an Imperialist, it is because the destiny of the English race, owing to its insular position and long supremacy at sea, has been to strike roots in different parts of the world. I am an Imperialist and not a Little Englander because I am a British Race Patriot.' Rather than an old-style imperialist, however, he was foremost a colonialist who believed in empire as a means of acquiring Anglo-Saxon dominion of the globe. 'The British State,' he continued, 'must follow the race, must comprehend it, wherever it settles in appreciable numbers as an independent community. If the swarms constantly being thrown off by the parent hive are lost to the State, the State is irreparably weakened. We cannot afford to part with so much of our best blood. We have already parted with much

of it, to form the millions of another separate but fortunately friendly State [the USA].
We cannot suffer a repetition of the process.'

11 *Oxford Dictionary of National Biography*, 'Lord Lothian'.

12 Melville, Cecil F., *The Russian Face of Germany* (London, 1932), pp. 4–120.

13 Quoted in Fielding, Keith, *The Life of Neville Chamberlain* (London, 1946), pp. 347–8,
   p. 183.

14 Howard, M., *The Continental Commitment* (London, Maurice Temple Smith, 1972),
   pp. 120–1.

15 William C. Bullitt's report to President Franklin D. Roosevelt, quoted in Adamthwaite,
   Anthony P., *The Making of the Second World War* (London, Routledge, rev. 1979), pp. 181,
   206–7.

16 Churchill, Winston, speech in the House of Commons, 22 February 1938.

17 Churchill, Winston, speech in the House of Commons, 24 March 1938.

18 *Austen Chamberlain Diary Letters*, ed. R.C. Self (Cambridge, 1995), p. 505.

19 Henderson, Sir Neville, *Failure of a Mission* (London, 1940), p. 152.

20 The German war machine was not up to full strength in 1938, but neither were British
   military defences or alliances considered adequate to resist aggression by Germany and
   one or more allies.

21 Kelly, Scott, 'The Ghost of Neville Chamberlain: Guilty Men and the 1945 Election' in
   Conservative History (Autumn 2005), pp. 18–24.

22 William C. Bullitt's report to President Franklin D. Roosevelt, quoted in Anthony P.
   Adamthwaite, *The Making of the Second World War* (London, 1989), pp. 206–7.

23 Viereck, Peter, *Shame and Glory of the Intellectuals* (New Brunswick, 2007; first pub.
   Boston, 1953) p. 204.

24 Cooper, Duff, *The Second World War – First Phase* (Charles Scribbner, 1939), pp. 217–8.

25 Ibid., p. 219.

26 Eden, Anthony, speech in the House of Commons in answer to the prime minister's
   statement, 3 October 1938.

27 The *British War Bluebook*: 'the Prime Minister's Broadcast Talk to the German People on
   4 September, 1939', no. 144.

28 There were, however, ten times as many forced sterilisations in Germany in the period
   1933–45 than in the USA between the 1900s and 1945.

29 *Tatiana*, pp. 76–7.

30 Charles's other grandfather, by marriage, was Josiah Wedgwood.

31 Kelves, Daniel J., *In the Name of Eugenics: Genetics and the Uses of Human Heredity*
   (Berkeley, 1985), p. 9.

32 Darwin, Charles, *The Descent of Man*, p. 20.

33 Ibid., p. 123.

34 Although Darwin was not himself an atheist, claiming that he had never 'denied
   the existence of a God' and regarded himself as agnostic, there appears to have been
   a circle of scientists and natural philosophers around Darwin who championed a
   scientific rationalist materialist agenda. However, Darwin emphasised what he saw as
   the superiority of the Anglo-Saxons over other races in his work, which can have done
   nothing to prevent his followers from developing more extreme views on race.

35 Pearson, Karl, *National Life from the Standpoint of Science*, lecture, 1900.

36 Ibid., p. 23.

37 Ibid., pp. 30–4.

38 Proctor, Robert N., *Racial Hygiene: medicine under the Nazis* (Harvard, 1989), pp. 235–8.

39 Proctor, Robert N., *Nazi War on Cancer* (Princeton, 1999), pp. 161–3.

40 Ibid.

41 Ibid., p. 4.

42 Ibid., p. 138 and also see Cocks, Geffrey, *Pschotherapy in the Third Reich: The Goring Institute*, p. 57, and DeGregori, Thomas R., *Origins of the Organic Agriculture Debate* (Wiley-Blackwell, 2003), pp. 59–61.

43 Cited in, ibid., pp. 138–9.

44 *The Political Examiner* on the marriage of Princess Mary to her cousin the Duke of Gloucester in July 1816.

45 Darwin, Charles, *The Descent of Man*, p. 118.

4

THE GERMAN RESISTANCE MOVEMENT

The state was above and outside justice and morality. The individual and the community alike had to subordinate themselves to it completely. In the new formula, 'Right is that which is useful to the people,' the principle abhorred by all good men was openly proclaimed: 'The end justifies the means.' The idea of individual right peculiar to Christianity as well as the Germanic peoples was denied by (sic) him. Man was no more than a part, a member, and a functionary of the state; he was to be remodelled as a collective being, and to forgo any right to an independent personality. This conception of the state was fulfilled in The Single Party; its main feature was the formation of an authoritarian political will, which imposed itself by means of propaganda and violence.

Carl Friedrich Goerdeler[1]

Opposition to the Nazis preceded their political victory and continued until their fall. Even when war broke out and quick victories led to an increase in Hitler's popularity, there was still an opposition among ordinary people as much as German politicians and diplomats. 'Germany MUST lose this war, or we are heading for a fate infinitely worse than defeat,' confided Helen Biron. Her three brothers were in the army, recalls Tatiana Metternich, 'The Western Powers should have stopped Hitler last year'. She went on:

They never understood the Nazis didn't want power because the country was well or badly off: they only wanted power. They are building up the dark face of Germany … The Germans tend to love false gods. Once instilled with the idea that they are fulfilling a mission, nothing can stop them. The Nazis have upset all conceptions of good and evil. They use the same weapons as the Communists: first insult, then calumny, then murder. Blomberg [former head of the army] was forced to marry his mistress, then discharged for doing so. Fritsch [Blomberg's successor] was accused of being a homosexual, then thrown out of the Army. Now they lie about the Jews and Poles, tomorrow it will be the turn of the Church and then all those in their way ... It will never stop unless we lose the war.[2]

The German resistance movement was not represented by a coherent or a consistent group, but was a loose alliance of persons with sundry motives of diverse social and political backgrounds, ranging from high-ranking aristocratic army officers and politicians to churchmen and avowed Christian socialists. Some of the military conspirators were more anti-Hitler than anti-Nazi, and convinced that the Führer would bring Germany to ruin through his military adventures. Some offered and withdrew their support to various plots according to changing circumstances and the fluctuating chances of success. Others, however, such as Carl Friedrich Goerdeler, Hans von Dohnanyi and Hans Oster showed their disgust of the whole Nazi regime and its policies by actively defending their Jewish compatriots and assisting their escape from Germany. They made several overtures towards the British government during the 1930s, but the response was negative on the whole and deeply disappointing to them. This was because Britain's policy of appeasement was not only influenced by a principled desire for peace, but also because it was influenced and promoted by a group of people who thought that a strong Germany facing East was preferable to a strong Soviet Union facing West.

Frustratingly, the first efforts of the movement were, therefore, resisted by elements in the British Establishment who wanted to keep on good terms with the dictatorship that they wanted to overthrow. Some of the dissidents were members of the party who had either become disenchanted or had hoped to purge its more unsavoury elements from the inside. Tatiana Metternich recalls:

> We learnt gradually that when courage, especially civil courage, was conspicuously lacking, all other qualities collapsed with it: there was no room for kindness, consideration or fidelity. The exceptions, those of independent thought: the happy go lucky, the chivalrous, bonded together in instinctive solidarity. They at first hoped to change things from within. When they realised the impossibility of doing this, the final decision to overthrow Hitler in spite of the war began to take concrete form.[3]

The Bismarck brothers Otto and Gottfried were among these. Both came to despise Hitler and the party they had joined. At a function early on in the regime, Prince Otto von Bismarck waited in line to voice his concerns to Hitler. Ahead of him Hitler erupted against those Germans who protected Jews. Barely disregarding what he had just heard, Bismark launched into his prepared speech:

'Mein Führer, there is a rumour that certain extreme elements in the party contemplate terroristic activity against a section of the population [the Jews]. Out of moral principles and also because of deep concern expressed by our neighbours, this would be highly inadvisable.' He repeated, 'Highly inadvisable.' Thereupon a storm of vituperation burst over their heads. 'Everyone thinks themselves entitled to an opinion …' and on it went. The Bismarcks went home, deeply thoughtful, Otto still muttering, 'Ghastly! Ghastly!' The mask was soon to fall … As far as the Bismarcks were concerned, they now knew that any order concerning the Jews came direct from Hitler, and any hopes they harboured of restraining extreme elements within the party, were dispelled forever.[4]

The Civilians

Early conspirators included officials from the German Foreign Office such as Adam von Trott zu Solz and Erich Kadt – both former Rhodes Scholars – and Hans Bernd Gisevius from the Ministry of the Interior. One of the leading members of the movement was Carl Friedrich Goerdeler (1834–1945), Mayor of Leipzig and former Reich Commissioner for Price Regulation, an office he resumed in 1934–35, using it as a means of criticising rearmament and Nazi racial policies. Ulrich von Hassell was stationed with the Foreign Office in Rome, the son-in-law of Admiral Tirpitz, he was a lawyer and diplomat. He opposed the Axis agreement and joined the resistance during the war. Hans-Bernd Gisevius was senior official at the interior ministry. A diplomat and intelligence officer, he compiled evidence against Himmler for use after the war and was involved in secret talks with the Vatican. Hans von Dohnanyi was a highly placed lawyer in the Reich justice ministry. In 1934 his objections to Nazi injustice, particularly the Night of the Long Knives, led him into resistance circles. He became a member of the *Abwehr* at the invitation of Hans Oster. In 1942 he facilitated the escape of two Jewish lawyers and their families to Switzerland disguised as *Abwehr* agents. Dohnanyi was arrested in 1943 but not tried and executed until after the 20th July plot.

Dr Otto John was a lawyer who worked for Lufthansa, which gave him the opportunity to travel widely and forge links with the British authorities. It also brought him into contact with Prince Louis Ferdinand of Prussia, who he introduced to other members of the movement. He was involved in the 20th July plot but managed to escape with the help of British Intelligence. After the war he appeared as a witness in the Nuremberg Trials and was appointed President of the West German Office for the Protection of the Constitution. Pastor Dietrich von Bonhoeffer was an early opponent of Nazi anti-Semitism and its interference in the churches. In 1933 he made an anti-Hitler radio broadcast warning against an idolatrous cult of the Führer.[5] Then, in 1938, Bonhoeffer made contact with other resistance workers through his brother-in-law and school friend Hans von Donanyi of the *Abwehr*, which he joined in 1941 as cover for his activities. Although an avowed pacifist he eventually agreed the assassination of Hitler was necessary.

Jakob Kaiser was a trade union leader and friend of Carl Goerdeler, who joined the German resistance in 1934. Although he was arrested in 1938 he continued his anti-Nazi activities after his release. He went into hiding following the 20th July plot. Dr Justus Delbrück, a lawyer who was a member of military intelligence, was a brother-in-law of Dietrich and Klaus Bonhoeffer and brother to Max Delbrück, a Nobel Prize-winning micro-biologist who emigrated to the USA in 1937. Ernst von Harnack had been a high-ranking government official and administrator through the 1920s and 1930s until his dismissal in 1932; he was arrested in 1933 and again in 1945. Joseph Wirmer was a lawyer who opposed the racist tendencies of the Nazis and worked for an alliance of the Centre Party and Social Democrats as a bulwark against extremism. As such he provided a useful bridge between the two groups within the resistance movement. He was associated with Kaiser and in the 1940s was part of the circle around Goerdeler. He also opposed the concordat between the Catholic Church and Germany.

Many of these civilians were driven by strong Christian moral principles that prevented them from contemplating assassination as a legitimate means of ridding themselves of an oppressive regime, however repugnant. Jurist Hans-Bernd von Haeften of the German Foreign Office refused to agree to an assassination of Hitler on moral grounds and prevented his brother Werner from shooting Hitler with a pistol in 1944 because it was against the fifth commandment. Their high morals expressed at that time were both a strength and a weakness. They would not use Nazi methods to rid themselves of the Nazis. The Christian principles of Bonhoeffer and Dr Goerdeler, for example, would not allow them to support an assassination attempt on the Führer either.[6] By July 1944 many had changed their minds, but by then Germany was under direct attack and the Allies insisted on unconditional surrender.

Goerdeler believed that 'Germany historically needs the monarchy' and would accept nothing but a monarch as the 'formal head of state, representative of the Reich, and commander-in-chief'. The personal oath of the armed forces could be made to a constitutional monarch who appointed the chancellor and state secretaries, but whose authority was wielded by his democratically elected ministers.[7] From 1938 the German constitution envisaged by the resistance included a restoration of the monarchy. This was not always spoken about openly, nor was it believed inevitable by all of the resisters, but it was an ever-present undercurrent. John Flournoy Montgomery wrote shortly after the end of the war, 'The monarchists, by no means the communists, were the only opposition of which Hitler was really and permanently afraid. It was, in fact, the only opposition which almost succeeded in killing him.'[8]

Military Opposition

There were a number of critics of Hitler in the armed forces who consid-
ered staging a putsch against the regime. Military opponents of Hitler included
Admiral Wilhelm Canaris and Colonel Hans Oster of the *Abwer*. Army chief of
staff Ludwig Beck was succeeded by Franz Halder. In 1938 Oster asked Colonel
General Beck – who had just resigned over the Sudeten Crisis – and General
Halder to support a coup against the regime. In the summer of 1938 messengers
were sent to Britain to ask for the government to stand firm on Czechoslovakia.
It was intended that, with a broad international front against Hitler's expansion
plans in place, the arrest of the dictator and the replacement of his government would be possible if he attempted to go to war against the wishes of the
German people. General Erwin von Witzleben was also involved in the 1938
plot, as was General Kurt Freiherr von Hammerstein-Equord, who planned
to attack Hitler in a frontal assault (he was to close down party headquarters).
While General Hammerstein made no secret of his intention of ambushing
Hitler given the chance, even those army commanders who were sworn opponents of all for which Hitler stood were reluctant to act against their oath and
outside of their code.

Colonel General Kurt von Hammerstein-Equord had been commander of the
Reichswehr (army) when Hitler assumed power. He regretted that he had not then
used troops to crush the Nazis. Bruning described him in 1939 as a man 'without
nerves'. Forced into retirement in 1934 he plotted to personally rid Germany
of Hitler. When the army was mobilised for the invasion Poland, Hammerstein
was recalled to command of 'Army Section A' on the German western flank.
He intended to lure Hitler to his headquarters in Cologne, giving as reason that
this would give the impression of a larger number of forces there than there was.
But Hammerstein had no intention of allowing Hitler to return and, in any case,
Hitler would not take the bait and did not visit his general.[9]

When Hitler became chancellor the generals were ordered to co-operate by
Hindenburg. Some viewed National Socialism as a political experiment that
should be allowed to be given a chance. They regarded the Nazis as 'turbulent
but useful allies' who might well bring about rearmament and be good for the
officer corps. They believed that they could bring the experiment to an end at
any time. As time went on they continued to hold the 'deluded conviction that
they were still undisputed masters of the situation,' and it suited Hitler for them
to think that way. Conservative leaders both military and civilian assisted Hitler
in the belief that he could be controlled. 'Not until they had fitted the fetters on
their own wrists,' comments Wheeler-Bennett, 'did they realise who indeed was
captive and captor.'[10]

As the size of the German army was increased under the new regime, new
officers were trained and appointed whose rise was associated with Nazi policies,

and who owed their position to its leader. As a consequence, there was a portion of the officer corps who were never going to join with the old guard in opposing Hitler and plotting his fall.[11] The reluctance of the army to break their oath of loyalty to Hitler, whom many of them loathed, and take action against him, is explained by Prince Louis Ferdinand:

> Through the centuries my ancestors had educated their officer corps to be brave in the field and to take orders. This attitude had not changed after the Hohenzollerns had ceased to give orders and a president of a republic had stepped into power, nor after a former corporal had become the supreme warlord.

The army, Louis Ferdinand points out, was a sword to be used by anyone who ran the country, but not the army itself. Adherence to this policy made the overthrow of the dictator almost impossible.[12] A military putsch was unheard of in Germany, but the extraordinary situation demanded extraordinary measures.[13]

Plots

In the summer of 1938 the resistance movement sent frantic messages to Britain, asking that it stand firm on Czechoslovakia as a putsch was planned against the regime. This was in the event of Hitler attempting to carry out his plans to annex the Sudetenland against the united opposition of Britain and France, the inevitable consequence of which would be war. Ernst von Weizsäcker, under-secretary of state at the Foreign Office, sent messages to London – as did Beck and Oster and Goerdeler – but the response was disappointing. In August 1938 a British Foreign Office official claimed that Britain had not been given any reason to suppose that the German army would be willing or able to overthrow the regime.[14]

In September a coup was planned that included General Erwin von Witzleben, the commander of the Berlin area. Generals Halder and Beck, however, hesitated. They believed that it could not take place until Hitler made unmistakable moves towards war in order to ensure the support of the officer corps. It was generally agreed that Hitler must lose his life in order for the army to be released from their oath of loyalty. Before anything happened, Chamberlain announced his trip to Germany to meet with Hitler to avert war, which undermined the German resistance moves. Although the conspiracy was revived when talks appeared to have broken down.

Adam von Trott zu Solz visited London in 1939, where he had several meetings with Lord Lothian and Lord Halifax in an attempt to persuade the British government to abandon its policy of appeasement.[15] In October of the same year he also visited Washington on behalf of Beck, Goerdeler, Schacht and Leuschner to seek US support for the resistance. The response was disappointing. Another Rhodes

Scholar, Erich Kordt, who worked with his brother Theodor in the German embassy in London, was appalled at the lack of interest shown by the British.[16] Halder had secret talks with the British Ambassador Sir Neville Henderson to gain support for a coup should Hitler invade Poland, but the invasion took place without incident.

Trott visited London three times in 1939 and tried to get Lord Lothian and Lord Halifax to persuade the British government to abandon its policy of appeasement. His trip ended in failure. Unfortunately he had met members of the Milner Group who, unaware of their visitor's anti-Nazi sympathies, assured him of their friendship for Germany. They stated their understanding of Germany's desire to expand back into its pre-war political geography, becoming militarily and industrially strong to counter bolshevism inside its borders and resist it outside. Lord Lothian wrote a letter to Adam von Trott shortly after the fall of France in 1940. He called upon his old friend to work for a reconciliation between Britain and Germany. Trott was not sure to what Germany Lothian referred – Nazi Germany or one free of fascism – but considered any deal between the two countries while Hitler was in charge as an 'odious' prospect. He did not reveal the existence of the letter to anyone until he mentioned its contents to Marie 'Missie' Vassiltchikov on 20 July 1944, when it seemed obvious that the plot to assassinate Hitler had failed.[17]

The members of the resistance movement wanted some kind of assurance from Britain that, in the event they could wrestle power from Hitler and establish a new government in a putsch, it would not take advantage of the ensuing chaos to launch military attacks on Germany. They also wanted Britain to take a firm stand in relation to Nazi claims to that part of Czechoslovakia occupied by the Sudeten Germans, so that if Hitler attempted war the German military could, and would, move against him. After contacts with the British had borne no fruit, the conspirators switched their attention to the American president who they knew was a friend of Prince Louis Ferdinand and who had no sympathy for the Nazis. As a result, in the autumn of 1941, they approached Prince Louis' American friend in Berlin, Louis Lochner. Up to fifteen members met with him in the home of sympathiser and industrialist Josef Wirmer, representing the military and civilian wings of the resistance. They asked him to take a message to Roosevelt explaining their motives and political objectives, and requesting the president's help in achieving peace. They also sent a cover letter written by their mutual friend, Louis Ferdinand.

Lochner agreed at once, but before he had the opportunity to make the journey the Japanese attacked Pearl Harbor and Germany declared war on the USA. As a result Lochner was unable to leave for America until the following June. When he arrived in Washington he was met with a political brick wall. He was repeatedly unable to gain admittance into the White House to see the president, being told that his persistence was 'most embarrassing'. When he eventually had a meeting with Mrs Eleanor Roosevelt she revealed to him that it was now official

Washington policy that 'all doors were closed' to any dealings with Germans, even those opposed to the Nazi regime. The German resistance movement had been informed that the president's objective was the downfall of the Nazi regime and that his reaction to a constitutional monarchy under Prince Louis Ferdinand would be 'distinctly positive', but now Roosevelt and his administration had pulled up the drawbridge with Hitler's German opponents in Germany on the outside.[18] In 1942–43 Trott again attempted to change Allied attitudes to the prospect of a new German government following a successful coup, but was bitterly disillusioned by Anglo-American Allied indifference.

A memorandum was drafted by the internal German opposition in 1942 that appealed directly to the British government and its allies, regarding its reaction to a potential coup d'etat against Hitler and the likely attitude towards a post-Nazi government in Germany. It was sent via the Ecumenical Council of Churches to the lord privy seal, Sir Stafford Cripps, who was very interested in its contents and passed it to Churchill.[19] The memorandum commented on the destruction of human life and resources that had occurred, and suggested that even those who emerged victorious from the war would suffer from extreme poverty afterwards. It referred to a tendency towards totalitarianism, anarchy and the abandonment of all established civilised standards. The memorandum expressed deep concern that a Soviet victory over Germany would be a 'catastrophe' for all Europe and ultimately the world. The alternative would be the formation of a civilised German government to replace and oust the incumbent regime, with an aim of a decentralised federal Germany applying modern socialist principles and forging links with a federal Europe, each divested of its former nationalist and militarist tendencies. The authors of the memorandum claimed to represent high-ranking members of the armed forces and members of the German administration, as well as large numbers of members of the working class.[20]

The military situation at that time was still uncertain. German forces remained in possession of territory for a thousand miles inside Russia, so an offer from the German resistance movement could not be dismissed.[21] In May 1942 Hans Schönfeld and Dietrich Bonhoeffer, representing the resistance movement, had a meeting in Stockholm, Sweden, with George Bell, Bishop of Chichester, who related their proposals and concerns to Sir Anthony Eden back in the UK. Among the proposals was a repeal of the Nuremburg Laws and – if Britain agreed – the restoration of a constitutional monarchy with Prince Louis Ferdinand of Prussia as in Germany. Eden's response was not encouraging and merely called for the opposition to do something to bring Hitler down themselves.[22] Peter Hoffman remarks, 'too few people in influential positions believed that there really was serious opposition in Germany.' Furthermore, Churchill was wary of talking with the enemy partly due to his alliance with Stalin, but partly also due to bitter experience.[23]

Willem Visser't Hooft, Secretary General of the World Council of Churches, Geneva, acted as an intermediary with Theo Kordt, based in the German embassy in Bern, and British representatives. Pope Pius XII quietly arranged for a dialogue to by set up between the German resistance movement represented by General Beck, the lawyer Hans von Dohnanyi, Admiral Canaris and Hans Oster of the *Abwehr* and the British via D'Arcy Osborne, HM's minister to the Holy See, who passed on warnings of an imminent Nazi invasion of the Lowlands. However, no encouragement was forthcoming from the British.[24]

Unfortunately, the British had become suspicious of any approaches by persons claiming to represent a German resistance movement following the Venlo Incident on 9 November 1939. A Dr Fischer claimed to represent a group of disgruntled army officers who were planning a coup against Hitler, but in reality Fischer was a double agent working for the *Sicherheitsdienst* (SD), German security service, with orders to lure British agents into a trap. Neville Chamberlain was happy to support a coup that could end the war before it had begun in earnest, in spite of misgivings by one of the British Intelligence agents sent to meet with Dr Fischer at a cafe on the Dutch-German border. The two agents, Captain Sigismund Payne Best (head of 'Section Z' in the Netherlands) and Major Richard H. Stevens were captured in an ambush and dragged over the German border. A Dutch officer, Lt. Dirk Klop, was killed. A list of British agents in Europe was found in Best's possession and enough information was revealed under interrogation for much of Britain's intelligence presence in Europe to be compromised. Sadly for the real German resistance movement and hopes of an early end to the war, Winston Churchill associated contact with disaffected groups within Germany with Chamberlain's unsound judgement and the bitter compromise of Munich.

Another element in the distrust of the Western Allies of approaches by the German resistance movement was Vansittartism. Sir Robert (later baron) Vansittart had a deep distrust of the German nation as a whole, which he believed was intrinsically aggressive in character. He believed that the Prussian officer class and German industry must be crushed and destroyed and the population re-educated for at least a generation after the war. To negotiate with the resistance and support regime change would have been to leave that military class in place, risking the aggressive nature of German politics resurfacing at a later date. The German people, Vansittart claimed, had supported the Franco-Prussian War, the First World War and the Second World War, and could not be trusted not to support another war of aggression. Vansittart's ideas later influenced the Morgenthau Plan, which would have meant the annexation of the heavy industrial areas of Germany such as the Ruhr, the Saarland and Upper Silesia, and turning the rest of the country into a pastoral state, with no heavy industry or military capability.[25] Vansittart believed in alliance policy, particularly with France and the Soviet Union, in order to box in German expansionism – contrary to Chamberlain's insistence on British independence of negotiation and action or inaction. After the Nazi occupation of the Rhineland in 1936 he wrote candidly, 'We shall of course ... on no account whatever allow ourselves to be separated from France, in order to allow Hitler to conveniently overrun Europe. We know pretty exactly what awaits us in the future. Hitler's game is too grossly transparent to deceive anyone now.'[26]

A major impediment to progress was the presence of Stalin, who the Allies did not wish to alienate through a separate deal with German representatives – the possibility of which he was very aware. Furthermore, the presence of Russian spies in high positions of British Intelligence and the Foreign Office, such as Kim Philby, made a difficult job impossible.

Otto John sent a report to the British pleading for co-operation between the Allies and the German resistance movement. However, when it arrived at MI6, Philby prevented its circulation among those who could have done anything about it. Sir Stewart Menzies had for years wanted to meet Admiral Canaris and knew of the rivalry between the *Abwehr* and the SS secret service, but Anthony Eden forbade it because of Anglo-Soviet relations as Stalin was worried about a possible deal between the West and Germany. When Hugh Trevor-Roper wrote a paper about this rivalry in 1942, Philby prevented it leaving the building. The report recommended a clandestine co-operation with the German resistance would be useful and would not violate agreements with the Soviet Union and the USA.[27] Philby was a Russian agent and his position in MI6 allowed him to censor information unhelpful to the Soviet cause that might otherwise have landed on ministers' desks. He wanted, at all costs, to stop the Western powers coming to an understanding with anyone in Germany, however anti-Nazi they may have been.[28]

Philby devised a plot to assassinate Canaris in Spain. He was well aware of the admiral's role as a leading opponent of the Nazis and of his being in a position of power and influence in Germany, and passed this information to the Soviets. The Russians saw the possibility of a Germany free of Nazism as a possible (even probable) ally of Britain and America against them. Canaris proved very useful to the Western Allies: he spread disinformation in the Nazi camp, claiming that British military strength was considerably greater than it really was in 1940, which led Hitler to postpone Operation Sea Lion. Canaris also suggested that there would be no Allied invasion of Italy, even though when he knew it was about to occur and the Allies were actually approaching Anzio beaches.[29]

The attitude of the Allies was very frustrating for the conspirators. As the war progressed and stories of German atrocities multiplied, 'It became increasingly difficult for the Allies to distinguish between Hitler and his henchmen and the so-called "good Germans", and to agree on a policy that would enable a Germany purged of Nazism to be re-integrated into the community of civilised nations.'[30] The main impediment to Allied support for internal action against the Nazis was their insistence on unconditional surrender. Although it played into the hands of Göbbels' propaganda and dissuaded military leaders from supporting plots with uncertain outcomes, the complete defeat of Germany was thought preferable to a peace that could leave room for a new 'stab in the back' legend to surface afterwards.

When German air ace Major Heinrich Prinz zu Sayn-Wittgenstein entered 'the presence' of the Führer to collect the Oak Leaves to his Knights Cross in 1943, he was surprised when his handgun wasn't taken from him as it could have been possible 'to "bump him off" right there and then'. He later speculated that he might blow himself up when he next shook hands with Hitler, but was killed in action only a few days later. Princess Marie 'Missie' Vassiltchikov records, 'He often spoke of the agony he felt about having to kill people and how, whenever possible, he tried to hit the enemy plane in such a way that the crew could bail out.'[31]

The last throw was the 20th July plot – known to posterity as the Stauffenberg plot, after Wehrmacht officer Claus Graf von Stauffenberg – but its failure and the retribution that followed robbed Germany and Europe of the cream of political talent. It was without benefit, except that the act went down in history as a heroic stand by the German people against the tyrant who nearly plunged the world into oblivion. Too many people knew of the plot, however, and in 1941 Jakob Kaiser informed historian Friedrich Meinecke that their undertaking had been betrayed. With no small amount of fatalism Beck later confided, 'There is no use. There is no deliverance. We must now drain little by little the bitter cup to the bitterest end.' The need to act that had been delayed due to Beck's failing health became necessary before arrests were made.[32]

The original attempt to assassinate Hitler by the 20th July plotters had been scheduled for 11 July but was postponed. Marie 'Missie' Vassiltchikov records that on the previous day she had a bitter argument with Adam Trott about 'imminent events'. Trott being a true German patriot did not want to leave anything to chance and, like his fellow plotters, wanted everything worked out to the last detail including the type of Germany that was to follow the removal of their principle enemy, Vassiltchikov, on the other hand, argued for the 'physical elimination of the man' as soon as possible and the downfall of his regime, and let the future take care of itself.[33] Gustav Dahrendorf, a prominent German socialist and 20th July plotter, said:

> The revolutionary attempt of the 20th July, 1944, should not be considered as a badly managed undertaking by officers who had lost hope, and who wanted to escape from an awkward impasse, nor as an attempt of disgruntled, reactionary militarists to dissolve the link binding them to fascism. Both descriptions would be false and unjust. The motive force behind the preparations was a firm political will. There was only one aim, to liquidate fascism and end the war.[34]

Those Germans who were going to rebuild Germany after the war were almost completely wiped out following the 20th July rising. Hitler saved Stalin the trouble of making Germany's natural non-Nazi political and commercial leaders disappear.

The 'unwinding of appeasement', when the policy was abandoned in the UK, meant that distinctions between Nazis and other Germans, and encouragement of moderate elements in Germany to influence or assume government, no longer applied as they had done. When appeasement was abandoned, Social Democrat exiles in England were also abandoned and largely ignored. The casualties of the new policy included members of the German resistance in Germany as well as outside who were cut adrift even if they were listened to at times. This continued contact, however, merely gave the impression of a potential of real support.[35]

It is both easy and wrong to make retrospective judgements about persons of previous generations belonging to an age in which we do not live. We are shaped by our mental, emotional and physical environment but it is not our ruler. To have swum against the tide, out of moral conviction, in any place and at any time in history has always been extremely brave, but to have done so against the current of National Socialism and its *Gleichschaltung* earns the highest respect. In a time when fascism and Bolshevikism were sweeping Europe it took a special type of human being to stand against them in equal measure.

Jewish-born Kurt Hahn was founder of Salem School with Prince Max von Baden – for whom he was private secretary and biographer – forced to flee Germany in the 1930s, he lived in Gordonston in the UK. He was keen that the British understood the difference between Germans and Nazis and the risks and inevitable sacrifice of those who fought Hitler from within:

For this challenge, all Christian England and Christian Europe are waiting. I include Christian Germany and Christian Russia. All want to hear the Nazis indicted more often and as fiercely as ever. They want to hear their crimes mentioned without sparing us the authentic and terrible details which a reluctant and sluggish imagination finds it hard at all times to visualize and which many of us would fain be spared, so as not to disturb a peace of mind to which we have no right. They want to hear the watchword again and again: 'No peace with the murderers, no peace with their condoners who know better and never risk their lives to save hostages from being shot, prisoners from being tortured, Jews from being exterminated.'

They want to hear the German armed forces taunted with their servility. It would be only truth to add that our citizen armies would be turned into hosts of conscientious objectors were they ever ordered to carry out those merciless and fiendish practices which the German soldiers have now adopted as their routine duties. They want to hear the voice of great compassion, not only with Nazi victims outside Germany, but with millions of Germans who are now suffering and struggling under Hitler. They want to be informed if at any time our fighting forces have encountered a better Germany capable of redemption. They are anxiously hoping for a promise that discriminating and stern justice will be done by a victorious England from which a cleansed and liberated Germany has nothing to fear ... Christian Germany is waiting, and is, so far, waiting in vain that the light be lit in the West. Tension will grow and the moment may come when well-chosen words could release a revolution ... we should be under no illusion, nothing will spare us the necessity to invade and liberate Europe at the cost of a great number of precious lives. Until Germany is defeated, revolutions against Hitler are doomed to failure, but even though they are ruthlessly crushed, they may well hasten the final defeat.[36]

Notes

1 Carl Friedrich Goerdeler, 1943, from a manifesto of the new government intended for publication following the fall of Hitler. p. 84.

2 Metternich, Tatiana, *Tatiana* (London, rev. 2004; first pub. 1976), p. 103.

3 Metternich, Tatiana, *Tatiana*, p. 111.

4 Ibid., pp. 116–18.

5 Bonhoeffer, Dietrich, *A Testament of Freedom*, ed. Geoffrey B. Kelly (HarperCollins, 1995), p. 5.

6 Prussia, Prince Louis Ferdinand of, *The Rebel Prince*, p. 314.

7 Kruger-Charle, Michael, 'From Reform to Resistance: Carl Goerdeler's 1938 Memorandum', in *Contending with Hitler: Varieties of Resistance in the Third Reich*, ed. by David Clay Large (Cambridge, 1994), p. 77.

8 Montgomery, John Flournoy, *Hungarian History*, http://www.hungarian-history.hu/lib/montgo/montgo08.htm, p. 3.

9 Deutsch, Harrold C., *The Conspiracy Against Hitler in the Twilight War* (Minnesota, 1968), pp. 50–1.

10 Wheeler-Bennett, Sir John, *The Nemesis of Power: the German Army in Politics 1918–1945* (London & New York, 1953, rev. 1964), pp. 293.

11 Hoffmann, Peter, *Stauffenberg: A Family History, 1905–1944* (Cambridge, 1995), p. 141.

12 Prussia, Prince Louis Ferdinand of, *The Rebel Prince*, p. 314–5.

13 Meinecke, Friedrich, *The German Catastrophe*, trans. Sidney B. Faye (Harvard, 1950), p. 97.

14 Weinberg, Gerhard, *The Foreign Policy of Hitler's Germany Starting World War II* (Chicago, 1980), p. 396.

15 Trott was the son of a high official in the Prussian civil service. During 1932–33, he studied as a Rhodes Scholar at Oxford. Afterwards he spent time in the USA and China, but decided to return to Germany against the advice of friends. A truly brave man, he returned via Siberia in 1940 and joined the NSDAP as cover for his anti-Nazi activities. Trott was a friend of David (son of viscount) Astor, whom he met when he was at Balliol College, Oxford in the early 1930s. Son of a Prussian minister and a descendant of one of the founding fathers of the USA, in 1940, Trott joined the Nazi Party to use his membership as a cover for his secret activities against the regime, which included serving as foreign policy advisor to the Kreisau Circle. See especially Vassiltchikov, (Princess) Marie 'Missie', *The Berlin Diaries 1940–1945* (London, 1985) p. 23 and throughout.

16 They were both involved in Oster plot to assassinate Hitler in the event of an invasion of Czechoslovakia and warned Vansitart of German-Soviet negotiations.

17 Vassiltchikov, M., *The Berlin Diaries*, p. 201.

18 Klemperer, Klemens von, *German Resistance Against Hitler: The Search For Allies Abroad, 1938–1945* (Oxford, 1994), pp. 232–4.

19 In November 1938 Cripps had been a signatory to a letter to the London *Times* protesting at Nazi persecution of the Jews.

20 Hoffmann, Peter, *History of the German Resistance 1933–1945* (McGill-Queens University Press, 1996), pp. 216–7.

21 Ibid., p. 217.

22 Ibid., p. 218.

23 Ibid., p. 49.

24 Dippel, John van Houten, *Two Against Hitler: Stealing the Nazi's Best Kept Secrets* (Westport, Praeger, 1992), p. 104.

25 Hoffmann, Peter, *History of the German Resistance 1933–1945*, p. 115.

26 Roi, Michael Lawrence, *Alternative to Appeasement, Sir Robert Vansittart and Alliance Diplomacy* (Westport, Praeger, 1997), p. 132.

27 Waller, John H., *The Unseen War in Europe: Espionage and Conspiracy in the Second World War* (I.B. Tauris, 1996), p. 240.

28 Ibid., pp. 351–2.

29 Craig, John S., *Peculiar Liasons: in War, Espionage, and Terrorism in the Twentieth Century* (Algora, 2004), p. 192–5.

30 Vassiltchikov, (Princess) Marie 'Missie', *The Berlin Diaries 1940–1945*, p. 190. Princess Marie Vassiltchikov observed that, being patriots, the resistance movement hesitated to bring down the regime before putting in place well-worked out plans for its humanitarian successor to the last detail. She writes, 'I have never believed that such an interim government would be acceptable to the Allies who refuse to distinguish between 'good' Germans and 'bad'. This of course is a fatal mistake on their part and we will probably all pay a heavy price for it.' p. 190.

31 Vassiltchikov, M., *The Berlin Diaries*, pp. 140–1.

32 Meinecke, Friedrich, *The German Catastrophe*, trans. Sidney B. Faye (Harvard, 1950), pp. 101–2.

33 Ibid., p. 186.

34 Quoted in Schlabrendorff, Fabian von, *They Almost Killed Hitler* (Kessinger, 2005), p. 78.

35 Glees, Anthony, *Exile Politics During the Second World War* (Oxford, 1982), p. 44.

36 http://www.kurthahn.org/writings/sermons.pdf accessed 17 August 2011.

CONCLUSION

We accept that culture is international, but the Nazis confused distinct cultures with nationhood and race. They did not accept that each culture represents a collective response to a particular environment and common experience established over generations, which explains why colonial settlers and their offspring often 'go native'. This is not a sign of 'degeneracy' as the Nazis would have had it, but rather adaptation, survival and functioning social evolution.

Whereas it has been desirable to square Romantic, classical or Enlightenment values in order to establish a balanced civilisation, in the case of the Nazis it was achieved at the expense of civilisation itself. With them *Sturm und Drang* reached its stormiest and their interpretation of the Age of Reason was reasoning but entirely unreasonable.

One can easily compile a list of some of the certain and likely influences on Hitler and on the Nazi's mythic racism without it being comprehensive:

Immanuel Kant, Georg Freidrich Hegel, Arthur Schopenhauer, Freidrich Schelling, Freidrich Holderlin, Johann Gottfried von Herder, Arthur de Gobineau, Hans F.K. Gunter, Francis Galton, Karl Pearson, Arthur Moeller van den Bruck, Paul de Lagarde, Julius Langbehn, Fredrich Christoph Dahlmann, Heinrich von Treitschke, Heinrich Claß, Herder, Guido von List, Adolf Josef Lanz von Liebenfels, H.P. Blavatsky, Karl Maria Wiligut, Wolfgang Kapp, Houston Stewart Chamberlain, Ernst Haekler, Adam Alfred Rudolf Glauer, Alfred Rosenberg, Gottfried Feder,[1] Ernst Röhm, Erich Ludendorff,[2] Benito Mussolini and even Charles Darwin and Martin Luther.

This does not mean that Hitler and his followers were complex individuals, but rather he made use of any support and influence on his road to power.

National Socialism made use of modern philosophy and science as much as it made use of national tradition and myth. Scientific thinking of the 1930s, however, included social Darwinism, eugenics, and an increasing materialism throughout Europe and America, extending out to the European empires. Science is blind; it is has no intrinsic philosophy and contains no inherent morality. Its use is determined entirely by the morals, agenda and intensions of those by whom it is practised, who finance it and by whom it is applied. It is, however, fuelled by money and therefore business and government give it direction, not necessity or a mythical quest for truth. In Nazi Germany the money was on anything that squared with the party line and supported the preservation and triumph of the Aryan race.

The Nazis were concerned with physical fitness, environmental conservation, animal welfare, natural foods and medicine; they were interested in eastern religions and diet, northern European pagan beliefs and practices, nature religion and the celebration of the solstices, and getting back to a life in tune with nature. The Nazis were certainly not hippies, however. Their motive was not peace and love, but racial purity and dominance. They were Romantic modernists. Like other groups in western Europe and America they were interested in social Darwinism and eugenics.

Hitler appropriated many ideas and used many people in his pursuit of power. Though he discarded people and organisations (such as Röhm and the Theosophists) along the way, this was not before their use was over and ideas were assimilated. Paradoxically, the Nazis applied the latest technology, business practice and scientific thought in the advancement of a claim to a racially preeminent mythical *völkisch* historical identity. National Socialists were culturally conservative in regard to perceived decadent novelties in art, literature, theatre and architecture, but enthusiastic for the modern tools of Aryan dominance. For example, Himmler's Teutonic Knights travelled in the latest tanks with the most modern weapons of war at their disposal. This was a very modern barbarism rooted in the competitiveness of concepts like 'survival of the fittest' of the Aryan race, which was portrayed as much as a struggle for survival as of dominance of the united German tribes, if not more so.

Hitler's Western enemies must accept some of the blame for the rise of National Socialism and its core beliefs. Versailles and the resulting award of reparations, as well as a lack of sensitivity to moderate opinion in inter-war Germany, had their effect on German politics. However, a belief that Germany had been unfairly treated at Versailles led Western politicians to overlook some German transgressions of the treaty, especially given Germany's geographical position as a potential buffer to Soviet expansion. The timing was certainly out because by the time of appeasement statesmen of the like of Stresemann and Brüning were no longer in evidence, and Western leaders had to deal with Hitler and representatives of his regime.

Hitler made use of any and every German myth and national interest from Luther to Versailles, from folk myth to racial magic and even environmentalism. Luther was emblematic of subsequent German nationalism, he had written an anti-Semitic book in which he had appeared to have condoned attacks on synagogues and Jewish homes and businesses. Book burnings took place at his castle of refuge 200 years after the Reformation. In the 1930s book burnings returned and Luther's book found dark expression during *Kristallnacht*, which occurred on the reformer's birthday. Evil enters in through the flaws in human character, never where it is morally strong. The humiliation and blows to national pride at Versailles – and the economic ruin that followed – fed latent nationalist extremism together with fears of the relentless march of apparently Slavic-Jewish Bolshivikism.

As a secret or semi-secret society, the Thule Society could not be a direct political influence. It needed a front organisation supplied by the DAP (later the NSDAP) of which the young Adolf Hitler became the front man. It is not clear whether Hitler's new NSDAP outgrew its esoteric roots or whether it continued to use the man on the stage as a conduit for its quasi-mystical elitist xenophobic nationalism. More likely it was a sympathetic relationship, whereby from 1934 Hitler became the solitary prophet guarded by the black priesthood of Himmler's SS. The roots of National Socialism ceased to be and were suppressed as Hitler's personal power grew and the organisation he led spoke with a single voice. Nothing was lost however, everything useful was subsumed.

Hitler cast a spell over the German people, appealing to their darkest fears and deepest national desires. When the spell broke it was already too late; *Gleichschaltung* had already been put in place, oaths had been made to the Führer in person, and the dishonourable had made full use of unbreakable German honour. They had walked into the spider's web singing nationalist songs, scorning Weimar and Versailles, but now they were trapped. Hitler's first easy victories made many people relieved; perhaps the right man was in control after all. Carl Jung saw in Mussolini a man, even a man with good taste in certain matters, 'For example, that it was good taste to keep the king'. However, he saw no such humanity in Hitler who was, in his opinion, a kind of shaman or medicine man or myth, hardly there at all, 'like a mask, but there is nothing behind the mask'. Jung explains, 'When Hitler speaks he tells the Germans nothing new, but simply what they want to hear. Especially he is a mirror of that inferiority complex which is so markedly a German characteristic.' Hitler was, he wrote, virtually the nation, 'And the trouble about a nation it does not keep its word and has no honour, at least on the level of the collective unconscious. A nation as such, for all the claims of the totalitarian states, is a blind force.' Jung points out that a crowd never rises to the highest thoughts but those that everyone has become the dominant characteristics. Hitler represented the lowest common denominator of the German psyche, the blackest aspects of the nation.[3]

For Hitler the ancient Grecian city-state, with its apparent muscular philosophy and communal elitism, was an ideal template for Germany.[4] Athens and Sparta had particular appeal as indicated by the immediacy of Nazi spectacle and physical display, and their relationship with the natural world. Women in Soviet Russia were like men, expendable units of production, but also potentially their equal on the front line or in the factory. In Germany the woman was also a means of production, for the all-important perpetuation of the pure race. The Nazis both encouraged women to start and extend families through legislation and inducements such as tax allowances for each dependent child (while increasing taxes for the unmarried), generous family allowances and maternity benefits together with awards of medals to the mothers of large families, and also introduced measures to remove women from the workforce so achieving a drop in unemployment of German males and an arrest and reverse of a declining birth rate. The Nazis were not so much anti-feminist as pro-natal. The continuation and expansion of the German nation was dependent on young fertile females baring children as early and for as long as possible, rather than building careers. Nazi policies, whatever they may look like on the surface, were usually racially motivated.[5]

So what were the main differences that seemed to make our princes immune from the Hitler's spell? First and foremost, I would suggest, was their faith. They were all devoted Christians, and the teachings of Christianity do not mix with National Socialism. Christianity is international and demands loyalty beyond any temporal authority. Moreover, Otto, Rupprecht and Hubertus were Catholic with a special loyalty to Rome. Three were heirs and claimants to empty thrones. Monarchy has its own duties to people and place beyond any mere ideology. It also, in a sense, represents individuality and by extension individuality of thought and expression, forbidden under the Nazi regime. Several had doctorates and one – Rupprecht – was highly cultured and educated in the arts, having studied fine art as well as having been a high-ranking military commander. All four were internationalist in outlook and admirers of cultured civilisation. In short, they could not have been regarded by Hitler as anything but rivals, and he could not have been regarded by them as anything but a dangerous man with dangerous ideas – a curiosity – but with his paramilitary forces and extremist views, more of a frightening phenomenon than a politician.

Notes

1 Gottfried Feder was a member of the Thule Society and the DAP. He gave the speech that drew Hitler into the party. He was both anti-Semite and anti-capitalist. He had a small moustache that is thought to have been the inspiration for Hitler to cut his in the same way.

2 Although Ludendorff and Hitler were allies in 1923 and the general believed that future hope for Germany lay in the nationalist groups, he felt betrayed by the National Socialist leader: 'By appointing Hitler Chancellor of the Reich, you have handed over our sacred German Fatherland to one of the greatest demagogues of all time. I prophesy to you this

evil man will plunge our Reich into the abyss and will inflict immeasurable woe on our nation. Future generations will curse you in your grave for this action.'

3 Jung, Carl in *Jung Speaking: Interviews and Encounters*, ed. by William MacGuire and R.F.C. Hull (London, Picador, 1980), pp. 133–9.
4 The presentation of and symbolism associated with the 1936 Olympics expressed the propaganda that ancient Greece was an early example of Aryan civilisation and that Nazi Germany was its natural successor.
5 *Germany*, pp. 627–31, see also Mason, Tim, *Women in Germany, 1925–1940* (Oxford, 1976), pp. 96–101.

II

THE PALACE: HITLER'S ROYAL ENEMIES

5

PRINCE LOUIS FERDINAND OF PRUSSIA

The Hohenzollerns

Prussia was not traditional German land; it was itself a colonial settlement. It was a land of conquest beyond the easternmost German march. This was its tradition and the principal driving force of its ruling class. The Habsburgs were already rulers of Austria in the thirteenth century, but it was not until the sixteenth that a newly Protestant Hohenzollern, Grand Master of the Teutonic Knights from Swabia, became the first hereditary ruler of Prussia. It is not unlikely that the cohesion and attitude of the Prussian officer corps into the twentieth century derived from the special relationship of the Teutonic Knights and crusading aristocracy with their grand master, turned king, turned emperor. It was an empire of frontiersmen and borderers galvanised into a military machine primed for expansion in defence of Protestantism and a belief in a unique German elitism, derived from presiding over and displacing conquered peoples. The fragmentation of old eastern Franconia was viewed as an opportunity for magnates who were able to re-assemble the pieces in their own image.

Friedrich I (reigned 1688–1713), son of the Great Elector Friedrich Wilhelm, was the first Prussian king, called king in Prussia as he could not hold the royal title over territory within the empire. He ruled over a number of territories from Brandenburg in the west to colonial East Prussia, which differed radically economically and in religion. Catholicism was a sizable minority in the prosperous west, for example. Friedrich raised a standing army that grew massively under his son Friedrich Wilhelm I, who spent up to 80 per cent of the nation's revenues on military expenditure in peacetime. It was said in the late eighteenth century that Prussia was not a country with an army, but rather an army with a country. The king refined the administrative apparatus of the state and broke much of the independence of the nobles by introducing a meritocracy – whereby servants of the state could attain ennoblement through good service, but nobles could no longer expect to hold state offices in their own localities. Both he and his son, Friedrich II, made use of the Protestant faith and especially pietism to 'centralise ideological loyalty'.[1] During Friedrich II's reign Prussia developed considerable economic as well as military power, allowing him to rival the Habsburgs and take them on in their own back yard. In 1740 Friedrich invaded the province of Silesia, which he succeeded in keeping, and acquired territory in Poland so uniting the disparate parts of his domain as a single entity. It was during this period that Saxony, Württemberg and Bavaria asserted their own identities as autonomous states, while never succumbing to absolutism.

The dualism that followed the rise of Prussia divided the old empire along religious and economic lines. A largely Protestant North German Confederation was formed with Prussia as the dominant partner. This became the German Customs Union or Confederation. The 'year of revolutions', 1848, saw a major attempt to unify Germany. Disorder broke out throughout the German states. For the first time the King of Prussia made common cause with liberal German nationalists. On 21 March King Friedrich Wilhelm IV rode through the streets of Berlin dressed in black, red and gold, and installed a parliament with a liberal administration.

In 1848 in Frankfurt a liberal 'national' parliament loosely representing Germany drew up a document containing a doctrine of fundamental rights calling for an elected parliament under an emperor governing a Germany of federal states. In the following year it was decided to offer the imperial Crown to the King of Prussia with certain conditions including radical democratic reforms. The offer was rejected contemptuously by the Prussian king who, with the decline of liberal quasi-revolutionary fortunes, had no need to offer concessions to a powerless Frankfurt parliament. Besides which it was the royal position that reform must be granted from above not demanded from below – foremost it must be workable and benefit every section of society.

German unity was never a forgone conclusion and, when it had occurred in the past, was partial and incomplete. German was more a single language than a culture or anything like a political unit. The German Empire was more of a conversation than an association; more of a continent within a continent under light family management than an embryonic super-state. The many states of Germany grew organically and were assimilated into greater entities with local political ambitions. After the decline of the Holy Roman Empire and the brief French ascendancy, it was Prussia that sought to become identified with Germany, which was a Prussian hegemony by another name. The Habsburgs retained Austria and an empire outside of that of old Germany, but the new Germany had to be invented with all the myths and traditions that could be mustered in its support.

German academics in the late 1800s, for all their logical detachment, encouraged nationalism. Historian Heinrich Treitschke glorified war as German destiny and in his lectures poured scorn on Germany's neighbours. Furthermore, he had a particular distaste for Britain and its empire, calling for the pre-eminence of British sea power to be ended. One of his eager students was Alfred von Tirpitz, the future admiral, who was to oversee a naval arms race with the United Kingdom just prior to the First World War, which convinced the British that it would be wise to ally with France and Russia in an attempt to contain German militarism and maintain the balance of power in Europe. Treitschke emphasised German cultural superiority. His students included Tirpitz, Heinrich Claß (founder of the Pan-German League, the membership of which included a large number of university professors), Friedrich von Bernhardi and Carl Peters. Treitschke fed Germany 'the stream of rabid nationalism that engulfed his country in 1914'.[2]

Friedrich Meinecke claimed that unification under Otto von Bismarck came with a high price. According to contemporaries Jakob Burdckhardt, Constantin Frantz and Christian Planck the chancellor's blood and iron policy was 'destroying certain foundations of Western culture and the community of states and was a really deep-reaching revolution which was opening the prospect of further revolutions and an era of wars'. It 'let perish the finer and higher things of culture in a striving after power and pleasure'.[3] Meinecke suggested the Prussian soul had a 'two-fold nature' and that the higher and a lower principle were always struggling with one another. Nationalism and socialism, or *Macht und Geist*, power represented by Prussian militarism and spirit represented by the Germany of the great philosophers and composers.[4] Meinecke wrote:

> Must we not always be shocked at the precipitous fall from the heights of the Goethe era to the swamps of the Hitler period? Passionately we Germans ask ourselves how this was possible within the selfsame nation. We are reminded of Grillparzer's mid-nineteenth century words, which are both diagnosis and prognosis: 'Humanity – Nationality – Bestiality'.[5]

Union was not the triumph of German liberal nationalism, but of Prussian economic and military might and Protestant independence from its Catholic Austrian neighbours. Bismarck is remembered for forging German unity by means of three wars (1864, 1866, 1870), which resulted in the absorption of neighbouring German states – followed by the southern German states that had been excluded from the North German Confederation – into an overall federal state. All this was largely through economic clout and military alliance at the conclusion of the Franco-Prussian War. This war with the French was a patriotic 'German' war to unify previously disparate peoples with local loyalties, and in some ways may have been revenge for the French victory over Prussia at the Battle of Jena in 1806. However, during Bismarck's chancellorship, the deep divisions of religion and dynastic loyalties were revived. He was partisan towards the Protestants during the *Kulturkampf*, which threatened Catholic interests in the new German Empire and resulted in the formation of the Catholic Centre Party as the political wing of the Catholic laity.

Historians have tended to blame Kaiser Wilhelm for the fall of the Hohenzollerns and the demise of the imperial monarchy because he hesitated to abdicate when he could have handed his Crown on to one of his grandsons – untainted by the previous four years. This, however, ignores the principle of legitimacy and the dangers of precedent. How could he have willingly disinherited his son and heir and surrendered the rights and responsibilities of the Crown that he was sworn to uphold, and to an unsure future in the constitutional model of the UK, possibly as a tool of left-wing politics to which he was fundamentally opposed (especially following the fall of the Romanovs)? Furthermore, Prince Louis Ferdinand of Prussia was fully aware of his own responsibilities to the dynasty and the monarchical principle when he resisted suggestions that he should accept the Crown or represent his family while his father or elder brother lived.

Prince Louis Ferdinand

Countries which have never felt the horrible yoke of ruthless and lawless tyranny will never understand what physical and mental torture it means for those who live under such a regime.[6]

Prince Louis Ferdinand of Prussia was an extraordinary man, the more so because he actively sought his destiny among the ordinary everyday. He was the first in his family to be awarded a PhD and the first who felt the need and desire to pursue higher learning. In spite of being the second son of the German Crown prince and a grandson of the kaiser, Wilhelm II, he worked as a labourer on the Ford assembly line in Detroit for workman's wages and went on the road in the USA as a car salesman. He admitted that as a schoolboy he had 'leftist leanings' and was an enthusiastic supporter of the Weimar Republic. Although he came to the conclusion that monarchy was a desirable if not essential component of the smooth working of the state for the benefit of all its citizens, he never lost his rebellious streak and was a friend and supporter of Franklin D. Roosevelt and the Democratic cause in the USA. He was assiduous in his opposition to the rule of the Nazis in Germany, which extended to active participation in plots against Hitler. He was the preferred head of state to succeed Hitler following a successful coup and offered to give the order to the military high command to oust the dictator if the situation demanded.

After the end of the First World War and the fall of the kaiser, the family of the Crown prince, including himself, were guarded by the president of the Workers and Soldiers Council of Potsdam with about thirty soldiers who had made the journey with the express intention of making sure that the royal family came to no harm in the disturbances. Prince Louis Ferdinand recalls the confusion among his own family at the time of the November Revolution:

> The dejected mood of the grownups impressed me strongly. People who up until that day had been vested with every possible authority were unable to conceal their helplessness and despair. From our window I could see my uncles and aunts, all in a long row, walking up and down in front of the palace.[7]

The revolution of 9 November 1918, writes the prince, was neither a social upheaval nor was it directed against any ruling family in Germany. 'It was a revolution of hunger, caused by the desperate desire of the people for peace at any price, especially after President Wilson had declared his fourteen points. The great majority of the people had no particular grudge against the dynasties.' Germany had a 'lack of talent for revolutions' due to their obsession with order.[8] Louis Ferdinand observes that Germans have 'no talent for revolution' because of that obsession.

Prince Louis' grandfather, the kaiser, was exiled to Doorn in the Netherlands, which became, he recorded, a refuge for the imperial family, 'especially after Hitler turned Germany into a huge dungeon'.[9] Kaiser Wilhelm is remembered as an amiable exile who read lessons from Scripture to his family and staff on weekday mornings and was pleased to receive visitors. The prince's parents insisted, however, that they would stay in Germany if at all possible, which they did. In the 1930s dictatorships were state of the art. Democracy appeared to be an anachronism – unfitted to modern political realities and unequal to the needs of progressive nations, battling threats from the far Left. During a visit to Italy Louis Ferdinand met Il Duce (the fifth dictator he met), but found little real enthusiasm for fascism in the country. He writes:

> To fascists who tried to sell Mussolini's achievements to me, I used to answer, 'In Germany we do not need a dictator to make our trains run on schedule or to keep the streets clean'. (After Germany got her own dictator neither did the trains continue on schedule nor were the streets kept clean).[10]

Louis Ferdinand also met Hitler, whom he said only wanted to talk about the motor car industry. But it was less of a discussion, more of a monologue by the dictator. The prince's grandson and heir, Prince Georg Friedrich of Prussia, says that he has always been impressed by his grandfather's frank description of his encounters with Hitler, Mussolini and other fascists – especially the one with Hitler shortly after the dictator had taken over. In spite of his deep reservations, Prince Louis Ferdinand admitted that Hitler had a certain charisma which seems to have been the secret of his success.[11] Don Luis Ruiz de Valdivia remarked to Prince Louis Ferdinand in the 1930s:

I cannot understand what has happened to the German people since this Hitler came to power. During all the years I lived in Germany I never noticed any real anti-Semitism. I think it is all directed from above. They want some scapegoat. Maybe you and your relatives will be next after the Jews to be liquidated.[12]

De Valdivia told Louis Ferdinand that the prince's family had been supportive of the Jewish people in the past and that had been to the benefit of Germany, whereas in Spain the persecution of the Inquisition had driven out much talent and led, he thought, to the decline of Spain as a world power. Friedrich II of Prussia had written:

Catholics, Lutherans, Reformed, Jews and other Christian sects live in this state, and live together in peace. If the sovereign, actuated by a mistaken zeal, declares himself for one religion or another, parties spring up, heated disputes ensue, little by little persecutions will commence and, in the end, the religion persecuted will leave the Fatherland, and millions of subjects will enrich our neighbours by their skill and industry.

On 8 April 1930 Crown Princess Cecilie of Prussia was reported by the *Chicago Tribune* press service to be on board the steam ship *Ancona* bound for Argentina. Her intent was to plead with her grandson to give up his job as a labourer at the Ford plant in Buenos Aires and return for the celebration of his parents' twenty-fifth wedding anniversary. She also wanted to 'look over' the prince's new girlfriend, the daughter of the Argentine multimillionaire, Carlos Tornquist. Especially given the prince's recent 'adventures in Hollywood', where he'd had an all too public affair with the movie actress Lily Damita. Dynasty and politics further intruded on Prince Louis Ferdinand in 1933 when his elder brother, Wilhelm, renounced his rights upon his marriage to a commoner, Dorothea von Salviati, in 1933. Consequently Louis now became heir to his father's and grandfather's titles and to the responsibilities to the Prussian and German people.

On 8 November 1933 Prince Louis Ferdinand sent a telegram to Governor Roosevelt congratulating him on being elected President of the United States. 'Lining up with many millions of the world I want to congratulate Your Excellency for the most brilliant victory of common sense and democracy due to your wonderful courage and determination.'[13] The president elect replied, 'We had, indeed, a wonderful victory on Tuesday last,' and wrote that he and Mrs Roosevelt looked forward to seeing the prince over the winter. 'You must be sure to come and see us at the White House,' he concluded.[14]

Professor William E. Dodd, the American ambassador in Berlin, warned Prince Louis Ferdinand, 'If you don't try to be more careful with your talk, Prince Louis, they will hang you one of these days.'[15] In March 1938 Ambassador Dodd forwarded a letter from Prince Louis Ferdinand to President Roosevelt. He also

1. Dr Otto von Habsburg (second from left) and his brothers in the USA. (Photograph courtesy of the office of the late Dr Otto von Habsburg)

2. Dr Otto von Habsburg, Florida 1942. (Photograph courtesy of the office of the late Dr Otto von Habsburg)

3. Herzog Dr Maximilian von Hohenburg, taken by the SS when he first arrived at Dachau. When he was released his wife hardly recognised him. (Dachau Archive, by permission of HH Herzog Georg von Hohenberg)

4. Dr Otto von Habsburg. (Photograph courtesy of the office of the late Dr Otto von Habsburg)

5. Prince Hubertus zu Löwenstein and family. (With permission of HSH Princess Konstanza zu Löwenstein)

6. Prince Hubertus zu Löwenstein.
(With permission of HSH Princess
Konstanza zu Löwenstein)

7. Prince Hubertus zu Löwenstein. (With
permission of HSH Princess Konstanza zu
Löwenstein)

8. Crown Prince Rupprecht of Bavaria. (Private
Collection (by request))

10. Prince Louis Ferdinand with Franklin D. Roosevelt in 1929. (Eigentum des Hauses Hohenzollern, SKH Georg Friedrich Prinz von Preussen. Hausarchiv Burg Hohenzollern)

11. The friendship of the UK's King George VI and Queen Elizabeth (the late Queen Mother) with president F.D. Roosevelt and Eleanor Roosevelt. The royal couple's popularity in America was critical prior to the USA's entry into the war. (Wikimedia Commons)

12. The rides of Christian X of Denmark through the streets of Copenhagen were a recognisable gesture of defiance against the German occupation. (Wikimedia Commons)

13. A Dachau watchtower. Dachau concentration camp had several royal residents. (Wikimedia Commons)

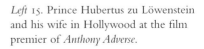

Above 14. Prince Hubertus zu Löwenstein and his wife.

Left 15. Prince Hubertus zu Löwenstein and his wife in Hollywood at the film premier of *Anthony Adverse*.

stated his belief that the prince was hopeful of becoming a citizen of the USA.[16] Prince Georg Friedrich of Prussia notes, 'Theoretically various possibilities may have been considered by my grandfather at that time but eventually I think it was his distinct sense of tradition which kept him from becoming an American citizen.'[17] Had he become a US citizen he may have been able to work against the Nazis from over the Atlantic much in the same way as Crown Prince Otto and Prince Hubertus. However his coming role as heir and unifying focus of the German resistance movement depended not only on his continued German nationality, but his continued domicile within the Reich.

In 1938 Louis Ferdinand married the Grand Duchess Kira, younger daughter of Grand Duke Kirill of Russia and Princess Victoria Melita of Edinburgh, a grand-daughter of Queen Victoria. Roosevelt responded to the news of Louis Ferdinand's wedding by inviting the prince and his new bride, Princess Kira, to spend part of their honeymoon as his guests, to which they replied from the SS *Bremen* in mid-ocean in the affirmative signing off, 'Much LOVE, KIRA and LOUIS'.[18] According to Louis Lochner of the Associated Press and long-time friend of Prince Louis Ferdinand, when the prince and his wife visited the USA as part of a round-world honeymoon trip in 1938 they were the house guests of the Roosevelts and had many chats with the president on the dangers of Nazism and its imperialistic and militaristic threats. 'The President and the Prince found themselves in com-plete accord,' he recalled.[19] Louis Ferdinand was asked by the president to take back a message to give to Ribbentrop suggesting a meeting between Hitler and the president together with Mussolini and the British prime minister, with the Azores as a possible location. The prince passed on the proposal, but it was not answered except with an accusation that he was having treasonous contact with an enemy of Germany.[20] On his honeymoon trip around the world he found no enthusiasm for Hitler or his regime. 'Is that madman in Berlin going to start a war?' asked General Windecker the German consul in Singapore. The captain of the SS *Potsdam* on which he was sailing barely concealed his 'cordial hatred of Nazism' and the *Japan Times*, which was close to the Japanese Foreign Office, published a derogatory arti-cle about Göring and other leading Nazis while the prince visiting that country.[21]

Writing to Prince Louis Ferdinand on the birth of his eldest son, President Roosevelt assured the prince that the 'great event' had made him very happy and sent his warm congratulations, commenting, 'With such delightful parents we can all look forward to great things for him,' and concluded with an invitation to 'come back and see us at Washington or Hyde Park [the family home] where a hearty welcome awaits you'.[22] HRH Prince Georg Friedrich of Prussia says that the years his grandfather spent in America definitely had a strong impact on him and his character:

Therefore he probably represented a type of man who was capable of a new beginning. Especially after his grandfather and his father had abdicated he seemed to be the only possible pretender for any eventual reintroduction. At the same time his personal interest in music and his artistic mind made him independent and created a link between the past and the future. He epitomized many aspects of Germany's history and always declared that he would have been ready if the German people had called upon him.

Prince Friedrich (Fritzi) of Prussia (a critic of the Nazi regime) was in London at the outbreak of war in 1939, and chose to stay on in England rather than return to Germany. In 1940 he was detained as an enemy alien and sent to an internment camp in Canada, but was released in January 1941 as a result of the intercession of Queen Mary. After serving in the Pioneer Corps, clearing the debris of the Blitz in London, he took up farming in Hertfordshire.

In November 1948 Prince Friedrich told Queen Mary that he had recently visited Castle Hohenzollern and enclosed a photograph with his letter. 'The Burg is well kept, a heavenly view for miles and miles, but the inside of the Burg is hideous. It is too cold to live in it during the winter.'[23] When he was invited to the coronation he sent his thanks to his 'dear aunt' Queen Mary recalling, 'You really don't know how much I was impressed by the great events through which we lived.'[24]

Prince Louis Ferdinand and the German Resistance

Prince Louis Ferdinand of Prussia was an obvious candidate for constitutional monarch in Germany. He took no part in the First World War as he was too young and so was untainted by the association. He had a PhD and had lived in the USA where he worked as a Ford worker, and was a friend of President Roosevelt. Curiously, in 1933 the US Consul General in Berlin, George Messersmith, believed that if an international crisis became unavoidable Hitler might make Prince Louis Ferdinand head of state in Germany with him remaining as chancellor, which Messersmith thought would be a good solution – it would lead to more moderate and saner government. Louis Ferdinand was, he judged, 'a very sensible and really a very fine boy'.[25] Hitler, however, had no intention of restoring the monarchy and Louis Ferdinand had no intention of being a puppet.

Louis Ferdinand was first approached by the embryonic German resistance movement through Otto John, a fellow Lufthansa employee, in 1937.[26] Louis Ferdinand told John that he would be glad to co-operate, 'provided his organisation had a sound platform and proceeded in complete secrecy'. John admitted that the opposition had made little headway up until that time because it was almost impossible to secure the co-operation of the army, 'The only body which could eliminate Hitler by force.' However, in November 1939 he was informed by John and Dr Klaus Bonhoeffer that General Franz Halder had been won over to their cause.[27]

Meetings 'camouflaged as musical or cultural evenings' were held at Prince Louis Ferdinand's house where he met leading anti-Nazis. These included Hans von Dohnanyi, Dr Justus Delbrück of the secret service, Christian trade union leader Jakob Kaiser, Social Democrat Ernst von Harnack, churchman Dietrich von Bonhoeffer and Dr Joseph Wirmer of the Catholic Centre Party. Of those who visited the prince only two survived Hitler's purge after the famous plot of 20 July 1944.[28]

Louis Ferdinand was told that the opposition needed 'a stabilizing and unifying figure upon whom they could build,' especially in the immediate aftermath of a successful coup. He, they told him, was acceptable to both conservatives and progressives in the army and labour organisations. His experience as a Ford worker and his friendship with President Roosevelt were of particular benefit. The prince replied that he wanted to help, but his grandfather, father and elder brother had to be considered. Although his brother Wilhelm had officially lost his place in the dynastic succession due to his morganatic marriage, he still regarded himself as rightful heir. Besides which he was extremely popular in the military, whereas Prince Louis Ferdinand was distrusted by some army leaders who saw his lack of military experience and foreign left-wing associations as negative indications of his character and dynastic suitability.[29]

However, His Royal Highness Prince George observes that the years Louis Ferdinand spent in America definitely had a strong impact on him and his character, 'Therefore he probably represented a type of man who was capable of a new beginning'. After his grandfather and his father had abdicated he seemed to be the only possible contender for an eventual restoration. At the same time his personal interest in music and his artistic mind made him independent and created a link between the past and the future. He epitomised many aspects of Germany's history and always declared that he would have been ready if he had been called upon by the German people.[30] He then approached General Ludwig Beck who replied that it was unwise for them to meet at that time as the general was being watched by the Gestapo, and suggested that the prince should keep in the background, 'so as not to excite the curiosity of Hitler's men'.[31]

The invasion of France was a considerable setback for the opposition, as it was more difficult to topple a successful German leader than a failure or one who was demonstrably putting the Fatherland in danger. After the invasion of Soviet Russia, however, the spirits of the opposition leaders rose again. In 1941, at John's suggestion, Louis Lochner wrote an article about Louis Ferdinand's close relations with Roosevelt, which was intended for circulation among top German military commanders to encourage active support for regime change.[32]

As detailed in the previous chapter, in the autumn of 1941 up to fifteen members of the resistance movement met with Louis Lochner in the home of sympathiser and industrialist Josef Wirmer. They asked him to take a message to Roosevelt explaining their motives and political objectives and requesting the president's help in achieving peace, together with a cover letter written by their mutual friend Louis Ferdinand. Lochner agreed at once, but before he had the opportunity to make the journey the Japanese attacked Pearl Harbor and Germany declared war on the USA. As a result Lochner was unable to leave for America until the following June. As we already know, when he arrived in Washington he was met with a political brick wall.[33]

In July 1942 he met Dr Goerdeler, the man in whom, 'countless men and women from all layers of the German populace opposed to Hitler placed their hopes'. Goerdeler said that it was high time to stop the war and that only by removing Hitler could reasonable peace terms be obtained. As assassination was against his principles he intended to visit commanders at the front to convince them of the necessity of taking action to overthrow the Nazis. He advised the prince to remain at home in *Cadinen* and keep as quiet as possible. As a possible future constitutional head of state, the opposition were keen to protect him – he was one of their most valuable assets. It was as a consequence of the importance of the prince's dynastic position, which ensured that no one revealed his involvement even under torture; it is to their credit and because of their bravery that Hitler's most dangerous royal enemy and intended replacement survived the war.[34]

In an interview with General Hammerstein, Louis Ferdinand told the soldier he thought it high time the army moved against Hitler and that he was ready to issue the order in his right as heir to the German throne if necessary, to compensate for a lack of 'civil courage' (*Zivilcourage*) by the German military caste. Hammerstein agreed that only the army could do it, 'But,' he continued, 'they will never do it.' He said that they didn't have the civil courage to do it: 'I don't see the slightest chance of such action. The German army will be defeated utterly, and only then will Hitler fall.' He told the prince that he appreciated his readiness to co-operate, but neither General Beck nor he were able to do anything, certainly at that time at least. 'The only advice I can give you,' he said, 'also in the name of Beck, is to go back into hiding at your country place and keep alive!' The general's pessimism was an 'awful blow' to Louis Ferdinand and the conspirators, but they had no alternative but to keep up hope.[35]

In March 1943 John met with the prince in Berlin and told him that contact had been made with Field Marshal von Kluge, but without any immediate success. A group that included John, Kaiser and Dietrich Bonhoeffer appealed to his patriotism and asked if he would be prepared to give an order to act to the generals in the expectation that they would obey a leading Hohenzollern. Louis Ferdinand replied that he was willing to give that order if the situation so demanded, but he would have to consult with his father first, as the Crown prince was the legitimate heir and because General Beck was devoted to him. As a consequence, an order from his father had far more chance of being obeyed than any he might give without first being sanctioned by the head of the house of Hohenzollern.[36] He went to see his father that evening while Ewald von

Kleist sought an interview with General Olbricht, second-in-command of the home forces, to ascertain his views on action to be taken. The Crown prince's reaction was not encouraging as he not only refused to give his authority to an order that might save the Fatherland, but strongly advised his son to steer clear of subversive movements. 'Other people', he said, had lately approached him with similar suggestions, but none of the schemes proposed seemed to him sufficiently sound to warrant even a chance of success. This reaction was deeply disappointing to Louis Ferdinand given the situation in Germany, which had a ruling class 'made up largely of ruthless criminals'.[37] Meanwhile General Olbricht had told Dr Goerdeler that for the moment he could not act and therefore any order from Louis Ferdinand or his father would be a 'useless risk'. Neither was General Kluge willing to make any commitment to take action at that time. Goerdeler saw that there was not much the prince could do except return to his family and stay in the background.[38]

After 1943 Prince Louis Ferdinand did what he was told; he remained quiet and waited. The generals involved in the 20th July plot of 1944 evidently left the prince out of the loop, either to protect their principle asset in the event of failure or because the pressing events of Soviet and Western Allied offensive action forced a revision of the planned composition of the immediate post-Hitler administration, which may not have included a Hohenzollern for the time being. One might be cynical and postulate that when the prince's name failed to gain them access to president Roosevelt or reverse the Allied insistence on unconditional surrender, the plotters moved on without him. There were rumours that not only had the plotters intended a restoration of the monarchy, but that a coronation had been prepared in Konigsberg in 1944. Furthermore, although the prince referred to his activities as indirect, HRH Prince Georg Friedrich of Prussia says, 'Even if my grandfather's role remained "indirect" he and his family were permanently threatened throughout the last years of the Nazi regime. From well informed sources [members of the family and others] I have been told that his commitment went much further than what is generally known.'[39]

After 20 July 1944 two Gestapo officers visited Prince Louis Ferdinand at his home near Elbing. They asked him where he had been and to whom he had spoken in the previous two weeks. He told them that he had just returned from Golzow where he had been arranging quarters for his family, who needed a change of climate. Believing that 'the truth is the best lie' he also revealed that on 20 July he had visited Field Marshal von Küchler and enquired whether they thought the field marshal was involved. 'No, not him,' they replied, 'he's alright as far as we know.' The prince told them that his life was an open book and his friends and acquaintances were well known to the local Gestapo officer, who agreed that they were. After his visitors had been provided with wine and cigars and the prince had signed a protocol and toasted their health, they left apparently convinced that their host was innocent.

After the war Prince Louis Ferdinand was offered British citizenship as he was a descendant of Queen Victoria, but he declined as his dedication to his country was undiminished. He ardently wished for the re-unification of Germany, but did not lose his well-developed sense of humour. 'When a deputy of the GDR government once visited him in the 1980s at Hohenzollern Castle in order to ask whether the coffins with the remains of King Frederick the Great and his father Frederick William I could be taken from there back to Potsdam,' recalls Prince Georg Friedrich of Prussia, 'He patiently listened to his proposals and accepted every detail until he finally added, that the only precondition of this enterprise would be the reunification of Germany ...'[40]

Notes

1 Fulbrook, Mary, *A Concise History of Germany*, p. 80.
2 Vivian, Herbert, *Secret Societies Old and New 1927* (Kessinger, 2004), p. 205.
3 Meinecke, Friedrich, *The German Catastrophe* (Beacon Press, 1972), p. 13.
4 Ibid., p. 105.
5 Ibid., p. 53.
6 Prussia, Prince Louis Ferdinand of, *The Rebel Prince*, p. 224.
7 Ibid., pp. 39–42.
8 Ibid., p. 42.
9 Ibid., p. 49.
10 Ibid., p. 120.
11 Interview with Prince Georg Friedrich of Prussia, August 2010.
12 Prussia, Prince Louis Ferdinand of, *The Rebel Prince*, p. 72.
13 Telegram from Prince Louis Ferdinand of Prussia to Franklin D. Roosevelt, 8 November 1934. Franklin D. Roosevelt Library, PPF 110.
14 Letter from Franklin D. Roosevelt to Prince Louis Ferdinand of Prussia, 9 November 1934. Franklin D. Roosevelt Library, PPF 110.
15 Prussia, Prince Louis Ferdinand of, *The Rebel Prince*, p. 253.
16 Memorandum from Hon. R. Walton, Assistant Secretary of State, Washington, 23 March 1938. Franklin D. Roosevelt Library, PPF 110.
17 Interview with Prince Georg Friedrich of Prussia, August 2010.
18 Radio message to Pultney Bigelow, 22 May 1938. Franklin D. Roosevelt Library PPF 110.
19 Prussia, Prince Louis Ferdinand of, *The Rebel Prince*, p. 148.
20 Ibid., p. 148–9.
21 Ibid., pp. 280, 291.
22 Letter to Prince Louis Ferdinand, Potsdam, Germany, 23 March 1939. Franklin D. Roosevelt Library, PPF 110.
23 RA/QM/PRIV/CC45/1612. All extracts from private letters in the Royal Archives, Windsor Castle, reproduced by kind permission of HM Queen Elizabeth II.
24 RA/QM/PRIV/CC45/1100 I.
25 George S. Messersmith to William Philips Under Secretary of State in Washington, 14 August 1943, p. 10; George S. Messersmith papers 1907–1955, Ms 109, 125500, Box 2, F16; Special Collections Department of the University of Delaware: http://www.lib.udel.edu/ud/spec/findaids/html/mss0109.html.
26 Prussia, Prince Louis Ferdinand of, *The Rebel Prince*, p. 311, Otto John was second legal advisor for Lufthansa and a friend of Hans von Dohnanyi, who was in turn a friend of the prince's piano teacher and another member of the opposition movement.

27 Prussia, Prince Louis Ferdinand of, *The Rebel Prince*, p. 311.

28 Ibid.

29 Ibid.

30 Interview with Prince Georg Friedrich of Prussia, August 2010.

31 Prussia, Prince Louis Ferdinand of, *The Rebel Prince*, p. 313.

32 Ibid., p. 313.

33 Klemperer, Klemens von, *German Resistance Against Hitler: The Search For Allies Abroad, 1938–1945* (Oxford, 1994), pp. 232–4.

34 Prussia, Prince Louis Ferdinand of, *The Rebel Prince*, p .316.

35 Ibid., p. 314.

36 Ibid., p. 316–7.

37 Ibid., p. 317–8.

38 Ibid.

39 HRH Prince Georg Friedrich of Prussia, interview with the author, August 2010.

40 HRH Prince Georg Friedrich of Prussia, interview with the author, August 2010. In November 1948 Prince Friedrich of Prussia, who had been a wartime exile from Hitler in England, wrote to Queen Mary of Great Britain shortly after a visit to Castle Hohenzollern: 'The Burg is well kept, a heavenly view for miles and miles, but the inside of the Burg is hideous. It is too cold to live in it during the winter.' Royal Archives, Windsor Castle, RA/QM/PRIV/CC45/1612.

6

CROWN PRINCE RUPPRECHT OF BAVARIA

The Wittelsbachs

Bavaria was ruled by the Wittelsbachs from 1180 until 1918, dukes and counts palatine – i.e. with a right to direct rule and complete control of all justice. Their kingship only began in 1805, however, at the Treaty of Pressburg, following which the Bavarians promoted the continued independence of small states in the face of the competing nationalism of Prussia and Austria. The electoral palatinate by the Rhine was awarded to the family in 1214.

Although Bavaria eventually joined the Prussian-German Federation following the Franco-Prussian War, it never lost its individual identity and retained much of its sovereignty within a federal context. Its preoccupations with its own separate identity were based on a highly developed cultural identity of which a political identification was a natural consequence.

Crown Prince Rupprecht

Crown Prince Rupprecht of Bavaria was an early opponent of Hitler and his sometime ally General Ludendorff. He went into exile when the dictator came to power and remained in Italy (for the latter part in hiding from the Gestapo) until liberation. Much of his family meanwhile, and unbeknown to him, were captured by the Nazis following the 20th July plot under the *sippenhaft* ('kith and kin' – collective responsibility) laws and send to Dachau and Sachsenhausen concentration camps. Crown Prince Rupprecht of Bavaria was a student of the fine arts who particularly favoured Renaissance and Eastern art and travelled widely in the Far and Middle East and Italy. He also studied international law and trained as a soldier, becoming as near to a professional army officer as is possible for any prince. In short, he was a true Wittelsbach and took his role as heir to King Ludwig III of Bavaria very seriously.

The current Duke of Bavaria, HRH Duke Franz, only really got to know his grandfather after 1945. He remembers him as a rather strict old gentleman who, however, had a good sense of humour and a particular empathy with young people. 'He was,' the duke says, 'highly educated and had a deep understanding of culture,' which greatly impressed him and influenced his own appreciation, discovery and collection of works of art.[1]

Crown Prince Rupprecht was an able wartime commander rising to field marshal. As the general commanding imperial troops opposing the British Expeditionary Force at the first Battle of the Somme, he regretted the terrible loss of British lives. On 15 September he wrote:

> Our losses in territory may be seen on the map with a microscope. Their losses in that far more precious thing – human life – are simply prodigious … It saddens us to exact the dreadful toll of suffering and death that is being marked up on the ledger of history, but if the enemy is still minded to possess a few more hectares of blood-sodden soil, I fear they must pay a bitter price.[2]

He did reflect afterwards that during the battle the Allied powers had succeeded in destroying what was left the pre-war professional German army. The Germans were forced to withdraw.

Duke Franz makes it clear that his grandfather was not limited to the titular role of a princely regimental commander, but served on the Western Front. He was not confined to a headquarters away from the action, but actively involved in planning and fighting the war at the front – such as the Battle of Lorraine on 20 August 1914, when the Crown prince's army feigned retreat and lured the French forces into a trap before counter-attacking.

> He cannot, however, be dismissed as a 'militarist': after years of war his personal experience of bloodshed at the front informed and shaped his opinions. He was particularly sickened by the use of poison gas. Unfortunately, he was unsuccessful in convincing the *Oberste Heeresleitung* [military high command] of his arguments.[3]

He was also concerned about the behaviour of troops under his command. Duke Franz continues:

> Over an over again he tried to prevent looting and burning by German soldiers and gave orders to that effect. He saw no military advantage in a 'burnt earth' policy to harass the civilian population and destroy the resources of

conquered areas. His refusal to follow this policy was equally for military and humanitarian reasons.

Rupprecht was not only capable; he was pragmatic. In 1917–18 he wrote to his father and the kaiser with the opinion of a general in the field that a German victory was no longer possible. He urged the negotiation of an armistice from strength while his county's forces still occupied large areas of enemy territory. In July 1917 he wrote to Count Georg von Hertling, the German chancellor and former Prime Minister of Bavaria, urging him of the necessity of opening peace negotiations based on a return to the pre-war status quo with the exclusion of claims of compensation. He believed that peace should be made with Russia by the beginning of 1918 at the latest. He also questioned submarine warfare against Britain and told the chancellor that the aerial bombing of London was entirely mistaken and could only lead to an increase in bitterness against Germany and reprisals.[4] He called for the opening of peace talks based on a restoration to the Allies of all the territory that it had acquired on the Western Front, while retaining all that had been acquired in the East.[5] Rupprecht came into conflict with generals Paul von Hindenburg and Eric Ludendorff, whose uncompromising direction of the war was based on entirely military objectives. Needless to say, Rupprecht disagreed with General Ludendorff's plans for a large-scale offensive in 1918, which he claimed would fail, thus wasting an opportunity to secure a peace with some honour and little compromise.

Rupprecht's disagreements with the military policies of Ludendorff were further exacerbated by the latter's insistence that, after the end of the war, the politicians in Germany who had negotiated with the Allies had stabbed the unconquered German army in the back. This was done, he claimed, by their making peace with the Allies on unfavourable terms and disowning the kaiser and military high command to further their own personal political ambitions. In November 1918, it was said, the German army was unbeaten and in enemy territory. But this ignored Ludendorff's admission on 8 August 1918 that his demoralised troops could no longer be depended upon and that peace was needed quickly. On 26 September, after the collapse of their Austrian and Bulgarian allies, the German high command informed the kaiser that 'an immediate appeal must be made to president Wilson [of the USA] to mediate an armistice', of which Ludendorff claimed, 'No one would say it was too soon.' Prince Maximilian von Baden questioned the decision that would he thought be an admission of defeat, but he was overruled by Hindenburg and Ludendorff.

In autumn 1918 the German high command sought a peace with the Allies who would not negotiate with the military or the kaiser (who they blamed for starting the war). Wilson, in particular, wanted a settlement with what civilian authority there was in Germany. As a consequence Hindenburg and Ludendorff appointed Prince Maximilian von Baden as chancellor, with the brief of negotiating an armistice. On 7 November 1918, Kurt Eisner, leader of the Independent Socialist Party, declared Bavaria a socialist republic and took over the state. King Ludwig was ousted and his son and heir serving his country on the Western Front was disinherited. Duke Franz says that it is evident that the Crown prince's main concern after the war was for all sections of the Bavarian population who were at that time in dire straits. Moreover, his mind was particularly directed to how in the chaotic political situation that then prevailed, the cultural inheritance and sovereignty of Bavaria could be protected. 'My great-grandfather, King Ludwig III of Bavaria never abdicated,' he continues, 'but only released the military and civil authorities from their personal oath of allegiance to the king so that the administration of the country could continue to be enacted.'[6]

On 10 November, Rupprecht protested against, 'the political upheaval which was brought about by a minority without the participation of the lawmaking authorities and will of Bavarian citizenry in the army and at home'. He demanded that the form of government, 'be decided by a national constituent assembly on the basis of free and general suffrage ...'[7] This personal commitment to the general will of the Bavarian people is key to understanding the Crown prince's continued refusal to consider a restoration of the monarchy that was not explicitly popular and legally obtained. He was first and foremost a believer in popular monarchy, acting not only in the interests of – but also with the consent – the Bavarian people. Duke Franz says of Crown Prince Rupprecht, 'Throughout his life he remained convinced that a constitutional monarchy was the best form of government for Bavaria.' His Royal Highness points out that as heir to the throne of his father Ludwig III, the sovereignty of Bavaria was of prime importance to him, and that the role of monarch implied a position that was above political parties.

Eisner was assassinated on 21 February 1919. The soldiers and workers councils took over the Bavarian government, and Russian-born member of the German Communist Party (KPD) Eugen Levine declared a soviet republic defended by Red Guards. An overtly communist Bavaria threatened the integrity of the German republic, so Frederick Eibert ordered the regular German army and 30,000 irregular *Freikorps* under Franz Epp, into Bavaria to reassert the dominion of the Reich government.

Rupprecht and his family returned and settled in Bavaria after the collapse of the revolution. The change of regime and the presence of federal troops, however, further eroded Bavarian independence and any hope of a restoration of its monarchy. Although there were several monarchist groups operating in Munich at that time, and the house of Wittelsbach (especially its Crown prince) remained extremely popular – if not more popular than even before the war, restoration served little practical purpose as far as the political ambitions of most members of the state government were concerned, apart from as a possible means of countering German centrism. Before the war, the German princes were allies of the

kaiser, not his vassals. After the war the states revolved around Berlin more completely than ever before.

For many Germans in 1918 – faced with the Allies' demands, internal starvation and unrest perceived as the result of excessive militaristic nationalism – a
rejection of an insular empire based on the old order in favour of something
more international and socially equitable seemed desirable. So representatives of
international socialism in its several forms, ranging from the pre-war model to
the more violent extremes of Bolshevism, squabbled over what was left of the
German economy and government. A Russian émigré like Eugen Levine could
even assume the leadership of a soviet Bavaria and its worker's councils – if only
for a short while. The Versailles conference however, with its harsh conditions
of reparation and the acceptance of war guilt, restored feelings of nationhood
(in its different forms) and a siege mentality began to prevail that promoted and
fed extreme nationalism. 'Us and them' did not only mean Germany and the
rest of the world, but real Germans (or Bavarians, Prussians, etc.) and those alien
forces and ideas that had – in the view of nationalists – threatened to ruin the
country forever, such as international communism and foreign interference. So
monarchism as a sentiment representative of national independence, if not an
achievable political reality, became as much an ideal among patriotic liberals as
their right-wing opponents. Heinrich Held, the leader of the peasant wing of the
Bavarian People's Party stated, 'Under the monarchy I was … under suspicion of
being anti-monarchist. Only from the first day of the Revolution on did I openly
acknowledge my monarchical conviction.' In Bavaria monarchism and federalism, as against the intrusions of a centralist republic, went hand in glove. In 1920
Held addressed the Reichstag claiming that being federalist did not mean being
an enemy of the Reich however. 'The Federalist conviction,' he said, 'can be more
advantageous to the Reich than centralism that makes everything the same.' He
went on to point out that it was the 'distended sausage skin' of Prussia that was
'in the end called the Reich', to which he and fellow federalists objected.[8] The
Weimar Republic suddenly began to look un-German.

In 1920 unrest continued in Germany. About 50,000 communists formed
themselves into a red army and occupied the Ruhr until put down by the *Freikorps*
on the orders of the government. A right-wing coup (the Kapp Putsch) gained
temporary control of the Berlin government until a General Strike brought it to
an end. In 1921 King Ludwig died and Rupprecht succeeded to his father's rights,
if not his throne. There was a moment when the Crown prince considered taking
the Crown and sounded out Hindenburg as to the likely response of the Reich
authorities. In the same year the *Freikorps* were dissolved, which led many to join
Hitler's paramilitary SA, swelling its numbers and increasing its political influence
through its physical presence.

While the National Socialists dreamed of the overthrow of the Weimar
Republic and the active reversal of the Treaty of Versailles point by point, in 1922

Crown Prince Rupprecht offered his personal thoughts about the Washington Conference. He said that he did not know whether disarmament or the limitation of arms was possible, but he believed that warfare could be made more humane. For example, he called for a complete ban on aerial bombing behind the lines, commenting, 'I believe bombing villages, towns and cities is inhuman. A few soldiers may be killed, but many civilians and the inhabitants generally are the victims.'[9] He also called for a complete ban on the use of gas and chemical weapons, stating that during the First World War he was absolutely opposed to the use of gas and expressed himself strongly to that effect. 'The general argument for abolishing bombing,' he said, 'holds good for gas. Civilian inhabitants, too, are the victims.'[10] Similarly he wanted bans on long-range guns that could hit targets far behind enemy lines and submarine blockades (illegal under international law), which threatened civilian populations both on the home front with starvation (as in Germany up until Versailles) and with losses at sea. 'We did not want the [1914–18] war,' he said, 'I knew what war would be like.'[11] He hoped that Germany could be represented and co-operate in future disarmament conferences that may follow on from the Washington Conference. Duke Franz comments:

> He rejected the use of modern weapons of mass destruction – gas for example – for strategic as well as humanitarian reasons. He also objected to the use of aerial bombardment, such as from Bar-le-Duc in June, 1916. He could not, however, convince the High Command or the Kaiser with his arguments. He believed such measures were militarily pointless and foresaw that they could only lead to reprisals. And so it came about.

Prince Rupprecht believed that his Crown would eventually be restored to him and many agreed, especially as he was, as *Time* magazine put it, 'known to be a thoroughly trustworthy and practical man and as such is respected'. A king in waiting he may have been, but there were several political groups in Bavaria that thought him valuable as a pawn to advance their own fortunes. Rupprecht was under no illusions and all too aware of the dangers of getting too close to any one party. He commented to a British officer, 'If offered a throne, I might sit on it for three weeks. Why should I do that to please a party?' He said that he wanted to establish his position on something 'less precarious than a tightrope', and questioned what he could offer his country while the 'stranglehold' of the Versailles conditions remained upon her.[12] Rupprecht was never lured into action in pursuit of his throne, but was rather known for his reserve:

> Although after the death of Ludwig III in 1921 as well as during periods of political instability, as in 1933, there were those who expected the Crown prince and his followers would restore the monarchy in Bavaria, he rejected this. He did not want to restore the monarchy by means of another coup d'état,

because he was of the opinion that such an action could not bring about lasting success. Moreover, he feared that it would have led to bloodshed among
the civilian population.[13]

In 1922–23 French and Belgian troops occupied the Ruhr and took over the
industrial region (which was the key to economic recovery) after the German
government defaulted on reparation payments. Although the government called
for passive resistance to the takeover, it later gave in to international pressure.
Local passive resistance led to the French sending their own workers to work
the mines, and passive resistance ended. The French occupation and the end of
passive resistance to it were a national humiliation by which extreme nationalist
groups, such as the National Socialist Workers' Party, gained much popular support that they would not otherwise have been able to count on. As a consequence
of these events, the German economy collapsed and massive inflation ensued,
so driving even more people into the arms of the extremists. During 1923 there
were also brief communist takeovers of Hamburg and Saxony. The response of
Adolf Hitler, leader of the National Socialist Workers' Party, inspired by the Italian
Fascists' 'March on Rome' (by which Mussolini came to power with apparent
ease), was to call for 'grand manoeuvres' and plan a German 'march on Berlin'.

In early 1923 a monarchist plot was revealed by Ludendorff's associates and
its leaders put on trial. Prince Rupprecht was in no way implicated. Indeed,
Rupprecht told Professor Fuchs, one of the leading plotters, that he would never
enter Munich at the head of machine-guns, as a restoration of that kind would
not be becoming to so ancient a monarchy. 'When he returned, so he had told
Fuchs, he would enter accompanied by schoolchildren and by young girls in
white.'[14] In September 1923 social unrest and violence threatened to de-stabilise
the Bavarian state. Consequently, the prime minister, Eugen von Knilling, introduced martial law and appointed Gustav von Kahr as *staatskomissar* (a position
with dictatorial powers), who, with military and police heads *Reichswehr* General
Otto von Lossow and Colonel Hans Ritter von Seisser, formed a political trium-
virate to neutralise extremists groups and restore order.

Hitler and General Ludendorff decided to take advantage of the reaction
of disparate groups of disaffected German 'patriots' to the humiliation of the
Ruhr occupation. They planned a coup to coincide with the anniversary of the
November Revolution to rid Germany of the politicians and their republic,
who they said had stabbed the German army in the back in 1918, betraying the
German people. The Weimar Republic, disliked by different groups for different reasons (in Bavaria for its centrist disregard of the autonomy of federal state
governments), could be portrayed as un-German traitors who had sold out the
country, ruined by the impossible terms or the Allies, for the gain of personal
political power. The conspirators counted on the acquiescence – if not active support – of nationalist and monarchist groups and individual politicians in Bavaria.

Approaches were, therefore, made to elicit their approbation of the establishment of a new Reich government in Berlin to bring about a national renewal and a restoration of national pride. Incidentally, in October it was reported in *Time* magazine that though Hitler had backed down in face of the opposition shown him by Dr von Kahr, 'He will continue to be a force to be reckoned with in Bavaria, because his military and political organization is said to be perfect,' and, it goes on to say, 'An agreement with von Kahr is by no means unlikely.'[15]

Hitler sent former Bavarian army captain, Ernst Röhm, twice to see Rupprecht to try to win him over with vague promises of a restoration of the monarchy, but the Crown prince would have nothing to do with the National Socialists. During the second meeting in early 1923 the uniformed Röhm, in a theatrical attempt to appeal to Rupprecht as a soldier, bent down on one knee to demand and then beg the prince's favour, but he was unceremoniously dismissed.[16] In November a Lieutenant Neunzert was also sent to Rupprecht to implore him to support the putsch with an offer of a regency, but Neunzert was swiftly ejected and the Crown prince sent a messenger to Kahr, Lossow and Seisser to reassure them of his opposition to Ludendorff and his Nazi allies.[17] He told them through his adjutant to put down the putsch 'at any cost', using troops if necessary. Hitler later confided that he 'hated' Rupprecht von Beyern.[18] Hitler's apparent monarchism was short-lived if it ever existed at all and appears to have been based on attempts to widen his support among the many groups that opposed the Weimar Republic. Hitler also claimed to be a Catholic and added the word 'socialist' to the name of the movement he led. But princes like Rupprecht and Louis Ferdinand of Prussia, Catholics like Cardinal Faulhaber, Archbishop of Munich, and the 3,000 priests who were imprisoned in Dachau concentration camp, as well as traditional German socialists, were among Hitler's most bitter opponents. As part of the conspiracy there was a plot to capture Rupprecht and his staff, together with the entire Bavarian government, at the unveiling of the monument to the Unknown Soldier in front of the war ministry building, but Hitler was dissuaded from carrying it out due to the enormous risks involved.[19]

Ludendorff and Hitler broke into a meeting in a Munich beer hall (the *Bürgerbräukeller*), attended by most of the Bavarian state government, whereupon Hitler fired a gun into the air, announced that the November Revolution was at an end and arrested the entire audience. When von Kahr, Lossow and Seisser refused to agree to joining Hitler's new Reich government, he threatened them with execution by his own hand and said that he would march on Berlin there and then.

During the putsch, Cabinet member Franz Matt was having dinner with Rupprecht's friend, Cardinal Faulhaber and the Papal Nuncio, Monsignor Eugenio Pacelli, the future Pope Pius XII. Once he knew of the putsch, as the sole representative of democratic authority still free, Matt organised a government-in-exile at Regensburg and ordered the police and armed forces to remain loyal and put down the coup.

During a march to link up with Röhm – whose unit had taken over the war ministry – forces led by Hitler and General Eric Ludendorff met with Munich police at Oderplatz. The police opened fire on the rebels and in the skirmish that followed Ludendorff was captured, Göring was wounded and Hitler made an ignominious escape before being captured later.

The period between the French and Belgian occupation of the Ruhr and the Beer Hall Putsch was filled with turmoil. The Weimar government responded to the nationwide unrest and communist insurgency, but it could not prevent a rapid succession of events that threatened to engulf it and spread chaos throughout the country. The government appeared to have been outmanoeuvred by foreign enemies. Central government had failed; it had (it appeared) lost control and could no longer guarantee the prosperity and security of the Reich. Gustav Kahr flirted with the possibility of a putsch to take over the federal government, but his actions must be seen in the context of the times. Bavaria had already suffered communist rule, civil war and its aftermath. For those who considered themselves as patriots, a government of national emergency that promised to restore the monarchy and provide stability would have had enormous appeal, especially if it were portrayed as a truly German solution to the Reich's political problems. Extremists of Left and Right could be dealt with in due course. In the meantime, however, Hitler and his followers, who comprised a not insignificant strength of numbers, needed to be kept quiet. Not for the last time, Hitler was underestimated. Kahr largely failed in his own ambitions because of this underestimation.

Duke Franz says of Rupprecht's relationship with the National Socialists, 'To my grandfather it was clear that a person like Hitler would not allow a division or sharing of power even if there were real or potential monarchists among the National Socialists, Röhm for example. He was personally of the opinion that the NSDAP would be incapable of rule.'[20] In November 1923 von Kahr proposed that Rupprecht should accept the post as chief executive of the Bavarian government that he had recently been obliged to vacate, but despite being urged to accept the offer during a meeting of leading dignitaries, including the philosopher Oswald Spengler, the Crown prince refused.

The Dawes Plan was introduced, which arranged for more manageable reparation payments on a sliding scale and a succession of US loans, which lead to a lowering of inflation to manageable levels and a stabilising of the German economy. The French withdrew from the Ruhr in 1925, further improving the fortunes of the Weimar Republic. The Wall Street Crash, however, led to the US loans being called in and Germany's economic woes returned with a vengeance. The National Socialists' rise in popularity and their electoral successes followed on from the economic downturn of the late 1920s.

Hitler took out a libel action against the newspaper *Munchener Telegramm Zeitung*, which had reported that Rupprecht had refused to sign a Nazi/nationalist-sponsored public manifesto against the Young Plan and that Hitler had threatened him with a public offensive and threatened monarchy in general. Hitler denied the report and said that his attitude towards monarchy was a personal matter. Rupprecht's aide Count Soden, however, said that in a telephone conversation a representative of Hitler told him on behalf of his leader that 'the sharpest public attacks would be waged against the Crown prince unless he signed the document drawn up by Herr Hitler'.[21]

In 1930 Rupprecht refused to become a patron of the annual rally of the *Stahlhelm*, which royalist leader Count Antoni Arco-Valli described as 'a so-called Prussian patriotic organisation coquetting with the idea of dictatorship in Germany'. He said a Prussian *Stahlhelm* dictatorship would find no support in Bavaria. Asserting Bavaria's independence as a state in its own right, he said that Bavaria must be able, for example, to conclude alliances with Austria even against Prussia. He went on to suggest a Bavarian-Austrian Federation as a possibility.[22]

Most royalists in Bavaria, reflecting royal opinion, wanted a restoration of the monarchy, but not secession from the Reich – a Bavarian king presiding over a state legislature within a federal Germany, rather than an independent Bavaria, or a centrist German republic into which Bavarian autonomy had been subsumed. 'Crown Prince Rupprecht believed,' says Duke Franz, 'the sovereignty of Bavaria was best served in the context of a federation of states that constituted the Empire by consent.'[23] The rise of Hitler following the 1932 election, however, changed everything. Worse than a single state was a single state presided over by a single party and a single leader – and one who had no sympathy with Bavarian autonomy or the Bavarian monarchy.

In 1932 Rupprecht wrote to Hindenburg to try to persuade him to deny power to Hitler. A coalition of political groups in Bavaria believed that Rupprecht could be induced to become a bulwark against the Nazis, suggesting that the prince be offered the temporary post of *staatskommissar* with powers to restore order and establish an independent Bavarian state. Erwein Freiherr von Aretin, Rupprecht's close confidant and an anti-Nazi, had a leading role in negotiations with the Bavarian government under Held. Before this could happen, however, Hitler became chancellor, appointed Franz Ritter von Epp as *imperial state holder* in Bavaria and the Bavarian parliament was dissolved.[24] Duke Franz said:

> With the *Gleichschaltung* by the National Socialists from 1933 a *Reichsstatthalter* was imposed on Bavaria and the other German states, replacing the state parliament and prime minister. With that, the independence of all organisations in Germany was at an end because even small organisations and ecclesiastical groups were subsumed into National Socialist organisations. The Crown prince could only reject this because any care of the established culture of Bavaria supported by associations that were traditionally associated with the house of Wittelsbach, became impossible. This was one of the reasons why Crown Prince Rupprecht was not prepared to make any concessions to the

new rulers. His reserve was interpreted as opposition and he was excluded from public life. My grandfather and my father Herzog [Duke] Albrecht were monitored by the Gestapo because the Nazis were aggravated by their popularity and position as the soul of opposition to National Socialism in Bavaria. Also, as a way of intimidating them personally some members of their inner circle were arrested. An official invitation to the Crown prince could lead to repressive measures against the hosts.

Although generally reluctant to assert his rights as King of Bavaria, after Hitler's appointment as Chancellor of Germany in 1933 drastic measures were considered necessary to block the affects of National Socialism. Not only was the usually reserved Crown Prince Rupprecht willing to consider accepting the throne or at least the title of General State Commissioner if it were offered, but also members of the SDP openly considered a monarchic solution as a way of 'blunting' a centrist National Socialist Germany.[25]

Royalist groups could not compete with the National Socialists because, though monarchy could provide an element to government that was 'above the parties', it had difficulty appealing to those beyond its normal constituency. 'Royalists could not muster the diverse protest constituency that Hitler commanded with his appeal to dissatisfied "patriotic" Germans from all walks of life.'[26] So, while monarchy offered stability and national cohesion, it was overshadowed by the revolutionary zeal of a strong, yet ordinary man on a mission of national renewal.

What the Wittelsbachs represented and offered, however, was continuity, legitimacy and a Bavarian identity. During a speech Rupprecht summed this up, 'We are Bavarians ... We forced no foreign war upon the people. We are part of the people, of the soil. We are accustomed to think in centuries and in the interests of Bavaria. Do you think such a bond can be broken by ephemeral forms of government?'[27] Robert S. Garnett Jr observes that, 'Throughout the Weimar period, Rupprecht's highly respected if largely undefined position in the eyes of most Bavarians remained one of the Wittelsbach monarchists' most potent moral advantages.'[28]

After 1933, Rupprecht refused to recognise the legitimacy of the new federal government under the Nazis. His palaces were not decorated with swastikas on festive occasions and he would not allow the *Berchtesgaden* to be used to entertain special guests of the chancellor.[29] In one last desperate attempt to avoid the catastrophe of Nazism, Rupprecht sent an emissary to Hitler to tell the chancellor he was sure that he would see the necessity of a restoration of the monarchy. The emissary went on to tell him that he could not, of course, remain as Reich chancellor in the restored monarchy, because his continued presence 'would be an obstacle to the unification of the German people'. In exchange Hitler was promised rewards, including a dukedom. Hitler rejected the offer and later exclaimed that it had been Rupprecht and his fellow princes who had always been the cause of the disintegration of the German people throughout history, and boasted, 'never has there been a stronger and more integrated unity of the German races than that which we have achieved under my leadership'.[30] In 1934 Rupprecht warned British King George V about Hitler, saying that he was convinced that the German leader was insane.[31]

Crown Prince Rupprecht had close allies against the Nazis in the two principal representatives of the Catholic Church in Bavaria: the cardinal archbishop of Munich, Michael von Faulhaber, and the papal nuncio and future pope, Pius XII. On 21 November 1938, *Time* magazine reported that in Munich two Sundays before:

> Michael Cardinal von Faulhaber, Germany's No. 1 anti-Nazi prelate, preached in his cathedral on 'The God-Given Rights of Personality,' to the accompaniment of rude whistles (which he ignored) from Nazis in his congregation. Last week, at the height of Germany's pogroms, Cardinal Faulhaber asked for police protection for the Catholic clergy. Instead he received, from District Leader Adolf Wagner, a snarl: 'If Faulhaber mends his ways, he will be protected better than the police can protect him.' Thereupon a Nazi mob ganged up to the Cardinal's palace, smashed all the windows within stone's throw.
>
> Meanwhile, Archbishop Michael J. Curley of Baltimore encouraged his Austrian colleagues and excoriated their Nazi enemies from a Washington pulpit in a way no German bishop would dare. 'The madman Hitler and the cripple-minded Göbbels,' he cried, 'cannot silence the gentle and humble and courageous Cardinal Archbishop of Munich, nor can they silence the brave Innitzer [Archbishop of Vienna] ... No decent person can condone the actions of the madman Hitler and the cripple-minded Göbbels ... If Hitler does not like what I say about him and his cripple-minded Minister of Propaganda, let him take up the matter with Secretary of State Hull.'
>
> On the anniversary of the coronation of Pope Pius XI, von Faulhaber preached a sermon complaining about the Nazis' disregard of the concordat between Germany and the papacy, and their heathenism. He noted that there were many in Church circles who were then saying, 'we were hanged without the concordat, and with the concordat we are first drawn and quartered and then hanged.' Afterwards large crowds cheered the cardinal when he left and Crown Prince Rupprect who they also greeted with, 'Long live Rupprect'.[32]

In the latter 1930s Crown Prince Rupprecht became aware of the danger of impending war at the latest following the German invasion of the Sudetenland. Duke Franz reflects that he was one of those who held the opinion that this would be the last time that it would be possible to stop German expansion and prevent war, 'He was surprised why nobody, above all the British, acted at this time.'[33] The Wittelsbachs' uneasy truce with the Nazi hierarchy ended in 1939 when a resistance movement led by monarchist Catholic lawyer Adolf von

Harnier was uncovered. The Wittelsbach properties were confiscated by the state and Rupprecht went into exile in Italy as the guest of King Vittorio Emanuele.[34] Duke Franz explains:

> After 1933 my grandfather undertook several trips, some of them to Italy and there were other opportunities to communicate with King Victor Emanuel III. In 1939 the Italian king invited Crown Prince Rupprecht on (what was offi- cially) a hunting trip, which enabled him to leave Germany. A passport and visa were granted to him to go to Italy in December 1939 probably because the authorities did not want to disturb the treaty of cooperation between the two countries. The family were to follow at the invitation of Queen Elena.
>
> The return of the royal family to Germany in May 1940 was refused on Himmler's orders, as was the case with other princes of German royal houses. Prince Heinrich was not able to start his military career and also had to remain in Italy.

A good relationship developed in the years when Pope Pius XII was papal nuncio in Munich. In 1921 Pacelli had performed the marriage of the Crown prince and princess and he certainly was highly esteemed by them.

While in Italy Rupprecht remained mentally active and kept in touch with the Allies, suggesting that after the inevitable defeat of Germany he could help restore order and assist in its rebuilding following a restoration of the Bavarian monarchy over territory that was to extend to much of the Austrian Tyrol. He said, 'With the continuous long tradition of our dynasty and my own authority I hope to protect [the defeated Germany] from chaos.'[35] He 'was very frank in expressing his dislike of Hitler', and often said that, 'The only hope for Germany was to be beaten and crushed for a long time.' In 1940 he had feared that Hitler would win, but recently said that he had received certain information secretly from Germany which led him to conclude that Germany had lost the Battle of the Atlantic.[36] A secret British document dated 20 January 1942 reveals:

> The Crown prince complains of the food in Italy and remarks on the intense hatred of Italians for the Germans. The Duce has completely lost his popular- ity though he still has a grip on the administration of the country. The Crown prince favours a political subdivision of Germany after the war with possibly a monarchic union between South Germany and what is left of Austria.[37]

Duke Franz observes:

> It is known that during his exile my grandfather dealt with questions relating to the re-organisation of government and its form after the expected collapse of the Third Reich. He wrote a diary, and in Florence he composed a work of

political theory, *Remarks about the state, its form and duties with special consideration of Germany*. Between the spring of 1943 and 1945 he sent several memoranda to the American and British governments about the future form of the government of Bavaria among other things, including some to President Truman. Although it cannot be proved that my grandfather's ideas and observations had any influence on these governments, at the Potsdam conference a plan that included a super German state (*Donaukonföderation*), which corresponded with the Crown prince's own position.[38]

After 20 July 1944, Hitler had Rupprecht's family arrested on his personal orders and removed to concentration camps. Rupprecht, however, escaped capture by the Gestapo and went into hiding in Florence until he was liberated by the Allies.[39] Duke Franz describes his family's ordeal:

With the outbreak of war I was five years old. In 1939 my parents emigrated, together with us two children, via Yugoslavia to Hungary where we were able to live until 1944. We were taught at home because the danger of being spied upon (*Bespitzelung*) made it impossible for us to be educated in a public school. But we were able to be together with our parents and those close to us, which for a child was certainly of utmost importance.

In autumn 1944 our family was arrested by the Gestapo and abducted back into the Reich into different concentration camps. In Sachsenhausen-Oranienburg, the first camp, we met my father's stepsisters. My step-grandmother, however, was separated from her daughters. We did not meet her again during that time.

Because we were classified as 'special prisoners' we could stay together with our parents. On the intervention of my father our nanny, who had been arrested with us, was allowed to leave the concentration camp. However, Countess Bellegarde who taught my father's step-sisters, had to remain. As a child of ten years perhaps one experienced and processed the type of things that we got to see a little more lightly than it affected the adults.

We were taken into *sippenhaft* (kith and kin) custody on Hitler's personal orders. We did not, as so many other prisoners, have to work nor were we starved to death. Neither were we sent on a death march, because we were above all hostages of the Nazis.

The system of 'kith and kin' arrest was introduced by the Nazis using the precedent of their interpretation of ancient Germanic custom whereby an entire family was outlawed for the crime of one of its members.[40] Duke Franz continues:

After the Stauffenberg plot they arrested the family members to force my grandfather to leave his hiding place in Italy. However, he only got to know about the destiny of his family in 1945.

We were liberated by the American army on 30 April 1945. Crown Prince Rupprecht was still in Italy and tried to acquire permission to return to Bavaria, which was only approved in November. Crown Princess Antonia was seriously ill had been held prisoner under cruel conditions in Jena, more dead than alive. There, by chance, she was discovered by an officer from the Luxemburg army.

Only in November could Crown Prince Rupprecht return to Bavaria to settle there as a private citizen. In the new Federal Republic of Germany he had very little direct political influence. Throughout his life he remained convinced that a constitutional monarchy was the best form of government for Bavaria.

From his return in 1945 he was regarded by all sections of the population as a prominent and upright national figurehead who had a stabilizing effect on the country during this time of upheaval.[41]

In 1945 Rupprecht wrote to Queen Mary (19 August) asking her to intercede with King George VI to restore his 'only home' of Leutstetten in Bavaria, which had been requisitioned by British forces following the fall of the Nazi regime. His principal residence(s) in Munich was 'completely in ruins'. He reminded the queen of their earlier meeting in 1934, 'Very sad and tragic events lie between that day and today, but may I notwithstanding turn to Your Majesty for help.' Rupprecht briefly explained that his family had been, 'persecuted by the National Socialists for the past 12 years' and his wife and children had been incarcerated in various concentration camps during his own exile in hiding from the SS in Italy. He added that his wife was in hospital as her health had been 'badly shaken by all the terrible suffering she went through'. The letter was followed by another from Leutstetten thanking the queen as he was now restored to his property and he had heard from an American officer the identities of the persons responsible.[42]

In 1945 Pope Pious XII favoured a restoration of the Habsburg dynasty over a Catholic state in central Europe. This idea was viewed sympathetically in a number of countries and by the British government, who believed that the re-establishment of a popular monarchy in Austria promised an effective bulwark against the spreading tide of communism.[43] Neither Rupprecht's proposals, nor the pope's, came to anything. Duke Franz comments, 'In general, Crown Prince Rupprecht regarded the pope's direct influence on international politics as minimal. Anyway, after World War II, as after World War I, the Americans were not prepared to see a return of the central European monarchies.'[44]

Who is to say whether as King Rupprecht could have steered his country away from the totalitarian disaster that engulfed it in the 1930s, or could have healed and rebuilt it better and sooner than was done. History reminds us that revolution can be a road to tyranny. Revolution in England led to Cromwell, in France Robespierre and Emperor Napoleon, in Russia Stalin and in Germany Hitler.

In lands of faith, birth is not an accident but a divine appointment and duty. For the deeply religious Crown Prince Rupprecht of Bavaria (as with other wartime princes, such as Otto von Habsburg of Austria-Hungary and King Christian of Denmark) it could be said that his life was his country and its well-being, and he devoted his whole life to its service.

Notes

1 Interview with HRH Duke Franz of Bavaria, 2 June 2009.
2 http://www.firstworldwar.com/source/somme_rupprecht.htm from a report by Crown Prince Rupprecht during the first Battle of the Somme.
3 Interview with HRH Duke Franz of Bavaria, 2009.
4 *The Times.*
5 Rickard, J. (6 November 2007), *Crown Prince Rupprecht of Bavaria 1869–1955*, http://www. historyofwar.org/articles/people_rupprecht_bavaria.html.
6 Interview with HRH Duke Franz of Bavaria, 2009.
7 Garnett, Robert S., *Lion, Eagle and Swastika: Bavarian Monarchism in Weimar Germany 1918–1933* (New York and London, Garland Publishing Inc., 1991) pp. 79–80.
8 Garnett, *Lion, Eagle and Swastika*, p. 132, citing a speech from the Reichstag on 29 October 1920.
9 *Washington Post* interview with Crown Prince Rupprecht of Bavaria by correspondent Cyril Brown, Munich, 2 January 1922, appeared 4 January, p. 2.
10 Ibid., pp 2–3.
11 Ibid., p. 3.
12 Ibid., p. 89.
13 Interview with HRH Duke Franz of Bavaria, 2009.
14 *The Times*, 19 March 1923.
15 'Regime of Dictators', *Time* magazine, 8 October 1923, http://www.time.com/time/magazine/article/0,9171,727551-1,00.html.
16 Petropoulos, Jonathan, *Royals and the Reich: The Princes Von Hessen in Nazi Germany* (Oxford, 2008), p. 72.
17 Ibid., p. 103.
18 Petropoulos, Jonathan, *Royals and the Reich: The Princes Von Hessen in Nazi Germany* (Oxford, 2008), p. 72.
19 Hanfstaengl, Ernst, *Hitler, the Missing Years* (New York, Arcade, 1994), pp. 89–90.
20 Interview with HRH Duke Franz of Bavaria, 2 June 2009.
21 *The Times.*
22 *The Times*, 1930.
23 Ibid.
24 Hanfstaengl, Ernst, *Hitler, the Missing Years*, pp. 89–90.
25 Garnett, *Lion, Eagle and Swastika* (New York, Garland, 1992), pp. 307–14.
26 Ibid., p. 328.
27 Ibid., p. 87.
28 Ibid., p. 92.
29 Petropoulos, Jonathan, *Royals and the Reich: The Princes Von Hessen in Nazi Germany* (Oxford, 2008), p. 73.
30 *Hitler's Table Talk*, ed. Hugh Trevor-Roper, pp. 560–1.
31 Petropoulos, Jonathan, *Royals and the Reich: The Princes Von Hessen in Nazi Germany* (Oxford, 2008), p. 73. At the meeting, the Crown prince was presented with a 'Saint Walburga box' which he later told Queen Mary that he was going to pass on to the Saint's convent. He continued to communicate with Queen Mary, asking her to receive his daughters sent to be educated in England, and in 1938 let her know that he hoped to visit again himself in the following year. RA/QM/PRIV/CC45//917, 1148 and 1170.

32 *The Times*, 14 February 1938.

33 Interview with HRH Duke Franz of Bavaria, 2 June 2009. Members of the embryonic resistance movement in Germany were equally surprised and disappointed by the British response, which was contrary to the warnings and wishes of the movement as expressed in meetings with British officials. See chapter on Prince Louis Ferdinand and the German resistance.

34 Petropoulos, Jonathan, *Royals and the Reich: The Princes Von Hessen in Nazi Germany* (Oxford, 2008), p. 73.

35 Interview with HRH Duke Franz of Bavaria, 2 June 2009.

36 TNA FO 371/29929/0016.

37 TNA FO 371/33219/0011.

38 Interview with HRH Duke Franz of Bavaria, 2 June 2009.

39 Ibid.

40 See Hoffmann, Peter, *The History of the German Resistance 1933–45* (Cambridge, Mass, 1977) pp. 519–20.

41 Interview with HRH Duke Franz of Bavaria, 2 June 2009.

42 RA/QM/PRIV/CC46/464 & RA/QM/PRIV/CC46/475.

43 http://www.vaticanbankclaims.com/hapsburg.pdf.

44 Interview with HRH Duke Franz of Bavaria, 2 June 2009.

7

HUBERTUS ZU LÖWENSTEIN-WERTHEIM-FREUDENBERG

Following Hitler's assumption of power in 1933, Prince Hubertus zu Löwenstein-Wertheim-Freudenberg left Germany and was forced into exile after a tip-off from a local police captain concerning his imminent arrest. He was already one of National Socialism's most bitter enemies.[1] In his doctoral thesis on Italian fascism in 1931 Löwenstein asserted that:

> Every totalitarian regime, be it of Left or the Right, was inherently contrary to the basic laws of society among Christian peoples of the Occident. Whenever there was a fundamental violation of human rights, and if all legal means were of no avail, there was a right to resist which went beyond law: indeed every individual would then have 'not just the right, but the duty to revolt'.[2]

The German prince believed that although fascism had not upset the balance of power in Europe, Nazism in power would mean another war.[3] As a consequence, he espoused the republican cause in Spain in spite of his royal and Catholic background and beliefs. He wrote that if the fascist powers were successful their next victim would be Czechoslovakia and other central European states, until the fascists were strong enough to turn against the eastern and the western democracies.[4] 'The future of Europe,' he explained, 'will depend on the Spanish campaign. Spain fights for all of us. A defeat of fascism would mean the beginning of the end of the fascist world plot.' In his autobiography the prince points out that on 28 March 1939 Madrid surrendered. 'Five months later Warsaw was bombed, and the Second World War began.'[5]

The SRG, or *Reichsbanner*, which the prince joined, was specifically and demonstrably loyal to the German republic. Formed in 1924 with the explicit aim of standing against the enemies of the German republic, it was comprised of members of all the democratic parties of the Weimar Coalition and recognised by the black, red and gold colours. At its inception it had 3 million members, which grew to 5 million by the time of its prohibition in 1933. In 1933 Hitler became chancellor and assumed power in Germany. Löwenstein writes:

> The German nation was not robbed of its freedom, it was sneaked away from it: the power of the state was neither given to the Nazis by the German people, nor did the Nazis obtain it by a revolution. That power was embezzled after it had been given to them by the president, when they solemnly undertook to respect the constitution.[6]

He points out that the 'easing off' of the world economic crisis at the beginning of 1933 was of political benefit to the Nazis, whose propaganda convinced a large section of the population that unemployment was being overcome solely due to the efficiency of Hitler's government. Löwenstein notes that the political situation in 1933 was favourable in other ways: the Lausanne Conference in 1932 had set the total German reparation debt at three billion marks, but payments were no longer required; the Rhineland was no longer occupied; the return of the Saarland assured and opposition to voluntary union with Austria had lessened. Thus, the National Socialists took credit for the achievements of the previous regime, which made Hitler more popular and undermined the position of the political opposition.[7]

Fr Rudolf Löwenstein, the prince's grandnephew, recalls that he took a genuine interest in what both he and his brother had to say:

> Always very courteous and precise in his manner of speech. He would ascertain exactly what the situation was, before commenting and considering what was said. He was very much a gentleman in his treatment and great respect for others. His general knowledge was on a very large scale indeed, and he was able to converse on almost any subject at all; religion, politics and history were very much areas where few could hold a candle to him.[8]

HSH Princess Konstanza zu Löwenstein, the prince's daughter, observes that although as a young man Löwenstein was not of sporting appearance, 'Pictures of the time' portray him as a typical intellectual, fine featured with glasses and hair waxed. 'He never lacked for courage,' for he was emboldened by the two most important people of his political activity, if not of his life: his young wife Helga and fellow *Reichsbanner* activist Volkmar Zühlsdorf. According to Zühlsdorf, Helga's political involvement was notable. Born Norwegian and raised in Germany, she married Löwenstein when she was 19 (he was 23) and the marriage lasted until his death fifty-six years later. She was fluent in several languages and well travelled, whereas he was more introverted. They complimented each other perfectly.[9]

Löwenstein, a member of a branch of the Wittelsbach family, was born and raised at Schönworth near Kufstein in the Austrian Tirol. He was the son of Maximilian, Prince of Löwenstein-Wertheim-Freudenberg, and was the grandson of an English privy councillor, Lord Pirbright. Educated in Munich, Geneva, Berlin and Hamburg (where he completed his doctorate on the Italian and German constitutions), Löwenstein was politically a Christian Democrat and supported the Weimar Republic. He had no political affiliation until he was preparing his doctoral thesis in 1930, however, when unemployment was rising, the republic was being assailed from all sides and there was violence in the streets.[10] He had urged the Bavarian government to resist Hitler's centrism and supported the *Reichsbanner* (black, red and gold) (a Social Democratic multi-party paramilitary organisation that supported the republic) as a foil to the SA and the Bolsheviks.[11] 'The Red Prince', as Göbbels called him, was regarded by the Nazis as a dangerous enemy.[12] Löwenstein's 'major weapon' against Hitler, reveals Princess Konstanza, 'was his mind'. He began a career as a journalist when he was 22 and on 12 July 1930 he wrote an article for the *Vossischen News* entitled *The Third Reich*. It was described by Sten Nodalny as 'a merciless exposure of National Socialism'. Princess Konstanza says that 'Hitler fumed', and Göbbels referred to Löwenstein as 'This Red Prince, who writes for the Jewish press'. 'Although Göbbels misinterpreted the political colours of my father (because at this time anything not brown was red!),' comments Princess Konstanza, 'the fury over his views was undoubted. For in the article, he concluded that although Fascism itself did not threaten peace, a power seizure by the National Socialists would mean a second world war.'[13]

Löwenstein left for Austria in 1933, his exile was brief because the Gestapo wanted to kidnap the prince and his wife and take them back to Germany, following their prey across the border. They escaped thanks to the intervention of an Austrian army platoon who guarded them. As a consequence the young couple left Austria and motored through Switzerland and France to Holland, where he met the historian and philosopher Johan Huizinga, who told Löwenstein that he believed fascism was an international disease, 'It could break out anywhere.'[14] From Holland they travelled to England, the homeland of Löwenstein's maternal grandfather, where he had meetings with Lord Chelwood and Sir Austen Chamberlain. In 1935 Löwenstein actively sought a meeting with Winston Churchill and on 5 May wrote to the politician at Morpeth Mansions in London, enclosing a letter of introduction written by John Eppstein, political secretary at the League of Nations Union. Eppstein points out in his letter that not only was Löwenstein a well-known opponent of the Nazi regime in Germany, but that he had found the information that he has provided to be 'substantially accurate and objective'. He also informs Churchill that the German prince has a lot to say about the movement of public opinion in the USA as regards Germany having spent several months lecturing in North America.[15]

In America the prince campaigned relentlessly for a German cultural alternative to that in place in the German homeland. He stated in 1935 that the real Germany survived, but only outside of its borders as the spiritual and intellectual Germany.[16] So Löwenstein became an exile, one of many intellectuals who were forced to leave Germany and Austria:

> Princess Konstanza points out that between 1933 and 1941 around 300,000 people left Germany and neighbouring countries. Amongst these were about 30,000 intellectuals, of whom around 2,500 were writers. That this was a great loss for Germany and a great gain for other countries was highlighted in an article entitled 'Hitler's gift to Britain' which reported that by 1995, in England alone, 19 Nobel Prize winners had originated from this group.

In the USA Löwenstein found not only fellow German exiles of like mind, but also a public receptive to his message of freedom and democracy, and the cultural independence of refugees from foreign oppression. He became Carnegie Visiting Professor of International Relations, and founded the German Academy of Arts and Sciences in Exile and the American Guild for German Cultural Freedom, whose members included Thomas Mann, Sigmund Freud and Albert Einstein.[17] Princess Konstanza says that one of the most important aims was to keep German culture visible, 'Building on this came the founding of the German Academy in Exile. Its goal was to make those dispersed representatives of the "other" Germany visible.'[18]

The Foundation of the American Guild for German Cultural Freedom was an attempt to compose a uniform picture of Germany's intellectual emigration abroad, especially in the USA. Princess Konstanza says:

> The American Guild had as its aim to offer assistance and political support to destitute exiles, many of whom were destitute poets, actors and academics whose greatest loss was their own language. Even lawyers had no chance of finding work in a foreign land. Hardly any of the emigrants, for example, Einstein or the conductor Klemperer, or even already famous authors, (such as Feuchtwanger, Weig, and Mann), whose works had been translated into several languages, could find work in their own profession.
>
> In a short time a host of personalities arrived and were supported the Guild, among them Oswald Garrison Villard, who made his two storey offices available. The chairman of the organisation was the governor of Connecticut, Dr Wilbur L. Cross, and senator Robert Ferdinand Wagner was a board member. Many prominent Americans joined.

German-born Wagner was co-sponsor of a bill to admit 20,000 refugee Jewish children to the USA from Nazi Germany. However, the bill was blocked by 'patriotic' groups and rejected by Congress in February 1939. Princess Konstanza continues:

Through the efforts of the Academy the world was made aware that there was another 'Germany'. Thomas Mann asserted that it was in this way that they could serve the German name from outside its borders. Volkmar Zühlsdorff wrote that the greatest success of the Academy was that, despite all the evils of the Regime, the work of the Academy and its members, kept an acknowledgment of the 'other Germany' alive in the eyes of the world.

The initiative and energy to found and support the Academy and the charisma to bring people together stemmed from Lowenstein himself. After his exile it was his only possible means of fighting Hitler.[19]

At a dinner in New York Einstein confided to the Catholic prince, 'In view of such harmony in the universe which I, with my limited human mind, am able to recognize, there are yet people who say there is no God. But what really makes me angry is that they quote me in support of such views.'[20] Löwenstein wrote that the exiles represented the real Germany, which was 'the land of knowledge and research, the land of philosophy and humanity; not the land of barbarism, pernicious ideology, bondage and the jackboot'. This cultured liberal Germany stood in stark contrast to Hitler's Reich and was intended to replace it after the Führer's inevitable fall.

On 23 April 1936 he landed in Los Angeles to attend a dinner in his honour 'for the relief of victims of Nazism' in the Victor Hugo restaurant in Hollywood, presided over by John Joseph Cantwell, bishop of Los Angeles.[21] The Hollywood Anti-Nazi League had been founded by Dorothy Parker, Donald Ogden-Stewart, Fritz Lang, Oscar Hammerstein and Frederick March. It published the anti-Nazi magazine *Hollywood Now*. Chief among Löwenstein's contacts in Hollywood was the left-wing anti-Nazi Rudolf Breda, of whom the prince commented dryly:

> Breda 'sold' communism to the wealthy Hollywood magnates by working on their bad social consciences until they were cringing with contrition ... The complete religious and metaphysical desert in the minds of the motion picture colony made Breda's game easier. Marxism with its promise of earthly salvation came in handy as a substitute for religion. If one could embrace it without giving up one's accustomed way and standard of living, all the better.

Peace movements in the USA and Europe prior to the Second World War largely had their origins in Moscow. There was a cynical manipulation of Western youth – that took advantage of their Christian morality, natural rebellion, pacific leanings and their fear of war – by Soviet leaders who held no such pacific principles. Full advantage of US isolationism was taken with spectacular success. During the Nazi-Soviet Pact even Chamberlain was depicted as a warmonger. After the war the peace movements continued to be pushed by communists with the intention of undermining the Western will to resist communism and defend its values by force of arms. The 1949 International Peace Conference used a lithograph of a dove by Pablo Picasso as its symbol. It had been acquired from the artist by communist poet Louis Aragon, a member of the PCF French Communist Party, which was politically closest and most loyal of all the national parties to Russia west of the Iron Curtain. In 1951 *Time* magazine pointed out the irony of speakers at the Cultural and Scientific Conference for World Peace in New York's Waldorf Astoria in March 1949, decrying America and supporting the USSR's 'fight for peace' at the time of the Berlin Airlift and while Chinese communists 'marched toward Nanking'. The Soviet 'peace offensive', reported *Time*, was not harmless, 'The peace propaganda campaign was a coldly calculated master plan to sabotage the West's efforts to restore the world's free economies and to defend itself.'[22]

In Hollywood Löwenstein preached to actors and film makers, and influenced the likes of Fritz Lang, David Selznick, Marlene Dietrich, Greta Garbo and Charles Chaplin. The Hollywood League Against Nazism was established as a result. So impressed was the *Los Angeles Times* that Löwenstein was referred to as Hitler's 'public enemy number one', who may one day, it believed, become leader of Germany himself.

Löwenstein used his family connections to promote the anti-Nazi cause in the UK and formed a British guild, the Arden Society, with the archbishop of York as joint patron. Sir Victor Schuster, a director of the National Provincial Bank, provided a generous donation and was assisted by his brother, Prince Leopold, in gaining the support of a number of British aristocrats such as viscount Cecil of Chelwood.[23] Among the sponsors and those who served on the board were a good mix of aristocrats and artists. They included, for example, the Duchess of Atholl, Lady Violet Bonham-Carter, Walter de la Mare, the Earl of Antrim, Augustus John and the Master of Balliol College, Oxford. The prince found a wider audience when he spoke at the Royal Institute for International Affairs at Chelwood's suggestion. He also wrote to General Sir Reginald Wingate to suggest that a detachment of British troops should be sent to the Saar region of Germany in the hope that it could be kept separate from National Socialist Germany and provide a geographical location for a free Germany, unfortunately too late. The British Foreign Secretary, John Simon, told the House of Commons that the use of British troops to maintain order in the Saar was not contemplated, in spite of Britain's role as guarantor of the Saar Statute to protect the civil liberties of the population. Sir Reginald agreed with Löwenstein that Simon's statement was a stain on Britain's honour and arranged a private audience with King George V. Shortly afterwards he was able to inform Löwenstein that 'the policy was reversed' as the king had summoned Simon to the palace and made plain his displeasure at the slight on the honour of the Crown.[24]

In August 1937 Löwenstein left for Spain in support of the republicans against Franco's Fascists whose forces were augmented by Nazi and Italian contingents.

He saw air raids in Spain as an awful warning of future events and on the Aragon front he witnessed foreign fascist involvement first hand, 'From the forward trenches on top of a chain of hills I saw the battle waving back and forth. Nazi planes were flying overhead, Nazi tanks attacking the republican lines, heavy artillery opening up – again a prelude to the future.'[25] From Madrid he made a broadcast on short wave radio on a station called *Voice of Spain* entreating Germans to sabotage the Nazi military production and warning the USA and United Kingdom of the dangers of fascism.[26] He announced to a press conference on his return to England, 'What Madrid suffers today, Paris will suffer tomorrow, and the step from Paris to London will be even shorter.'[27]

The prince then left for the USA where he lectured in over fifty universities and colleges, using every available opportunity to tell his students that Europe had been for the most part of its history a 'commonwealth of culture and destiny', that Hitler's Germany was not the real Germany, and that, in his opinion, Europe should join together into a democratic United States of Europe. Löwenstein regarded appeasement as the 'surest way to war, as any totalitarian regime interprets it as democratic weakness'.[28] He included the Polish-German Agreement of January 1934 and the Anglo-German Naval Agreement of June 1935, as well as co-operation between French and German banks, as examples of this misguided policy. Löwenstein had written in May 1935, 'The weakness of England (or rather the weakness of the English government) is worth several army corps to the National Socialists, London may wake up only when planes bearing the *HakenKreutz* will fly over Piccadily Circus.'[29]

The Munich Agreement (29 September 1938), he later noted, not only did not prevent war, but made it inevitable. It weakened the opposition to Hitler's regime within Germany because the international condemnation of Hitler's ambitions on which the German internal resistance movement largely depended appeared to evaporate, 'Even if passive resistance at home did not cease (for what was immoral and evil could not be righted by such an agreement) Munich yet paralysed its impetus.' Löwenstein continues:

> The various groups of the resistance movement, agreed only in their rejection of the regime … were too weak to fight 'a war on two fronts': they could not fight against the totalitarian power of the national socialist state and the party machine, and at the same time against the Signatory Powers of the Munich Agreement, which were England, France and Italy.[30]

Following Munich, Hitler 'was able to purge the leadership of the general staff of "unreliable elements," and to consider further plans of aggression without hesitation'.[31] The National Socialist regime, Löwenstein writes, could not have dared go to war in September 1938, 'The armed forces under General Ludwig Beck and his successor, General Franz Halder [supported by the civil resistance including Carl Friedrich Goerdeler, former mayor of Leipzig], would have over-thrown Hitler by force.'[32]

In August 1939 the Ribbentrop-Molotov Pact between Germany and the Soviet Union damaged the internal opposition in Germany even further. Left-wing exiles in the USA and elsewhere were no longer inclined to criticise the Nazis, but saw the declaration of war by (capitalist) Britain and France on Germany, following the invasion of Poland, as an act of aggression and an 'imperialist undertaking' in line with German and Russian propaganda. Political demonstrations took place in the USA calling 'for peace', but in support of Hitler's Germany and Stalin's Russia. Löwenstein writes that up to June 1941, when Hitler attacked the Soviet Union:

> It was considered almost reactionary, indeed as 'war mongering' to criticize the crimes of the Hitler regime – an opinion which prevailed widely even in 'liberal' circles. The standards applied by these pseudo-liberals in judging the worth or otherwise of a system of government, therefore, were determined by its advantages or disadvantages to the Soviet Union.[33]

William Dothie, a British officer who had been a member of the British Expeditionary Force to France in 1940, recalled the implications of the alliance on the field of battle:

> One of the major factors contributing to the collapse of France in 1940 was Germany's Treaty of Friendship with the Soviet Union, which served to neutralise much of the anti-German feeling of the French working class. The effects were far reaching, extending into the civil service as well as the fighting forces, and giving the German's fifth column wide-raging opportunities to manipulate officials, organise confusion and spread false information.
>
> The complete breakdown in communications, which occurred can also be attributed in large part to this cause. The lack of reliable information about the movements of the BEF in the course of their retreat northwards, and the contradictory reports received by the Commander-in-Chief, Lord Gort, and by the Cabinet in London, because of the breakdown, all contributed to the debacle. In my opinion, the Soviet Friendship Treaty was one of the most important successes of German strategy in the early days of the war. It was of course discarded as soon as it had served its purpose.[34]

Tatiana Metternich recalled that a Spanish friend had told her that when he went to meet the Germans at the Spanish border after the fall of France, which the Germans called *Fall Gelb*, he had asked a German tank commander how they did for petrol. The officer had replied that they had filled up at petrol stations and even bought food along the way. 'It was like a holiday outing,' he said.[35]

On 7 November 1939 Löwenstein wrote to Wingate, 'It is terrible to see how right we were with all our predictions – that war was inevitable, if Hitlerism should stay in power, and that finally Nazism and Bolshevism would make common game.'[36] He warns that the future of Europe can be safeguarded only if Nazism is overthrown, democracy restored, and a 'new international order – a European Confederation – established'.[37] He is relieved, however, that one of his 'eldest plans' – the formation of a German government in exile – is 'nearing completion' and councils that this group should be represented in the USA in order to win over the millions of German Americans subject to Nazi propaganda, 'who by no means are Nazis, but who see for the moment the Hitler government as the only existing German representation'. Although Löwenstein was himself a prince, as a Christian Democrat he cautions Wingate against the rising view in the UK that after the war Germany should be dismembered and the monarchies re-established, which was a view that Löwenstein believed to be creating an unfortunate impression in the USA. With a backward look at the origins of discontent in Germany and how this idea (if it became policy) would be received there he wrote, 'The German people will never revolt against Hitler (and this revolt is vital to shorten the war and preserve Europe from Bolshevism) if they have reason to fear, that after the war, would come another or worse Versailles, a treaty which would dismember the country.' The constitution of the Germany of tomorrow, he stated, 'must be created by a National Assembly, and not by outward pressure.'[38]

After Pearl Harbor and Germany's declaration of war, Löwenstein went to live in Newfoundland. Unable to fight for the USA or against his homeland, he had offered his services to the Chinese government against Germany's ally Japan. The Chinese ambassador in Washington replied, 'Certainly your present activities in lecturing and writing are far more useful to China, to free Germany, and to humanity in general than your services as a soldier on Chinese soil can possibly be.' He also applied for front-line service with the American Red Cross and Field Services, but was told that only US citizens would be considered. He succeeded in being appointed special correspondent to England by the *New York Herald Tribune*, but did not receive his promised UK visa before the liner upon which he was booked sailed without him. The ship was sunk with no survivors and the spared prince returned to writing and lecturing.[39]

Much of his work during the war years was concerned with a future post-war Germany within a rebuilt Europe with a new political vision. In his article, *Outlines of an equitable peace*, written in December 1941 and published in the following year, he proposed a European commonwealth with a European parliament of two houses and a supreme court. He also proposed a system of international schools funded internationally. His plentiful ideas all depended on the successful outcome of the war. 'The sooner the German army could be turned against the Hitler government the better,' he wrote.[40]

According to Löwenstein, the third blow to the German resistance movement after Munich and the Nazi-Soviet Pact was the demand made for unconditional surrender adopted at the Casablanca Conference 14–24 January 1943. 'Unconditional surrender proved to be the most welcome gift which national socialist propaganda could have received. From now on it was able to tell the German people, with apparent veracity, that there was no choice but to fight to the bitter end.' German political refugees denounced the demand which, they thought, could only unnecessarily prolong the war and would take away the incentive for the German people and military to depose the dictator.[41]

Löwenstein was particularly keen to inculcate on the Allies the importance of not treating all Germans as enemies, or especially Nazis, as if they were synonymous. He wanted to convince them that the insistence on unconditional surrender was not only wrong, it was counter-productive as it discouraged opposition groups from attempting to oust Hitler by force and robbed them of much of the support upon which they might otherwise have counted. He also proposed a post-war Germany that was not treated as a rightfully vanquished enemy: its industry and economy destroyed, and its political administration and geographic boundaries determined by the victors without reference to the inhabitants.

Löwenstein told an audience at Bowdoin College in the USA that if the new post-war democratic order was to be lasting, 'Germany must not be dismembered or humiliated. It must be permitted to re-enter the family of nations quickly as a partner with equal rights.'[42] He thought that an unjust peace played into the hands of the Nazis, but unfortunately the Roosevelt government was obsessed by the fear of a 'soft peace' – one without vengeance.[43]

This he believed directly affected the chances of an internal coup by the German Generals against the Nazi regime. In May 1944 he voiced his forebodings, 'No German group would be willing to start a civil war as long as the price were unconditional surrender, interpreted by millions as meaning the dismemberment and economic destruction of their country.' He warned that opposition leaders would be mindful of the danger that a civil war might 'precipitate the breakdown of the Eastern Front,' and thereby lead to a successful Russian invasion and communist takeover of Germany. 'Time is running out,' he predicted, 'Unless Germany is soon taken out of the war, the end will come only after complete exhaustion with millions of casualties on all sides as the "victory of democracy," would prove a short armistice only, until at the Elbe river, the Third World War would begin.'[44]

Although the Allies sufficiently changed their policy towards Germany and it was dismembered, Löwenstein's vision of a Germany united with and within a united European community bore fruit. 'Today I walked through Berlin,' he broadcast optimistically from ruined West Berlin in 1945, 'People dared to raise their heads again and use their tongues as God meant them to. There was no whispering anymore, no furtive looking for spies and secret agents. Even the pavement felt different from what I remember it back in 1933 … life is safe once more, and love is again hallowed.'[45]

Princess Konstanza recalls:

In October 1946 a small group of people left New York aboard a liberty ship bound for Bremerhaven. After 13 years in exile, my parents returned home two days prior to my father's 40th birthday. Most of the luggage consisted of documents: the cases contained the archives of the Academy, and not as we children hoped, mountains of chocolate!

My parents and Zühlsdorff felt that all these papers should be brought back to their proper place now the fight with Hitler was at an end.[46]

The greatness of a man like Hubertus zu Löwenstein cannot be measured in organisations founded or by political activities, but in his unceasing efforts to exorcise his country of the twin spectres of fascism and communism in the interests of the German people and the world in general. Although an enthusiastic supporter of the German republic he was very much of his line and an example of Wittelsbach preoccupations with culture and concern for the people. In fact, it was probably because of his princely background that he was such an enthusiast of a system of government that seemed to offer so much for ordinary people. He was, it seems, a true example of nobility, not only of the nobility of blood, but also of virtue. Princess Konstanza comments:

My father will always be described by some as 'The Red Prince', an idealist, a Don Quixote or adventurer by other Germans. He was clearly an outstanding person. He struggled as an individual against injustice, believed in the strength and meaning of the individual within the political arena. He was an old school aristocrat and yet something quite different from other aristocrats.[47]

Princess Konstanza believes that her father's deep interest and profound knowledge of history was largely due to the influence of an inspiring education by the good schools that he attended, and of his father who was also very interested in the subject. His wife – also a great influence – was very bright and politically minded, having been unconventionally educated at a progressive school (*Wikersdorf*), now considered to have been at the forefront of modern educational practice. The princess points out that when Löwenstein went to Berlin to work at a journalist he mixed with large numbers of intellectuals and people in the know, with whom he had discussions and learnt much about politics. He was very influenced by his professor in Hamburg and came under the spell of the poet Stefan George and his ideas of an elite that could save Germany from barbarism. Princess Konstanza says, 'My father felt a deep sense of duty towards European history and Germany and was disgusted by the primitive thinking of the early Nazi movement.' Other princes were far less interested in the politics of Berlin and some would have been horrified by Löwenstein's friendship with Social Democrats and communists. Löwenstein met Grand Duke Otto von Habsburg while in exile in New York, they were as one in their attitude towards the Nazis, but their visions of post-war Germany and Austria were very different, says Princess Konstanza. Dr Otto had fought for the independence of Austria from Germany, whereas Löwenstein was for a union of the two countries within a truly democratic framework. He didn't meet Prince Louis Ferdinand until after the war in 1946. Princess Konstanza comments, 'They also had very different understandings of post-war Germany, but became friends nevertheless.'[48]

Notes

1 The policeman, Captain Ranfft, said without looking up from the file in front of him, 'The Berlin climate is not too healthy for you right now. How about taking a little vacation somewhere in the South?' He then affixed exit visas to the prince and princess' passports and remarked that it would probably take between ten days and two weeks before the climate got really rough. Löwenstein, Hubertus zu, *Towards a Further Shore* (London, 1968), p. 118.

2 *Hitler's Exiles*, p. 9.

3 Löwenstein, Hubertus zu, *Towards a Further Shore* (London, Gollancz, 1968), p. 80.

4 Löwenstein, Hubertus zu, *A Catholic in Republican Spain* (London, Gollancz, 1937), p. 109.

5 Löwenstein, Hubertus zu, *Towards the Further Shore*, p. 200.

6 Löwenstein, Hubertus zu, *What was the German Resistance Movement?* (Grafes, Bad Godesburg, 1965) p. 32.

7 Ibid., pp. 33–4.

8 Correspondence with the author, November 2009.

9 Information provided to the author by HSH Princess Konstanza zu Löwenstein, from a speech made in Berlin.

10 Löwenstein, Hubertus zu, *Towards a Further Shore*, pp. 22–6.

11 Ibid., p. 79. The *Reichsbanner* was banned in March 1933.

12 On 20 February 1933, after Hitler had become Chancellor of Germany and Hermann Göring had instructed the police in Prussia to shoot first and ask questions later, Löwenstein announced at an election meeting: 'Today Germany has ceased to be a state of law.' Ibid., p. 110.

13 HSH Princess Konstanza zu Löwenstein, speech.

14 Ibid., pp. 128–9.

15 Chartwell Trust, The Sir Winston Churchill Archive Trust, CHAR 2/307. See also, *Towards a Further Shore*, pp. 192–3.

16 *Hitler's Exiles*, p. 21. There was a real danger that the West could mistake Nazi Germany for the real thing. American Louis Lochner commented to Prince Louis Ferdinand of Prussia, 'The longer this Nazi business lasts, the less difference will people abroad make between the Nazis and the German people.' Louis Ferdinand, *The Rebel Prince*, p. 268.

17 Zühlsdorff, Volkmar, *Hitler's Exiles* (New York, Continuum, 2004), p. 19, 24.

18 HSH Princess Konstanza zu Löwenstein, private correspondence and speech (*Rote Prinz*).

19 Ibid.

20 *Towards a Further Shore*, p. 156. Einstein was also recorded as saying, 'Being a lover of freedom, when the revolution came in Germany, I looked to the universities to defend it, knowing that they had always boasted of their devotion to the cause of truth; but,

no, the universities immediately were silenced. Then I looked to the great editors of
the newspapers whose flaming editorials in days gone by had proclaimed their love
of freedom; but they, like the universities, were silenced in a few short weeks. Only
the Church stood squarely across the path of Hitler's campaign for suppressing truth.
I never had any special interest in the Church before, but now I feel a great affection
and admiration because the Church alone has had the courage and persistence to stand
for intellectual truth and moral freedom. I am forced thus to confess that what I once
despised I now praise unreservedly.'

21 Ibid., p. 175.

22 *Time* magazine, 17 September 1951.

23 Ibid., p. 102.

24 Ibid., pp. 146–7.

25 Ibid., p. 194.

26 Ibid., p. 197.

27 Ibid., p. 200.

28 Löwenstein, Prince Hurbertus, *Towards the Further Shore*, p. 34.

29 Löwenstein, Prince Hurbertus, *Towards the Further Shore*, p. 157.

30 Löwenstein, *What was the German Resistance Movement?* p. 43.

31 Ibid.

32 Ibid., p. 45.

33 Ibid., pp. 46–7.

34 Dothie, W.H., *Operation Disembroil: Deception and Escape, Normandy, 1940* (London, Robert
Hale, 1985), p. 156.

35 *Tatiana*, p. 114.

36 Ibid., CHAR 2/368.

37 Löwenstein continually returned to this theme in his books and speeches and can be
regarded as one of the foremost proponents of a European common market followed by
political union. He did not, however, suggest that the UK should be part of this great
experiment any more than anyone else at the time. In Zurich in 1946, in the interests
of peace and common prosperity, Winston Churchill enthusiastically endorsed the idea
of a United States of Europe, based on a partnership of France and Germany, but also
including smaller countries whose voice would carry equal weight. This union should, he
said, be supported by Great Britain and the Commonwealth as well as the USA and the
Soviet Union. Britain, however, was never intended to be a member. Churchill famously
said that given the choice between Europe and the open sea, Britain should always
choose the open sea. See Churchill's speech to the academic youth of Zurich in 1946 at
wwww.europa-web.de/europa/02wwswww/202histo/Churchil.htm. European economic
and political union had been proposed in the 1920s by Aristide Briand, Prime Minister
of France, as a way to guarantee future peace. It was supported by German Chancellor
Gustav Stresemann, who had himself envisaged eventual European economic integration.

38 Ibid.

39 Löwenstein, Prince Hubertus, *Towards the Further Shore*, p. 248.

40 Ibid., p. 249.

41 Ibid., pp. 49–50.

42 *Towards the Further Shore*, p. 261.

43 Ibid., pp. 260–1.

44 Ibid., p. 270.

45 Ibid., p. 261.

46 HSH Princess Konstanza zu Löwenstein, speech (Rote Prinz).

47 Ibid.

48 HSH Princess Konstanza zu Löwenstein, private correspondence with the author.

8

HABSBURGS AND HOHENBERGS

The Treaty of St Germain in 1919 dissolved the Austro-Hungarian Empire, recognising the sovereignty of its successor states including the new Republic of Austria. It imposed reparations on the Austrians and left the country impoverished, particularly Vienna. It did, however, forbid any union of Austria with Germany without the agreement of the council of the League of Nations. There were two questions US Consul General in Berlin, George Messersmith was told, on which Hitler's friends could make no impression on him: the anti-Semite question and the Austrian situation, on both of these Hitler was implacable, He described Hitler's anti-Semitism as a religion and that Hitler 'wants to see the Jew wiped out', and he 'wants to bring about the "*Anschluss*" at all costs'.[1]

Dr Otto von Habsburg

His Royal and Imperial Majesty Dr Otto von Habsburg (lately deceased after the writing of this chapter) was the eldest son of the last emperor, Karl (Charles) of Austria-Hungary and Zita of Bourbon-Parma. The saintly Karl did his best to bring the First World War to an early conclusion and indeed was beatified following his untimely death in exile. He and his family were forced out of Austria after the war and, apart from a couple of attempts to regain the throne of Hungary, lived abroad in Switzerland and Madeira where the emperor died, leaving the young Otto as rightful claimant to an empire.

Otto said that his political outlook was very much influenced by that of his father. While in exile on Madeira Karl drafted an Austrian constitution based on a Danubian Federation, an idea that particularly influenced Otto. Karl's peace efforts failed, Otto believed, because of 'irrational Italian territorial greed and the obstruction of Austrian politicians'. The emperor concluded that the successor states could not survive economically without close co-operation and because of their multi-ethnic populations. Karl foresaw that with the fall of the monarchy a power vacuum would develop with Germany on one side and the Soviet Union on the other. The successor states, dominated by political elites, were not viable due to the distribution of nationalities across the region, leaving only agglomerations in which one nation would be dominant possible. The emperor's position was that the collapse of the monarchy was an impediment to lasting peace.[2]

In the winter of 1932/33 Otto von Habsburg visited Berlin ostensibly to attend a course given by (anti-Nazi conservative) Professor Serving, but really to assess the Nazi threat. This visit was arranged by Centre Party member, Count Galen.[3] Hitler hated the Habsburgs more than any other dynasty in Europe and thought them decadent. During his stay he met many people and engaged in some deep political debates, including with the Strasser brothers. He also read Hitler's *Mein Kampf*, after which it became absolutely clear to him what would happen if Hitler came to power. Above all he saw it as his responsibility to protect his native country, Austria, against the 'power-hungry' Hitler. In Austria itself, the assembly of the Eisernen Ring was instituted under the presidency of Otto's cousin Herzog Maximilian von Hohenberg who was his emissary in Austria. 'Austrian self-confidence had been shaken by the breakdown of the monarchy and the dispersion of the Crown lands. It was seen to be essential that Austria regain its strength and eventually organise its opposition to a potential German invasion.'[4]

John Flournoy Montgomery recalls in his book on Hungarian history:

> The restoration of the Hapsburgs [sic] in either Budapest or Vienna was very much feared by Hitler … To Hungarians and others in central Europe, restoration would have been a magnet that would have attracted millions of other former subjects, jeopardizing Hitler's power, as well as the Little Entente. Mussolini had that in mind when he favoured a monarchy for Austria, but this went by the board when he and Hitler were pushed together.

Reflecting on the role of the Western Allies in the abolition of the Austro-Hungarian monarchy he comments, 'Had the old Austro-Hungarian monarchy, which we helped to destroy, been in existence during Hitler's rise, what a different situation there might have been!'[5]

Otto was first approached to meet Hitler by Prince August Wilhelm of Prussia.[6] On a visit to the Crown prince, Wilhelm of Prussia, Otto was invited to August Wilhelm's house for a private talk. When he arrived he found the prince in the uniform of an SA officer, which he didn't appreciate at all.[7] The prince spoke highly of his party and its leader, whom Otto referred to pointedly as Herr Hitler. Otto had the advantage of already having read *Mein Kampf* and knew all about Hitler's aims, racist agenda and plans to incorporate Austria in the Reich. When he was told that Hitler wanted to see him, he answered that he was avoiding political meetings although he had had meetings with Democratic conservatives. Later Göring extended another invitation, which was also rejected.[8] The Hohenzollerns, he said, shared the illusion that Hitler would reinstate the monarchy once in power, 'I was certain that Hitler was only using them as a means to attract monarchist voters.' He was probably the last non-Nazi to be received by Hindenburg, who wore his Austrian imperial uniform and decorations.

Otto believed, 'Inevitably Habsburg and Hitler would be locked in a battle for their common Germanic homeland.'[9] The choice for many in Austria was voiced as 'H or H' – Habsburg or Hitler – it being assumed that it had to be one or the other. On his next visit to Germany in 1933 he was warned by a Croat member of the Gestapo to get out of the country if he wanted to avoid arrest.[10] Otto was always mindful of the second sentence of *Mein Kampf*, 'German Austria must return to the great German motherland ... One blood demands one Reich!' Brook-Shepherd writes, 'Vienna provided a natural target for Hitler and an easier one' than Hungary, which was later to become allied to Germany anyway.[11]

On 19 March 1934 *Time* magazine reported that if Otto was restored to the throne it would bring certain advantages to Austria. 'The minor squabblings of Heimwehr, Christian Socialists, and Dollfuss Front members would end once they had a common figure to rally round. There would be a new, possibly a more glamorous figure to draw impressionable youth from Adolf Hitler.'[12]

Mussolini provided a temporary impediment to a Nazi takeover of Austria. When he was still the most powerful dictator in Europe he was determined 'as a matter of vanity, as well as of policy, to reassert that dominance over any challenge from that brown-shirted upstart in Berlin.' In 1934 an attempted Nazi putsch in Vienna resulted in the assassination of Austrian chancellor and convinced nationalist Engelbert Dollfuss, but not regime change. Mussolini ordered Italian forces northwards the moment he heard of the attempted coup and placed them menacingly on Austria's borders to dissuade any further foreign interference in the internal affairs of his neighbour. In 1935 this policy was further strengthened by the Stresa Pact between Italy, Britain and France; an agreement shattered by Italy's belligerent attitude towards Abyssinia. Up until which Italy had been regarded by the UK government as one of the countries with which Britain was least likely to have a war – alongside France and the USA.[13] Following the assassination the British ambassador to Vienna, Walford Selby, believed that the British government should have made a more positive declaration about the preservation of Austrian independence. He also urged closer ties with France and a continuation of rearmament.[14]

In 1935 Otto received a deputation from Vienna bearing an 'address of allegiance signed by many Austrian monarchists, and a bag of earth taken from the grounds of Castle Warttholz'.[15] The disparate monarchist elements of Austrian society were difficult to quantify or organise into a common unity. Many supporters considered themselves and their beliefs to be above politics. It was not until 1936 that Otto was able to set up an umbrella organisation that focused monarchists from wide social, political and ethnic backgrounds, called the 'Iron Ring' (*Eisernen Ring*), under the overall presidency of Otto's cousin Herzog Max von Hohenberg and the executive presidency of Baron Friedrich von Weisner of the Foreign Office. Both men were later to be incarcerated in concentration camps. By his strong emphasis on non-partisanship, Wiesner built a successful movement by incorporating socialists, by placing value on youth work and by winning support from numerous Jews who hoped for protection against Hitler's anti-Semitic programme by a restoration of the Habsburg dynasty. Meanwhile, Hohenberg was tireless in holding meetings, liaising with the Austrian government and updating his emperor on the latest developments. He had a talent, remembered Dr von Habsburg, of bringing together people who otherwise had no common purpose.[16] Max Hohenberg became the readily identifiable representative of Otto in Austria.[17] He unsuccessfully attempted a restoration of the Habsburgs in 1936 and 1937.[18]

Otto revealed that it was clear almost from the outset that an *Anschluss* of Austria and Germany could not be prevented – German pressure was too strong and its military too powerful. Still everything was tried to strengthen the anti-German movement. A few days before his assassination in an attempted Nazi putsch, Engelbert Dolfuss confided in Karl Winter, deputy mayor of Vienna, 'Austria could only now be saved by a restoration,' and that he intended to bring about a return of the Habsburgs as soon as possible.[19] Dolfuss said that only a Habsburg could keep Hitler from taking over Austria, but he was assassinated the next day.[20] Ernst Karl Winter saw in Otto someone who was 'without any baggage who might be capable of uniting all Austrians in a single popular front'. It was, he thought, the last way out' for Austria and wrote a book on the subject, *Monarchie und Arbeitershaft*, which was banned.[21]

Dolfuss' successor as chancellor, Karl von Schuschnigg, lacked the spirit and unerring nationalism of his predecessor. He leaned towards monarchism, but was fearful of alienating foreign leaders who had objections to an Austrian restoration based on their own politics or perception of their own national self-interest and public opinion. He was also a devotee of all things German; all things, that is, except Hitler and the Nazis, whom he abhorred as much as feared. Gordon Brook-Shepherd points out that Austria was itself divided at this time into patriotic nationalists who believed in an Austria with its own national, political and cultural identity, and those who thought that Austria's German identity was linked to a greater Germany united with the Reich as one homeland for the German people. Much of the popularity for this cause, explains Brook-Shepherd, was because of the confusion during the early years of the republic. For many socialists union with Germany meant an *Anschluss* with German socialism, whereas the far Right viewed union as the fulfilment of a Greater German destiny. Most, however, were somewhere in the middle.[22]

Unfortunately for Schuschnigg, Mussolini's energetic defence of Austrian independence did not last, particularly when his attention turned to territorial conquest and he required the approbation of his fellow dictator in the north.[23] Mussolini had thought a strong Habsburg Empire could counter Hitler's ambitions, but Otto would not deal with him. He had refused to meet Hitler and Göring and later turned down other invitations from the Nazis. He similarly avoided a face-to-face meeting with Il Duce.[24] The Italian invasion of Abyssinia estranged Mussolini's Stresa allies and left Austria without the foreign support it needed. Schuschnigg visited several European capitals, but found little concrete support and was required to promise not to engage in anti-German policies. Only Czechoslovakia expressed any real empathy for Austria's predicament. The possibility of a Danubian Federation of Austria, Hungary and the countries of the Little Entente was discussed but the idea was denounced by Berlin and so quietly dropped.[25] Worse still, the vice-chancellor, Prince Ernst Rüdiger Starhemberg, who had headed the paramilitary *Heimwehr*, harboured Nazi sympathies at that time and had been present during the attempted Munich Putsch. In 1936 Admiral Horthy, the regent of Hungary, who had prevented the restoration of Otto's father the Emperor Karl, visited Vienna and visited the tombs of the Habsburgs. He was, however, snubbed by the nobility and naval officers who refused to attend a gala opera in the regent's honour.[26]

In July 1936 Schuschnigg signed a Treaty of Friendship with Germany that at the same time recognised Austrian sovereignty and that she was a German state and should act accordingly. In a separate and secret protocol an amnesty for thousands of Nazi prisoners was agreed, the ban was lifted on the Austrian Nazi Party and right-wing pan-German nationalists were admitted into the Austrian Cabinet.[27] Encouraged by Mussolini, who had moved closer to Berlin, Schuschnigg was deluded into believing that the German leadership was trustworthy. This so-called 'Gentleman's Agreement' was signed without Otto's prior knowledge, although Schuschnigg had agreed to keep him informed of any proposed constitutional changes.[28] Göring announced that Germany was not able to continue in its purchase of Austrian iron ore, but by spring 1938 purchase would no longer be necessary.

All over Europe democracy was seen as a spent force, unable to adequately tackle contemporary economic or social problems or resist the spread of international communism. Most European dictatorships were authoritarian rather than fascist, but elements within each country looked to fascist Italy or later Nazi Germany for inspiration. Rather than regard these right-wing regimes as potential allies Hitler looked upon them as rivals to be extinguished one by one or neutralised at his leisure.

Brook-Shepherd observes that, 'There was little doubt in Otto's mind that Austria had now set herself on the slippery slope to extinction.'[29] Inconclusive meetings followed in France to discuss a possible restoration of the Habsburgs to forestall a Nazi takeover of Austria. Then on 7 January 1935, near Zürich in Switzerland, Otto met with Schuschnigg face to face. There was agreed the *Einsiedln* Protocol, whereby the Austrian chancellor promised, 'to carry out the restoration as soon as possible in the coming year ... even if this should eventually lead to a serious European conflagration.'[30] Otto impressed on Schuschnigg that an *Anschluss* and the threat of a European war were inextricably linked and that, should war come, the Austrian people would not be able to hold their heads up if they had not resisted the Nazis, 'however hopeless the military odds'.[31] Schuschnigg further promised that any aggressive action by Germany would be resisted by force of arms. There could, however, be no acquiescence to an Austrian restoration by Hitler although the Austrian chancellor hoped (against declared German intentions) for his approbation of such a move. The German Foreign Secretary informed Schuschnigg that a restoration would be the best way for Austria to commit suicide.[32]

In January 1937, with a barely disguised allusion to the Nazi threat to his homeland, Otto wrote to the civic leaders of 1,500 Austrian towns and villages that had bestowed upon him the freedom of their boroughs, 'I welcome the fact that the people of Austria have found their way back to the martial spirit, and with their brave new Army, which takes up the heritage of a glorious tradition, have created an instrument to protect them from becoming the prey of warlike ambition.'[33] Unfortunately, though the commanders were willing, their prime minister in Vienna refused to give the order to resist the German army in 1938 for fear of spilling German blood.

On 16 December 1937 *The Times* reported that Otto received a delegation of monarchists, including some working-class delegates who, as socialists, had taken part in the armed resistance against the suppression of the Socialist Party in 1934 at Vaduz in Lichenstein, five miles from the Austrian border. They told their archduke that a potentially large body of public opinion had been canvassed and had responded favourably to a possible restoration, though they believed the opposition of foreign powers, notably Germany, made it impossible at that time irrespective of the will of the people.

Papen suggested to Schuschnigg that he should go to Germany to hold frank discussions with the Führer. He accepted when an Austrian Nazi plot to unseat him and call in German forces was uncovered. Their meeting on the Obersalzburg was attended by three of Hitler's generals and was full of threats about a new Spanish civil war beginning in Austria and complaints about Austrian provocation. It led to the signing of an agreement that included a list of concessions, such as admitting Austrian Nazis into the leadership of top institutions. Otto's reaction to what was clearly 'the beginning of the end', was to contact Schuschnigg with a proposal to replace him as chancellor if he felt he could not withstand further pressure. The situation was urgent and a restoration would have taken too long to implement, so the assumption of executive power in the current emergency necessitated few if any constitutional implications beyond the oddity of an Austrian president appointing his rightful emperor as chancellor.

Otto reflected on the situation, which he saw as a clear road to conflict and eventually outright war:

> At the end of this war, he predicted, the map of Europe would be redrawn again in the course of peace negotiations. It was most important for Otto to put Austria again on the map as a sovereign state. Nevertheless, a not insignificant question had already surfaced after the First World War: the concept of a southern state (involving Bavaria, western Austria and the Tyrol). He also asked himself the question: who had opposed and defended himself against Hitler and who had not? In Otto's mind, an Austria that had attempted to defend itself was of paramount importance if it was to emerge again after the war as an independent state. This was the background of his letter to Schuschnigg in February 1938, in which he asked him to hand over the chancellery.[34]

However, Schuschnigg rejected the offer following an announcement of his commitment to Austrian independence ('unto death') in a patriotic speech on 24 February 1938. As a response to continued Nazi demands, Schuschnigg asked permission from the president to hold a plebiscite on Austrian independence. The idea served to unite the disparate elements of Austrian society and rekindled optimism. It was to be short lived, however, as Hitler resolved to invade Austria before the plebiscite could take place in an operation code named 'Otto' after his bitterest Austrian foe. Although Austrian forces were mobilised they were then stood down. This was much to the dismay of Otto, who knew that Austria had at least to make some token defence to prove herself a victim under occupation, rather than a willing supporter of her own oblivion an a pan-German future that was both Nazi and expansionist. Schuschnigg, going back on his word, refused to shed German blood in defence of his country. From his exile in Belgium Otto tried to influence affairs in his home country and stir his countrymen to defiance. He even seriously considered flying to Austria to take over the government and lead the resistance against invasion, but the situation moved too quickly and it was already too late.[35] Otto pleaded for opposition to the Nazis and armed resistance in a protest published in Paris on 15 March 1938.[36] After the German takeover of Vienna, Otto was tried for treason in his absence and sentenced to death.

Hitler was livid that Otto refused any discussion with him in the winter of 1932/33 and that he had organised legitimate opposition within Austria. Immediately after the occupation the People's Court condemned Otto to death for high treason in his absence. A great many 'Legitimists' were arrested by the Nazis in March 1938 and were transported to Dachau, including the Hohenberg brothers, the sons of the Archduke Franz Ferdinand.[37] On 24 March 1938 *The Times* reported that the Archduke Joseph Ferdinand, head of the Tuscan branch of the family, had been arrested at Linz for declaring, 'I have written Goetz's [sic] words on my right hand so that I show them to every man to whom I raise my hand in the Hitler salute,' in a reference to the term of contempt ('*er kann mich im Arsche lecken*') used by Götz von Berlichingen in Goethe's play. As a result he was put under house arrest before being imprisoned in Dachau.[38]

When Otto lodged his formal objections to the Nazi takeover of Austria Göring responded with insults, calling him 'this comic boy'. The Nazi administrator Josef Burckel called him 'Otto the last'. In 1939 Otto further objected to the conquest of Czechoslovakia: 'I condemn with the utmost energy the violence with which Germany has subjugated Bohemia and Moravia. I condemn also the military occupation of Slovakia by a German Army.'[39]

In 1938 an SD (security service) report from Graz commented, 'Above all, the clericals and Legitimists must be viewed today as our truly active opponents.' The Catholic faith, patriotism and monarchism all worked together as catalysts for opposition. Radomír Luža writes:

> Undoubtedly Habsburg's followers perceived him as a living symbol of the distinctive Austrian identity. His early attempts to counter the occupation excited and motivated the early Legitimist groups and helped shape the process of national identification by presenting one visible Austrian alternative. By persistently urging that alternative in their underground publications, the Legitimists undermined the façade of political uniformity that Nazi propaganda strove to create. Their publications also motivated others to resist.[40]

After the outbreak of war William Bullitt the US ambassador to France, wrote to President Franklin D. Roosevelt to tell him that he had heard from a report handed to him by Otto von Habsburg of the danger of a German attack on South America. He continued by emphasising to the president the dangers of strict neutrality:

> I realize that it will probably be impossible for you to convince the people of the United States that they are menaced by Hitler. I cannot express to you my conviction that we are menaced in the most terrible manner by Hitler. If we do not change at once our Neutrality Act and supply France and England immediately with all the weapons of war that we can produce, we shall be insane. It is the considered opinion not only of our own military and Naval attaches in Paris, but also of the French General Staff that if the United States should continue to refuse to supply airplanes, arms and ammunition to France and England, France and England unquestionably would be defeated. It would be our turn next.[41]

In 1940 Otto received an invitation to meet President Roosevelt, which he accepted willingly. When he met the president on 10 March he found that he had a willing listener to all he had to say on the true nature and popularity of Hitlerism, and for Otto's idea for a federation of Danube countries. The latter was based on his father's insistence that the successor states were neither ethnically nor economically viable as separate states. Restoration was not mentioned, but rather Otto insisted that it should be for the people of Austria and Hungary to decide what form of government they should have. Roosevelt agreed that the USA would help re-establish Austrian and Hungarian sovereignty after the fall of Nazism. The president also offered his country as a place of refuge for the imperial family should the need arise. Otto delivered a speech to the US Senate outlining his vision of a Danube Federation of States. The Austro-Hungarian heir had barely returned to the family home at Chateau Steenokkerzeel in Belgium when the Germans invaded the country. On 9 May 1940 they received a phone call from the Belgian royal family with the message that, 'one should undertake a long walk'. This was the signal that the Nazis were on their way and they should make their escape. They went to Dunkirk, from where Otto headed for Paris, spending his time with his teacher and closest associate, Count Dagenfeld, to try to clarify the fate of Austrian refugees in the country with the residual government. 'It was agreed that these Austrians should gather near Libourne, from where a further escape route would be planned.'[42] On the night before the entry of the German army into the city Otto (under Nazi sentence of death) dined at the Ritz with US journalist and publisher Clare Booth Luce. Early next morning Otto left for Bordeaux where he was reunited with his mother. It was there that with the help of the Portuguese Consul General Aristide de Sousa-Mendes the family obtained the visas they needed to escape from France. The Consul General and his Spanish counterpart, Popper de Callejon, issued them transit visas, contrary to the orders of his government. 'Otto and [Count] Degenfeld worked day and night, bringing thousands more passports to these consuls for stamping. Otto only just evaded arrest by the Nazis. Finally, it became too dangerous as the German noose tightened across France.'[43] Before they left Otto obtained promises from the Portuguese and Spanish authorities there that any Austrians left without visas would be given permits before the Germans arrived including several hundred socialists and communists resident in southern France. Aristide de Sousa-Mendes issued thousands of visas and travel documents to refugees that included the entire Belgian Cabinet, the Luxembourg royal family and the actor Robert Montgomery, contrary to the orders of his superiors. He was made one of the Righteous Among the Nations by Israel for helping about 12,000 Jews escape from the Nazis. Many years later Otto von Habsburg wrote to Antonio Moncada Sousa Mendes, 'I wanted to say to you in writing how eternally grateful I am to your grandfather. At a time when many men were cowards, he was a true hero to the West.'

The family made their way to Lisbon where the fugitive Otto was politely asked to go abroad with his family at the earliest opportunity. Otto had intended to go to England where his brother Robert von Habsburg had set up an Austrian Office, flew with the RAF and had the ear of Winston Churchill – who Otto believed could pull Britain through those darkest days in 1940, especially as London had become the diplomatic as well as literal front line against Nazi tyranny for displaced European exiles. The family travelled to the relative safety of America however. Upon arrival Otto sought visas for Austrian compatriots stuck in Europe, mostly Jews and socialists. When asked who these people were, he replied that they were mostly Jewish refugees, to which the official at the Department of Foreign Affairs responded, to the USA's eternal embarrassment, 'We already have enough Jews here; Hitler can keep them'. Unable to make headway, the heir approached the Battista of Cuba and Trujillo of the Dominican Republic who agreed to provide thousands of visas.[44]

When Otto arrived in Washington he was welcomed by Roosevelt who, aware of the Habsburg's concern over Austria's failure to defend itself and having some sympathy with it, suggested the raising of an Austrian military battalion to engage in operations against the Nazis and give credibility to the notion of a free Austria among Americans. Otto was painfully aware that Austrian soldiers would be used against the Allies and was keen that, as they hadn't struck a blow against the invaders in 1938, Austrians should be seen to wage war against the Nazis in the interests of their country's liberation. Without informing the Cabinet, Roosevelt and Secretary of War Stimson decided in 1942 to establish an 1,000-man Austrian battalion within the armed forces. Otto was appointed head of recruitment but numbers were low. A danger of splitting and/or alienating various Austrian and central European political groupings, however, was high and the scheme was dropped.[45] Unfortunately Otto's dream of Austrians fighting side by side with the Allies under their own command came to nothing. Although Otto and his family intentionally took a backseat and did not attempt to adopt any leadership role over the Austrian or Hungarian refugee community in the USA, there were enough divisions anyway to make coordination of their activities difficult – if not impossible – not the least because the socialists refused to talk to the representatives of the Fatherland Front, even though they had a common enemy. Yet Otto was well thought of by the president and therefore had considerable influence on behalf of his country anyway. Roosevelt wrote to Otto, 'The American people would be happy to see the people of Austria regain their place as an independent nation', thereby ensuring US influence relating to any post-war political geography. Roosevelt agreed in principle to Otto's request for three free Austrian consulates to be set up and recognised, and passed on the archduke's proposals to the State Department. Otto didn't just want Austria to be free, but the centre of a credible self-supporting federation of independent states. Churchill favoured the Habsburg vision for central Europe, 'I am extremely interested in Austria,' he wrote, 'and hope that Vienna may become the capital of a great confederation of the Danube ... the separation of the Austrians and

Southern Germans from the Prussians is essential to the harmonious reconstitu-
tion of history.'[46]

Both Churchill and Roosevelt were initially on Otto's side and Churchill
remained so as long as he could. At first the British tried to establish a non-
political Austrian Office in London, 'But secretly gave Austrian monarchists
financial support and helped some of the form a pro-Habsburg Free Austria
movement in Canada.'[47] In 1945 Anthony Eden's private secretary, Oliver
Harvey, commented that Churchill, 'is very definitely on the side of fallen royalty, Habsburg, Hohenzollern or Glucksburg', recording that he was afraid that
Churchill may rush to the rescue of the Habsburgs.[48]

Robert Keyserlingk writes that Churchill had always regretted the passing of
the Austro-Hungarian Empire and supported its re-creation in some form after
the war. 'Even after his monarchical-federation scheme lost his officials' support
he continued to cling onto it and was liable to enthusiastic pro-Austrian out-
bursts in public.'[49] Roosevelt evidently enjoyed Otto's company and treated him
both as an equal and a personal friend.[50]

Crown Prince Rupprecht of Bavaria also had a vision of a great Central
European state. Otto, Rupprecht and other princes did not meet together until
quite late. One wonders if a common royal central European strategy could have
influenced events positively post war. But their ideas would still have run into
the sand of Stalin's stated and hidden agendas. The establishment of a democratic
federation of central European states, including those of southern Germany, was
Anglo-American policy, but under the influence of the Soviet Union, which
Allied success depended upon, Roosevelt became more and more ready to make
concessions to Stalin. He saw Stalin as an actual and current friend, rather than a
potential future competitor and adversary. Among the Allies there was agreement
that Austria ought to be restored to its independent position with Stalin insist-
ing that the nation earn its freedom by assisting in the fall of the Third Reich.
Stalin supported the idea of an independent Austria at the expense of any central
European association standing in the way of the Westward march (literal as well as
metaphorical) of international communism. It was the promise of the federation
becoming a bulwark against the spread of communism that would have made the
idea popular in central Europe as much as with the Western powers. A deep fear
of communism and Slavic expansion was exploited by the Nazis. The federation
had appeal in every village west of the Soviet border.[51]

A plan emerged to divide Hungary from the Reich and enlist its help in
liberating Austria and its neighbours, and attacking Nazi Germany through
the Balkans.

Hungary

Hungary was led by the regent admiral Horthy who had twice resisted the return and restoration of the man he purported to recognise as his king, Emperor Karl. The Nazi net closed around the country steadily until it found itself directly in Germany's orbit. The government had allied itself with Italy and hoped to not only retain its independence but reclaim territory that had become part of Czechoslovakia and Romania. With the German-Austrian *Anschluss* and the pact between Italy and Germany, Hungary was left dangerously exposed. Hitler was then able to play the statesman revising not only the Treaty of Versailles but also that of Vienna, awarding Hungary rights over disputed territory pulling the country ever more within its orbit.

Baron Viktor Kuchina de Schwanburg recalled that in the late 1930s, when political influence in the region began to shift from Rome to Berlin, thousands of people began to 're-Germanise their names' from the Magyar equivalent and had their new names listed in the official newspaper because they considered that they would gain advantage given the political situation. Schwanburg, who used his Magyar name Kuchina, joined an anti-German alliance of people who felt 'Hungarian in their hearts' in opposition to official government policy. When Hitler invaded Poland and war broke out they decided to use every possible means – including force – to resist the Germans. There was an inner struggle among the Hungarian Resistance as it brought them into conflict with their own official representatives, but they were vindicated when Admiral Horthy got in touch with them towards the end of the war. Their movement had been considered illegal even though protected by the Hungarian constitution: the *Jus Restistendi* in the Golden Bull of 1222 resistance against tyranny 'is an obligation not an offence' wrote the baron. The founder and organiser of the movement was Dr Imre Alpary, who also used the name van Tromp.[52]

By 1943 the Hungarian government were in touch with the Resistance and negotiating peace with the Western Allies. They agreed to an unconditional surrender and a suspension of assistance to the Nazis until such time as the surrender could be realised and thereby made public. This meant that Allied aircraft flew over Hungary without hindrance and German supplies were diverted away. Otto wanted an Allied invasion of the Balkans to liberate Austria and Hungary as soon as possible and would have preferred that an Austrian-Hungarian division joined the Allied forces. Churchill proposed what was described as an Istrian 'dagger' planted at Triest and moving on to Austria and Hungary, where the authorities planned to declare an immediate unconditional surrender and put Hungarian forces at the disposal of the liberating troops to secure the country against their former German allies. Roosevelt was prepared to support the plan up until listening to Stalin's objections at Tehran in 1943. In the summer of 1944 Churchill still planned a landing of six seaborne divisions, but his plea to Roosevelt for essential

tank-landing craft was refused. Had the Allies landed and successfully liberated Austria and Hungary with the assistance of Hungarian forces, the map of
post-war Europe might have been different. When Otto questioned Roosevelt's
trusting and accommodating attitude towards the Soviet marshal, the president
replied that after the war the Soviet Union would be so dependent on US aid that
the Americans would be able to dictate terms as to the composition of post-war
Europe. Hitler ordered his forces to take over Hungary, which was transformed
overnight from a vassal state into a territorial possession under occupation and
remained so until the Soviet Red Army ousted the Nazis.

When the Allies did reach the Tyrol, a partisan group that included Otto's
brother Rudolf made contact with them. However, much to Otto's chagrin and
although a resistance group was set up in Vienna towards the end of the war, there
was no mass uprising against the Nazis that would have demonstrated Austria's
status as occupied rather than complicit.[53]

Post War

Otto returned to Austria in 1945, relieved that his country had been liberated,
but concerned that it could end up firmly in the Soviet orbit. A general election
took place that proved a failure for the Soviet-backed socialists, but elements of
the country's constitution that kept the Habsburgs from office and banned the
dynasty from the country were re-affirmed by Austria's new left-wing president
and the Habsburg's old enemy, Karl Renner.

In April 1945 Churchill made plain the government's position as regards a possible Habsburg succession, 'We should not actively intervene on their behalf, being at
all times resolved that in any case where we are forced for the time being to depart
from the ideal of non-intervention our guide is the will of the people expressed
by the vote of a free, unfettered, secret-ballot, universal suffrage election.' He then
added wryly, 'The principle of a constitutional monarchy [in Austria], provided it
is based on the will of the people, is not – oddly enough – abhorrent to the British
mind.' On 28 June 1945, Churchill wrote to Robert von Habsburg thanking him
for his letter of 26 May, enclosing a memorandum from his brother on the subject of South Tyrol, and assured him that his brother's memorandum had already
received the attention of the Foreign Office. However, the letter concluded, 'You
will of course understand that the policy of His Majesty's Government is to defer
to the Peace Conference the settlement of all territorial questions.'[54] In November
1945 Sir Alexander Cadogan, Permanent Under-Secretary for Foreign Affairs,
wrote to Churchill to remind him to ask the Foreign Office if he should see Robert
von Habsburg, who had asked for a personal interview. On 30 November the
prime minister was advised in writing not to see the archduke. Cadogan believed
that HM government was 'more or less committed' to the incumbent Austrian

government, which was 'anti-Hapsburg [sic]'. He thought that the Austrians might be 'a bit unscrupulous' about the way they made use of such an interview and he didn't believe that the interview would do much good anyway – it might even do harm. Churchill noted in the bottom, left-hand corner of the document: 'In the circumstances it would be better for me not to see him. I am sure that the arch-duke will understand. WSC.'[55] The world had moved on. Churchill, who had been a friend to the Habsburgs and their ideas, was powerless to help.

After the war Otto revived his ideas for a united Europe immune from future conflict or dominance by a single aggressive power, and became an active member of the EU. In London in 1967, Otto warned that there was an imminent danger of the rise of political castes in the form of 'the undue influence of political parties, bureaucratic communities and economic power concentrations' replacing the political influence of social classes. As a solution Dr von Habsburg suggested the re-establishing of the authority of the state against undue private influences and to secure individual freedom:

> Which can be achieved only if institutions are created which are a mixed form of government, that is to say, where the sources of authority are dispersed and permit a more effective system of checks and balances that the one devised by Montesquieu. Here the role of the monarchy, as a factor of community, stability, independence of the State, and as a judicial power in defence of basic rights, assumed a new importance.

In the modern world of globalisation and polyglot political economies the need for such checks and balances is even more urgent.

The last word goes to a patriotic Austrian hotelier. *Time* magazine reported Otto's departure from Austria on 15 April 1946:

> The same Tyrolean ultra-conservatism that Napoleon failed to break brought them out to cheer Otto and Robert Habsburg who drove through the country a few months ago in a Mercedes with the royal crown on the radiator. An Allied directive from Vienna last month expelled the pair. Hotel Owner Franz Huber mourned: 'I shall always keep my finest suite ready.'

Dr von Habsburg passed beyond sorrow in his sleep at 3.00 a.m. on 4 July 2011. God bless him. May he rest in peace.

The Hohenbergs: the Princes of Dachau

Duke Maximilian (Max), Prince Ernst and Princess Sophie von Hohenberg were the children of Archduke Franz Ferdinand of Austria-Hungary. Although the

Hohenberg brothers were not in line for anything – not even a defunct throne due to being the sons of a morganatic (unequal) marriage that meant their father's rights as the Habsburg heir could not be passed on to his children – they demonstrated in their behaviour and their high moral principles, and all that it means to be a prince.

Time magazine reported to its readers on 19 March 1934:

> Although Franz Ferdinand had three children, Sophie, Maximilian, and Ernst, the crown went to Franz Ferdinand's nephew, Karl, husband of sober Zita de Bourbon, who was one of the 18 children of Robert Duke of Parma. Curly-haired Otto, the acknowledged heir, was their eldest child. Maximilian, son of Franz Ferdinand, is very much alive, and carries on the family fertility by having produced four more Habsburg princelings since his marriage.[56]

At this time Max was deeply involved in patriotic and anti-Nazi politics as the personal representative in Austria of 'curly-haired Otto', his emperor. The Hohenbergs, together with Otto, had hoped for some support from France and Britain in support of Austrian independence as provided for in the Versailles Treaty and that of St Germain, but this was not forthcoming. Otto was under no illusions about the British, who he said they could not trust but had hoped that the French could be relied on. But he had not realised, he confided later, that the French had been 'bled white' by the First World War and so exhausted their support collapsed. The British, Otto discovered later, had been in no position to assist them due to a disarmament programme that had rendered the country so defenceless its government found it necessary to buy time.[57]

They were not only anti-Nazis but the vocal supporters of a Habsburg restoration. Following the *Anschluss*, which they had vehemently opposed, they were rounded up and placed in Dachau concentration camp. They had been members of the *Reichsbund der Österreicher* and Max was president of the (cross-party) monarchist umbrella organisation, the 'Iron-Ring' (*Eisernen Ring patriotischer Vereinigungen*); a group opposed to German-Austrian political integration and, as such, representative of the interests of his cousin the Crown Prince of Austria-Hungary, Otto von Habsburg. Ernst was further accused of having attacked a swastika sign in Vienna in 1938. Their views were well known and, with the annexation of Austria by Germany, their lives were in great danger. The family attempted to leave Austria when the German takeover began but were refused admission into Czechoslovakia by border guards under orders not to let anyone through. They returned to Austria and decided to loose themselves in Vienna among the anonymous, wealthy foreign guests at the Hotel Imperial. From there they made their way to the British legation with Ernst's English father-in-law, Captain George Jervis Wood, who pleaded for their asylum. There was no safety with the British, however, who would not grant them protection from their enemies. The ambassador, Michael Palairet, told his visitors that Franz von Papen and his associates were regular house guests. 'They're all civilised these Germans,' he exclaimed. At this Max told his eldest son that he had been 'angry beyond measure'. Former chancellor and vice-chancellor Papen had been appointed ambassador to Austria by Hitler following Dolfuss' assassination. In a conversation with US Ambassador George S. Messersmith at the German legation in Vienna, Papen confided that he had been charged with the mission of facilitating German economic and political control over south-eastern Europe to the borders of Turkey as Germany's 'natural hinterland', and said that 'getting control of Austria was to be the first step' in that process. He came to Austria, he said, to weaken and undermine its government, and that he intended to use his reputation as a good Catholic to gain influence with leading Austrians.[58]

According to British records the Hohenberg family were very reluctantly granted a short period of asylum because of telephone death threats made against Ernst and his family. Lucian Meysels refers to British diplomacy at this time as 'shabby' and writes that the Hungarian, French and Belgian embassies in Vienna all gave asylum to political refugees, even helping them escape abroad.[59] The situation for the Hohenbergs did not improve. When they returned to their hotel the manager asked them to leave because the arrival of Adolf Hitler was expected imminently.

Dachau

It had all started gradually. First they put yellow stars on the Jews. These were worn almost proudly. Or in mockery, pinned to their dogs' collars. Their friends sometimes wore them too, in defiance. People shook their heads when they saw it, as if brushing off a mosquito. Or unpleasant thoughts: 'Nein so was!'

Soon stars vanished off the streets. There was a rumour that lorries carried them away to an unknown destination. 'Where to?' Nobody knew.

Tatiana Metternich[60]

Dachau concentration camp, in which the three children of Archduke Franz Ferdinand and most of Crown Prince Rupprecht's family and other royalty were interned, was established in March 1933 and liberated in April 1945. In the twelve years of its existence it housed 200,000 prisoners from all over Europe, of whom 41,500 were murdered.

German-Jewish philosopher and historian Hannah Arendt writes, 'Totalitarianism strives not toward despotic rule over men, but toward a system in which men are superfluous ... Precisely because man's resources are so great, he can be fully dominated only when he becomes a specimen of the animal species man.'[61] This situation, she proposed could only be achieved in a concentration camp. Fr John M. Lenz describes a prisoner's arrival in the camp at Dachau:

After they had taken our pictures, we were marched cross into the *Jourhous* through the great gates with their iconic inscription *Arbeit macht frei!* – Work brings freedom! Here we were stripped of all our clothing and possessions and headed stark naked to the barber who soon made short work of our head and beards if any. A quick shower followed, after which the 'zebra' prison camp uniform and regulation wooden clogs were flung at us … There was a terrible finality about that moment. Our fate had been sealed … It was as though these new clothes signified the new 'naked' existence that had begun for us, an existence in which everything private, everything individual, was verboten. I was filled with an indescribable pain which reached to the very depths of my soul.[62]

'Individuality,' writes Arendt on totalitarian regimes, 'anything indeed that distinguishes one man from another, is intolerable.'[63] Colonel Walter Adam describes his own journey to Dachau: 'We were soon to learn the methods by which they set out systematically to break every vestige of free will. We were fortunate indeed if we arrived at the camp with no more than broken teeth and bleeding lips.'[64] 'It is the very nature of totalitarian regimes to demand unlimited power,' states Arendt. She continues:

Such power can only be secured if literally all men, without a single exception, are reliably dominated in every aspect of their life. In the realm of foreign affairs new neutral territories must constantly be subjugated, while at home ever-new human groups must be mastered in expanding concentration camps, or, where circumstances require liquidated to make room for others. The question of opposition is unimportant both in foreign and domestic affairs. Any neutrality, indeed any spontaneously given friendship, is from the standpoint of totalitarian domination just as dangerous as open hostility, precisely because spontaneity as such, with its incalculability, is the greatest of all obstacles to total domination over man.[65]

Lenz describes the camp in which he was imprisoned for six years:

Our actual prison compound was rectangular, about 600 yards long by 300 yards wide, bounded on all sides by a high wall, an electrified barbed-wire fence and a moat. Round the perimeter were seven brick watch towers, several stories high, with heavy machine-guns which were trained on the compound. We were often to hear the sinister rattle, especially at night.[66]

'KLD [*Konzentrationslager Dachau*]: The initials were everywhere,' Lenz continues 'stamped on our clothing, branded in the stools and printed on the vehicles. I think they must be branded on the very souls of all Dachau prisoners … KLD.'[67]

Former prisoner Hans Oertel points out another sign:

> On the roof of an outbuilding was written in huge white letters:
> *There is a way to freedom,*
> *its milestones are:*
> *Obedience, diligence, honesty,*
> *Order, cleanliness, sobriety,*
> *Truthfulness, sacrifice, and*
> *Love of the fatherland!*
> The inmates were assembled on the parade ground three times a day for several years to be shown these words. But this so-vaunted road to freedom did not exist.[68]

Oertel points out that very soon after its establishment prisoners started to be shot while trying to escape from Dachau. A camp guard was given three days' holiday and a special cigarette ration for every prisoner shot in this way. Soon the camp began accepting all sorts of category of prisoner and many Soviet prisoners of war did not even enter the compound. They were killed upon arrival outside the gates so they wouldn't be registered as prisoners.[69]

Tatiana Metterninch recalls:

> One Waffen SS officer, who had only known fighting at the front until 1943, wished to find out for himself whether these rumours [relating to concentration camps] were true. Thinking his uniform and *Ritterkreuz* coverage and pass enough, he walked into Dachau, the concentration camp near Munich. He was held up at once:
> 'What are you doing here?'
> 'I came to have a look.'
> 'Then you can just stay here.'
> He found himself locked up until the end of the war.[70]

Arrival

The Hohenbergs were kicked onto railway trucks bound for Dachau with other political prisoners. The SS smashed the faces of their charges with rifle butts as they made their way to Germany. It was a first taste of the beatings, psychological and physical torture that were part of camp life where individuality was stamped out with gratuitous violence and extreme humiliation. If individuality is key to civility, civilisation had no place to breathe in a Nazi concentration camp. Group was set on group and human beings picked clean of their humanity.

On 4 May 1939 the *New York Times* referred to unconfirmed reports that Prince Ernst von Hohenberg had died in a concentration camp, reflecting that in January 1938 he had 'smashed with an umbrella an illuminated swastika on the building of the German National Railway.'

When Hohenberg brothers arrived at Dachau in 1938 they were given the job of cleaning out the lavatories.[71] Duke Max was given the green triangular badge of a political prisoner whereas Prince Ernst was made to wear the red badge denoting a criminal due to his defacing of the swastika sign in Vienna, but more especially to humiliate him in front of the other inmates. Ernst had also gone into the German propaganda office to rip down all the portraits of Hitler that he could find.[72]

The SS guards got sadistic pleasure from addressing the brothers as their 'Imperial Highnesses'. They were given the most demeaning jobs possible. They were hooked up to the latrine wagon and given spoons with which to clean out the lavatories from early morning to night. They earned the respect of their suffering comrades, many of whom were communists, and they addressed each other with the familiar 'Du'. Even the worst guards grudgingly recognised that the Hohenbergs suffered their many indignities while maintaining an admirable attitude, which had been instilled in them from childhood, not to show what they really thought.[73] The sight of the brothers descended as they were from Charles the Great and seventy-one German, twenty Polish, eight French and Italian noble families, carrying excrement was ingrained in the memories of many Dachau prisoners.[74]

Dr Hans Gamper, a fellow inmate in Dachau, recalled that the Hohenberg brothers bore the burden of their captivity and the abuse they suffered manfully and without complaint. They were alike in character, very serious; he never saw either of them laugh. As a consequence of the strength and quality of their characters everyone in the camp had a very high opinion of them. One of Ernst's jobs in the camp was to scatter and sweep sand in front of the SS quarters on cold days, as the prisoners waited to leave on work details. This reminded Gamper of a song from 1919 about the Habsburgs reduced to sweeping the streets after the Revolution. The irony of its fulfilment in Dachau was not lost on him. Whenever VIPs visited the camp Hohenberg was called to the gate to be shown off to them while the other inmates were lined up on parade. For the Hohenberg brothers life on earth had been extremely hard, he wrote, and the way they had endured it was 'an example to us all'.[75]

Leopold Figl, future Austrian chancellor (first chancellor of post-war Austria), recalled from his time in Dachau that he saw the Hohenbergs with their two-wheeled cart full of human waste:

> Stripped of all titles and offices and with death before their eyes every hour of the day, they endured the most excruciating humiliation, not with the stoic pride of the 'master race', but with the unwavering, serene dignity of descendants of an ancient family meant to serve to rule and rule to serve. They shared with us their last bite and their last sip, and were the most charming of companions.

Everyone – communists, Home Guards, Defence Leaguers – would have walked through fire for them.[76] Up until they died they were joined together with their fellow sufferers in addressing each with the fraternal 'Du'.[77] A communist fellow inmate also commented, 'In the two was an invisible authority that was involuntarily accepted even by those of a different mindset from them.'[78] Pauli Hertha writes that the Hohenbergs frustrated their tormentors, 'They had a calm, cheerful, majestic dignity about them, an unshakable sense of humour, an unbreakable solidarity. If the system set group against group by encouraging one to look down on another, the Hohenbergs made it clear they were not looking down on anyone.'[79]

On one occasion Ernst saved an elderly Jewish man from certain death by catching the man's cap in mid-air that an SS guard had thrown in the direction of a line over which it was forbidden to cross. Not to wear one's cap was also forbidden, and both were punishable by death. In doing so the Hohenberg risked his own life, but returned the cap with a smile.[80] On another occasion Max saved a Romany man by hiding him beneath a sandbox until his would-be murderer, a raging guard, had gone. Years later the Hohenberg family received two geese from the man's family in remembrance of the act of charity.[81]

After Max and Ernst had been arrested and transported to Dachau, Ernst's mother-in-law Rosa Wood, Countess von Lónyay de Nagy-Lónya und Vásáros-Namény, approached ex-Ambassador Papen to ask for his help. Papen feigned friendship and said it had all been an unfortunate mistake and he would take steps to get them released. In fact he did nothing.[82]

Max's wife Elisabeth, daughter of Maximilian IV Fürst von Waldburg zu Wolfegg und Waldsee, went to see Göring to plead for her husband and his brother.[83] He appeared dressed entirely in white (like a master butcher she thought) with a large gold ring on his little finger and holding a monocle, which he made no attempt to use but apparently carried to look aristocratic. He greeted his supplicant and told her that he knew that she had come to petition him for two whom, he said, he had long thought to either imprison in a concentration camp for years or send to the gallows. He said that Ernst's case was hopeless as he was accused of having tortured an Austrian Nazi. The duchess managed to keep composed and calm Göring down without calling him a liar, and he advised her to write again on her husband's behalf because one day the doors will open for him.[84] The family thought it likely that Max's wife's plea eventually secured the release of her husband.[85]

In answer to a letter from Ernst's wife, Marie-Thérèse (Maisie) Wood, daughter of Captain George Jervis Wood and Rosa Countess von Lónyay, Heinrich Himmler confirmed that her husband and his brother were imprisoned in Dachau. He said the reason for their imprisonment was bound up in their 'terrible behaviour' against the National Socialists in 1934.[86]

Among those who worked for the release of the Hohenberg brothers were Queen Mary of Great Britain (who had entertained their parents at Windsor

Castle), the King of Sweden, the Duke of Luxembourg, the pope and some members of the German aristocracy. Captain Wood continued his petitions in spite of the obstruction of officials at the UK Foreign Office. Otto von Habsburg made representations to Queen Mary on behalf of his cousins via his confidant and her art expert, Finnish Catholic Professor Tancred Borenius of University College London, who was also art advisor to the princess royal. The queen did not hesitate, but asked her aide Major Chichester to take up the matter with the Foreign Office – however her intervention stalled because of departmental bureaucracy and the reluctance of officials to get involved.[87]

However, Jan Galandauer writes that the fate of the Hohenbergs raised concerns, especially among the aristocracy of various countries who made representations to the German government. On 28 June 1938 the German ambassador in England reported the intervention of British Foreign Minister, Lord Halifax, 'it is the result of pressure from assorted influential circles who wish to be informed of the fate of some Austrian personalities in which said circles have an interest'.[88] Among these personalities were the Hohenbergs. The intervention was very discrete, writes Galandauer, 'Halifax of course knew with whom he was dealing.' He emphasised that the Hohenbergs had no knowledge of his intervention and said that earnestly hoped that they were not subject to any trouble as a result of his expressed interest. Reinard Heydrich, chief of the security police, described Halifax's intervention on behalf of the brothers as 'a risky act'.[89] It would seem that Queen Mary's own intervention at the Foreign Office did fall on deaf ears after all.

Future head of the Austrian National Theatre, Dr Rudolf Kalmar recalled, 'They were harnessed to the sewage cart like roped animals. Their slave driver, a professional criminal, beat them mercilessly as they were chased from one latrine to the next where they had to shovel excrement into buckets and cart them away.' Fellow prisoner General Roland Müller remembered that they were stopped repeatedly by two SS men:

> Soon word got around that they were the two sons of Archduke Franz Ferdinand, assassinated in Sarajevo. On the cart was a ton of muck. The SS-men stopped them and made fun of them. They took a flat stone, had the two prisoners put their heads close to the pile of muck and then threw the stone into the pile so that the brothers' faces were splattered with excrement.

This was repeated every day for the amusement of the SS.[90]

Hellmut Andics, in *Die Frauen der Habsburger*, describes how the brothers were an unbending, unyielding and courageous example to the other prisoners. Despite their torn and filthy prison clothing, they expressed true nobility. They spent their free time in the muddy street with communist comrades and shared a few lumps of sugar. Every new prisoner was shown the Hohenbergs as examples of how one ought to behave in the camp. Everyone knew that they came of the best stock.[91]

They were not heard to complain and they accepted every humiliation impassively as if they were not affected at all to the immense respect of their fellows.[92]

When the brothers were discharged from Dachau they found themselves not released but in Flossenbürg concentration camp, where they were given the same degrading occupation as cleaners of the latrines that they had before but, as fellow prisoner Otto Oerlel remembers, they would not be broken, humiliated by this job or Ernst's association with criminals, whom he regarded as fellow victims of the Nazi regime. Another prisoner said angrily, 'Now these Hohenbergs are here in Flossenbürg carrying shit again, won't it ever stop.' Ernst was, Oerlel recalls, a person of outstanding character and behaviour who was always willing to help others, and an example to them all. His comradely attitude won attention and respect throughout the camp. As a communist Oertel had had no time for the aristocracy before his incarceration, but Prince Ernst so impressed him that he changed his attitude completely.[93] While in Flossenbürg Max and Ernst assisted fellow prisoner Dr Mittmeyer's attempt to contain an outbreak of dysentery after the guards isolated the camp, abandoning the prisoners to their expected fate. Using charcoal as a disinfectant and herbal mixtures as medicine, and burying the dead as quickly as possible, their efforts bore fruit. When the guards returned and the SS were surprised to find so many still alive.[94]

Shortly before Max was released on parole, the Gestapo tried to get him to incriminate himself by recording his life history on paper with the likelihood that anything he said would be used in a trial for treason. That this did not happen, thought to be largely due to likely international interest and unwelcome publicity before the outbreak of war.[95]

At the beginning of 1940 Ernst was moved from Flossenbürg to Sachsenhausen-Oranienburg concentration camp, where he remained until April 1943. From there he was allowed to write to his family once a month. A surviving letter including his address as No. 17 739, Block 5, Oranienburg-Sachsenhausen concentration camp, near Berlin, concludes, 'Every day and every hour, my thoughts are with you and I just hope you are not too concerned. I embrace you and send you a thousand kisses. Your Ernst.' Ernst's wife had tried to arrange a meeting with Himmler, but was unsuccessful.[96]

The Hohenberg family was not kept in concentration camps for the whole of the war but neither were they set at liberty after their release. They later learned that Hitler had personally ordered that no mercy was to be shown to them. HSH Princess Sophie von Hohenberg (de Potesta) reveals that after his return from Dachau Prince Max was forced to live in the family castle, Artstetten in Austria, under house arrest, and the life of Prince Ernst, who was only released in April 1943 'was made all but easy' by the Nazis.[97] Ernst was *freed* after a sustained campaign for his release. His activities were, however, severely restricted: he had to report to the nearest Gestapo headquarters every Saturday and he was instructed to take work in a Gestapo factory, his property was forfeit to the German Reich without compensation, and he was not allowed to work without permission. He had developed a heart condition in Dachau and fell into a deep depression about his situation and of Europe under the Nazis.

The brothers never talked about their experiences in concentration camps partly, one suspects, because it meant reliving painful memories, but also because they were made to take an oath on leaving and as princes and men of faith with unshakable principles, they never broke an oath once made. The abuse that they suffered undoubtedly shortened the lives of both men. Ernst died of a stroke in 1954 and Max only outlived his brother by eight years although they had both been in the very best of health in 1938 at the time of their incarceration.

Max's home at Artsetten was ransacked twice, first by Nazis and later by Bolsheviks. The brothers' property was confiscated by the Gestapo and although Max was able to win some concessions, none were to be forthcoming for Prince Ernst.[98] On 8 May 1945 the Russians occupied Artsetten but their plundering was limited because there was next to nothing left to plunder. Ernst and his wife Marie-Thérèse (Maisie) moved from apartment to apartment until, with the help of his old Dachau comrade Leopold Figl, he obtained a permit to visit his children. Eventually he got to his home at Radmer in the British zone and began a legal battle for its return.[99]

In 1945 Max was elected mayor (Burgermaster) of Artsetten by a unanimous vote and the Soviet occupying power confirmed him in his office although he thought it were more likely that they would shoot him at the time. He was re-elected in 1950. When he died even socialist journal *Arbeiter-Zeitung* paid full respect to the Hohenbergs in an obituary that recorded that they were both supporters of the Imperial House and correct citizens of the republic as well. 'Their convictions were monarchist, their lives, impeccably faithful to the law.'[100] These Habsburgs who weren't allowed to be Habsburgs showed what it meant to be a Habsburg, the newspaper concluded.

Their sister Princess Sophie married Count Friedrich von Nostitz-Rieneck and lived in Czechoslovakia, from where she encouraged her brothers to escape from the Nazis. Tragically that country wasn't safe from the Nazis either; one of her sons was killed on the Eastern Front and another died in a Soviet internment camp after the war ended.

How could such an abuse of humanity occur in modern times? For it has happened since in Bosnia, Cambodia and elsewhere, though not on the scale of systemised cold-blooded efficiency of the camps. Evil feeds on fear. Fear of the Jews, Slavs and Gypsies, as well as political prisoners and priests, led to their persecution and murder. That it was done or consented to out of fear does not excuse it in any way; fear merely facilitated the workings of evil.

Notes

1 George S. Messersmith to William Philips, Under Secretary of State in Washington, 14 August 1943, p. 6; George S. Messersmith papers 1907–1955, Ms 109, 125500, Box 2, F16; Special Collections Department of the University of Delaware; http://www.lib.udel.edu/ud/spec/findaids/html/mss0109.html.

2 Correspondence with Eva Dammerle and the office of HR&IH Dr Otto von Habsburg, 2009.

3 Brook-Shepherd, Gordon, *Uncrowned Emperor: The Life and Times of Otto von Habsburg* (London & New York, 2003), p. 80. I am heavily indebted to Gordon Brook-Shepherd for the information that he provides in his excellent book.

4 Correspondence with the office of HR&IH Dr Otto von Habsburg, 2009.

5 http://www.hungarian-history.hu/lib/montgo/montgo08.htm, p. 3.

6 Brook-Shepherd, *Uncrowned Emperor*, pp. 79–80.

7 Correspondence with the office of HR&IH Dr Otto von Habsburg, 2009.

8 Brook-Shepherd, *Uncrowned Emperor*, p. 80.

9 Ibid., p. 79.

10 Ibid., p. 81.

11 Ibid., p. 80–1.

12 http://www.time.com/time/magazine/article/0,9171,747168-2,00.html#ixzz0rmXZclnr.

13 Brook-Shepherd, *Uncrowned Emperor* (London, 2004), p. 80–3.

14 James, Robert Rhodes, *Memoirs of a Conservative 1910–1937*, p. 401.

15 *The Times*, 16 April 1935.

16 Brook-Shepherd, *Uncrowned Emperor*, pp. 86–7.

17 Correspondence with the office of HR&IH Dr Otto von Habsburg, 2009.

18 Opfell, Olga S., *Royalty Who Wait: The 21 Heads of Formerly Regnant Houses of Europe*, p. 33.

19 Brook-Shepherd, *Uncrowned Emperor*, p. 87.

20 Opfell, *Royalty Who Wait*, p. 33.

21 Heinz, Karl Hans, *E.K. Winter: ein Katholik zwischen Österreichs Fronten 1833–38* (Vienna, Böhlau, 1984), Vorwort, pp. 11013, cited in: Muhlen, Hermynia Zur, *The End of the Beginning: The Book of My Life*, pp. 266–7.

22 Brook-Shepherd, *Uncrowned Emperor*, p. 88.

23 Goring warned Mussolini that the Axis was at stake if he supported a restoration, Gulick, Charles Adams, *Austria from Habsburg to Hitler* (California, 1948), p. 1746.

24 Opfell, Olga S., *Royalty Who Wait: The 21 Heads of Formerly Regnant Houses of Europe*, p. 33.

25 Brook-Shepherd, *Uncrowned Emperor*, pp. 88–91.

26 Ibid., p. 96.

27 Ibid., p. 100.

28 Ibid., p. 102.

29 Ibid.

30 Cited in Brook-Shepherd, *Uncrowned Emperor*, p. 102.

31 Ibid., p. 104.

32 Ibid., pp. 104–5. Prior to the *anchluss* Hitler told Lord Lothian that an attempt at a Habsburg restoration would be 'brought to nought at once'. The Austrian government was, he told Lothian, a 'papal government' that did not enjoy the confidence of the Austrian people, Franklin D. Roosevelt Library Archive, report by Lord Lothian.

33 *The Times*, 2 January 1937.

34 Correspondence with the office of HR&IH Dr Otto von Habsburg, 2009.

35 Brook-Shepherd, *Uncrowned Emperor*, pp. 115–29.

36 Luža, Radomír, *The Resistance in Austria, 1938–1945*, p. 30.

37 Correspondence with the office of HR&IH Dr Otto von Habsburg, 2009.

38 *The Times*, 24 March 1938.

39 Quoted in *Time* magazine, 3 April 1939.

40 Luža, Radomír, *The Resistance in Austria, 1938–1945*, pp. 30–5.

41 Franklin D. Roosevelt Library Archive, letter to F.D.R. from William Bullitt.

42 Correspondence with the office of HR&IH Dr Otto von Habsburg, 2009.

43 Correspondence with the office of HR&IH Dr Otto von Habsburg, 2009

44 Correspondence with the office of HR&IH Dr Otto von Habsburg, 2009.

45 Opfell, Olga S., *Royalty Who Wait: The 21 Heads of Formerly Regnant Houses of Europe*, p. 66.

46 Brook-Shepherd, *The Uncrowned Emperor*, pp. 155–61. Crown Prince Rupprecht of Bavaria had his own vision of a Central European state, of which Churchill was also ready to consider. Otto, Rupprecht, Louis Ferdinand and other princes did not meet together until quite late. One wonders if a common royal central European strategy could have influenced events positively post war. However, their ideas would still have run into the sand of Stalin's stated and hidden agenda.

47 Ibid., p. 63.

48 Keyserlingk, Robert H., *Austria in World War II: An Anglo-American Dilemma* note 25, p. 230.

49 Ibid., pp. 63–5.

50 Ibid., p. 66.

51 Brook-Shepherd, *Uncrowned Emperor*, p. 162.

52 From a story of the Kuchina de Schwanburg family, including the personal reminiscences of the author, Baron Viktor Kuchina de Schwanburg (awaiting publication).

53 Three cousins enlisted in the US army to fight the Nazis and a fourth cousin flew with the RAF.

54 CHUR 2/140, Sir Winston Churchill Archive Trust.

55 CHUR 2/140, Sir Winston Churchill Archive Trust.

56 *Time* magazine, 19 March 1934. Duke Max and his wife went on to have twelve children.

57 See (and hear) www.youtube.com/watch?v=0912bz3DMwE.

58 See 'Franz von Papen (1879–1969) http://www.jewishvirtuallibrary.org/jsource/Holocaust/Papen.html. During the First World War Papen had been expelled from the USA for complicity in German sabotage plots and in 1916 negotiated to supply arms for a rising against British rule in Ireland.

59 Meysels, Lucian, *Die verhinderte Dynastie: Erzherzog Franz Ferdinand und das Haus Hohenberg* (Molden, 2000), pp. 163–4.

60 Metternich, Tatiana, *Tatiana* (London, rev. 2004; first pub. 1976), p. 117.

61 Arendt, Hannah, 'Total Domination' reprinted in *The Portable Hannah Arendt*, ed. Peter Baehr (New York, 2000), pp. 137.

62 Lenz, John M., *Christ in Dachau* (Roman Catholic Books, 1960), p. 30.

63 Arendt, Hannah, 'Total Domination' reprinted in *The Portable Hannah Arendt*, ed. Peter Baehr (New York, 2000), pp. 137.

64 Colonel Walter Adam quoted in Lenz, John M., *Christ in Dachau*, pp. 29–30.

65 Arendt, Hannah, 'Total Domination' reprinted in *The Portable Hannah Arendt*, ed. Peter Baehr (New York, 2000), pp. 136–7.

66 Lenz, John M., *Christ in Dachau*, p. 35.

67 Ibid., p. 33.

68 *Otto Oertel as a Prisoner of the SS*, pub. and ed. by Stephan Appelius (Library and Information System of the University of Oldenburg, 1990), online document http://oops.uni-oldenburg.de/volltexte/1999/686/, pp. 125–6, accessed 10 January 2010.

69 Ibid.

70 Metternich, Tatiana, *Tatiana* (London, rev. 2004; first pub. 1976), p. 117.

71 Bestenreiner, Erika, Franz Ferdinand und Sophie von Hohenberg, *Verboten Liebe am Kaiserhof* (Zurich, Piper, 2004), pp. 287–8.

72 Pauli, Hertha, *The Secret of Sarajevo: the Story of Franz Ferdinand and Sophie* (London, Collins, 1966), p. 304.

73 Bestenreiner, Erika, Franz Ferdinand und Sophie von Hohenberg, p. 287.

74 Galandauer, Jan, *Frantisek Ferdinand D'Este* (Pasek, Praha, Litomyšl, 2000), ch. 6.

75 Gamper, Dr Hans, 'Die Söhne des ermordeten Thronfolgers', Tiroler Nachrichten, 13 (January 1962).

76 The English translation the author has of this line in Galandauer, Jan, *Frantisek Ferdinand D'Este*, has it that 'they all would have gone to the oven for them'.

77 Meysels, Lucian, *Die verhinderte Dynastie*, p. 178. The use of 'Du' must be regarded as extremely special and extraordinary between people of mixed backgrounds and indicative of the deep bonds and brotherhood between camp inmates. The brothers continued to address fellow ex-inmates in this way throughout their lives.

78 Ibid., p. 176–8.

79 Pauli, Hertha, *The Secret of Sarajevo*, p. 305.

80 Ibid.

81 Meysels, Lucian, *Die verhinderte Dynastie*, p. 177.

82 Ibid., p. 166.

83 Elizabeth's father had a deep abiding dislike of National Socialism and resigned his presidency of the Württemberg horse-breeding association when Hitler's came to power in 1933.

84 Meysels, Lucian, *Die verhinderte Dynastie*, p. 169.

85 Bestenreiner, Erika, *Franz Ferdinand und Sophie von Hohenberg*, p. 289.

86 Reichsführer, Briefe an und von Himmler, *Krsg von Helmut Heiber* (DTV, Quelle R85 5.0102), p. 65.

87 *Glasgow Herald*, 12 August 1938, p. 8.

88 Galandauer, Jan, *Frantisek Ferdinand D'Este* (Pasek, Praha, Litomyšl, 2000), ch. 6.

89 Ibid.

90 Meysels, Lucian, *Die verhinderte Dynastie*, p. 179; and Galandauer, Jan, *Frantisek Ferdinand D'Este*, ch. 6.

91 Bestenreiner, Erika, *Franz Ferdinand und Sophie von Hohenberg*, p. 288.

92 Galandauer, Jan, *Frantisek Ferdinand D'Este*, ch. 6.

93 *Otto Oertel as a Prisoner of the SS*, pub. and ed. by Stephan Appelius (Library and Information System of the University of Oldenburg, 1990), online document http://oops.uni-oldenburg.de/volltexte/1999/686/, pp. 125–6, accessed 10 January 2010.

94 Pauli, Hertha, *The Secret of Sarajevo: the Story of Franz Ferdinand and Sophie* (London, Collins, 1966), p. 306; and Galandauer, Jan, *Frantisek Ferdinand D'Este*, ch. 6.

95 Meysels, Lucian, *Die verhinderte Dynastie*, p. 180.

96 Quoted in Meysels, Lucian, *Die verhinderte Dynastie*, p. 189.

97 Private correspondence with the author, August 2011.

98 The appropriation of Max's property for the benefit of the German Reich was reported in Austrian newspapers in 1941.

99 Bestenreiner, Erika, *Franz Ferdinand und Sophie von Hohenberg*, p. 290.

100 Pauli, Hertha, *The Secret of Sarajevo*, p. 307–8.

EUROPEAN ROYALTY AND THE NAZIS

Italy

Vittorio Emanuele III of Italy did little to prevent the fascist takeover of his country, or its membership of the Tripartite Pact. He was also complicit in depriving rightful monarchs of their inheritance. When Mussolini's Fascists marched on Rome in 1922 the king refused to sign a decree of martial law to stop them. The army was loyal to the king and some of the leading Fascists hesitated in acting against the wishes of the king. However, Vittorio invited Mussolini to Rome to form a government, probably in the hope that it would lead to a return of political stability after years of chaos. Democracy fell away without the king's support and Il Duce became answerable to the monarch, who could only dismiss his prime minister on the advice of Mussolini's own Fascist Grand Council. Although the king made a deal with the Fascists, who represented an alternative to anarchy to prevent his country being destroyed by civil war, the result was war anyway and eventually the invasion of Italy. His acceptance of the Crowns of Ethiopia and Albania and particularly his apparent acceptance of racial purity laws were unacceptable and indefensible.

However, in July 1943 the king was asked to resume his constitutional powers and immediately ordered the arrest of Mussolini, entering into negotiations with the Allies with whom the king was already in contact. He also resigned his assumed title to Ethiopia and Albania in favour of their rightful claimants. On 8 December he announced an armistice with the Allies. In 1944 Vittorio passed over most of his powers to his son and heir, Crown Prince Umberto, without formally abdicating.

Princess Mafalda

Princess Mafalda of Savoy was a daughter of King Vittorio Emanuele III of Italy and the wife of Prince Philipp of Hesse, Landgrave of Hesse-Kassel a supporter of the Nazis until he fell out with them and was, as a consequence, imprisoned in Dachau. Hitler disliked and distrusted Mafalda, believing that she was working against him. He called her the 'blackest carrion in the Italian royal house'. On 23 September 1943 the princess was arrested by the Gestapo for her subversive activities and as a hostage to keep her father quiet. She was eventually incarcerated in Buchenwald concentration camp where she was badly mistreated, and died in August 1944 as a result of an Allied bombing raid. She told a couple of fellow Italians in her last hours, 'Remember me not as an Italian princess, but as an Italian sister.'

Norway

Norway was invaded by German armed forces on 9 April 1940. The invaders were met with spirited resistance by Norwegians defending Oslo, who succeeded in sinking the heavy cruiser *Blücher* and damaging the pocket battleship *Lützow*. They forced the Nazis to delay their occupation of the Norwegian capital and provided an opportunity for the royal family, Cabinet and the majority of MPs to relocate to Elverum, where the *Sorting* (parliament) was briefly reconvened – unanimously passing a resolution granting full powers to the Cabinet to defend the country until the *Sorting* could meet again.

Nazi minister Curt Brauer called upon the king to appoint Vidkun Quisling as head of a German-backed puppet government, and for his subjects to cease all resistance to German forces. Norway was threatened with reprisals if he did not surrender. King Haakon informed Brauer that he could not make such a decision without consulting his government.

The king addressed his Cabinet with some emotion, aware that his own views would be influential:

> I am deeply affected by the responsibility laid on me if the German demand is rejected. The responsibility for the calamities that will befall people and country is indeed so grave that I dread to take it. It rests with the government to decide, but my position is clear. For my part I cannot accept the German demands. It would conflict with all that I have considered to be my duty as King of Norway since I came to this country nearly thirty-five years ago.

Haakon then offered to abdicate rather than stand in the way of the decision of the Cabinet, because he could never appoint a government in which he knew parliament and people had no confidence. Inspired by their king, the government advised him not to appoint Quisling, and broadcast that Norway would resist the invasion for as long as possible. German aircraft attempted to wipe out king and government through bombing attacks, forcing them to take refuge in the countryside in April 1940. The king and Crown Prince Olaf relocated again towards the north of the country with the help of his British allies on HMS *Glasgow*, where they stayed until the military position became impossible. In June they were again taken on board of a British warship and transferred at Tromsø to London, where the king set up a government in exile. The Nazis failed to get the *Sorting* to depose the king, who in his turn refused to abdicate his responsibilities to his people. Coins bearing the king's monogram were worn as a symbol of resistance throughout the occupation.

King Haakon of Norway was the younger brother of the King of Sweden. However, he was regarded as a great Norwegian king and an inspiration to his people. All true monarchs and loyal consorts are required to become their country, native or adopted, and live and die in its cause. This is more than symbolic; mystical in concept maybe, but all too palpable in application.

Denmark

Christian X succeeded to the throne of Denmark in 1910. During the Easter Crisis of 1920, Christian followed the nationalist line, which wanted a re-unification of Danish territory. This included the ethnically Danish city of Fensburg that had been lost to Prussia, but was part of Central Schleswig, which unlike Northern Schleswig had voted to remain German. The prime minister resigned over the issue and his Cabinet was replaced, causing a constitutional crisis that led to a climb down by Christian who lost much of his authority as a result.

When German forces invaded on 9 April 1940, Danish resistance was quickly overwhelmed by the better-armed and equipped Germans who outnumbered their Danish counterparts. The government quickly surrendered and was allowed some measure of control over domestic affairs. The 6ft 6in king, who was allowed to remain head of state, stayed in Copenhagen – he became a symbol of Danish resistance, riding his horse, Jubilee, though the streets without escort every day and showing himself to his people, acknowledging their good wishes as an act of defiance, while ignoring Nazi salutes. All of Denmark was his bodyguard, it was said. He continued his daily rides until he fell from his horse and was too injured to continue. '*Der rider en kong*' stated a popular patriotic song of the time, claiming that Christian was the freest Dane and was guarded by Danish hearts. In 1942 Hitler sent Christian a long telegram to mark his 72nd birthday. The king sent back the briefest reply possible, '*Meinen besten Dank. Chr. Rex*', which the dictator regarded as an insult. He recalled his ambassador to Copenhagen, expelled the Danish ambassador from Berlin and dismissed the Danish government. When the Nazis attempted to round up Danish Jews many of their compatriots assisted their escape to neutral Sweden. When Denmark was liberated Christian re-opened the Danish parliament (*Rigsdag*) although he remained an invalid from the effects of the fall from his horse. Throughout the war the Danish flag flew from Christian's castle at Amalienborg. According to legend the German authorities ordered it taken down, otherwise they would send a soldier to do it for them. The king replied that if that happened a Danish soldier would raise it again. When the Germans announced that they would shoot that soldier Christian replied, 'That Danish soldier will be me.' The flag continued to fly. As a sign of resistance, like the Norwegians, many Danes wore a badge (*kongemærket*) that included the royal insignia.

Sweden

King Gustav of Sweden did everything in his power to keep his country from war. He was on friendly terms with leading Nazis and congratulated Hitler on his invasion of the Soviet Union, but he was no anti-Semite. He used his limited influence with the German leader to try to get him to change his attitude towards the Jews and appealed to Admiral Horthy of Hungary to protect his country's Jewish population in the name of humanity.

The Netherlands

By the outbreak of the Second World War the Netherlands and its queen had a track record of standing up to outsiders wanting to interfere in Dutch affairs. When the Allies attempted to extradite Kaiser Wilhelm from his exile in the Netherlands following the end of the First World War, Wilhelmina called the Allied ambassadors to her presence and 'lectured them on the rights of asylum'. *Time* magazine reflected in November 1939 that no one had given Queen Wilhemina more trouble that Adolf Hitler, 'and from no ruler has the Führer taken, at times, such straight talk'. When the German guests and bridesmaids at her daughter's wedding had their passports confiscated Wilhemena asserted, 'This is the marriage of my daughter to the man she loves, whom I have found worthy of her love; this is not the marriage of the Netherlands to Germany.' The passports were returned. She also protested at the death sentence passed on Dutch citizen Marius van Der Lubbe for his alleged participation in the Reichstag fire by means of a personal letter to Hitler.[1]

When German forces entered the Netherlands in May 1940, Queen Wilhelmina intended to direct the resistance of her armed forces from the town of Breskens in Zeeland. She wrote to Pope Pious XII upon receipt of his telegram of sympathy and support, 'I sincerely thank Your Holiness for your message of concern about our welfare and for your prayers that justice and freedom will be re-established. Confiding in God, my people are resolved to contribute with all their strength to the accomplishment of final triumph.'[2] However, when she was en route on the British destroyer HMS *Hereward*, Zeeland came under heavy attack and the queen reluctantly sailed into exile in the UK, on the understanding that she would return at the earliest opportunity. In London she headed her government in exile. When it became apparent that her prime minister, Dirk Jan de Geer, was a defeatist who wanted to negotiate with Berlin, Wilhelmina successfully had him removed from power. The queen broadcast to her people to give hope and inspire resistance. Dutch defiance was expressed in her subjects' illegal celebration of her birthday. Greatly admired by Churchill, the queen was awarded the Order of the Garter in 1944. She had no love for politicians, but much love for the people who she wanted governed after the war by those who were active resistance workers. When she returned to the Netherlands she showed herself to her people as often travelling by bicycle as car.

Queen Wilhelmina's husband, Prince Bernhard of Lippe Biesterfeld, was German by birth but became naturalised shortly before his marriage in 1937, fighting with his new Dutch compatriots against the Nazi Blitzkreig after getting his family to safety. He returned to Europe to assist the resistance in preparation for liberation.

As Prince Bernhard of the Netherlands climbed down through the rubble of the entrance to an apartment block where he had just had dinner with David Bowes-Lyon during a bombing raid, which had partly demolished his dinner venue, he was heard to say: 'So kind. Most delightful evening.'[3]

Belgium

King Leopold III of Belgium and his family were held inside the country until 1944 when they were transported to Germany under SS guard. While in captivity an attempt on the royal family was made by their gaolers, who supplied them with cyanide in the guise of vitamins, which were offered as compensation for their starvation diet. They were later moved to Austria where they were liberated by US troops.

King Leopold's mother Queen Elizabeth was a patron of the arts and friend of Albert Einstein. During the German occupation she used her influence to save hundreds of Jewish children from deportation, for which she was named one of the Righteous Among the Nations by the Israeli government.

Monaco

Although Louis II was a friend of Marshal Petin and conscious of the principality's position close to Italy, his son Ranier was not so reticent. He joined the Free French Army as an artillery officer in 1944 and took full part fighting off the German counter-offensive in Alsace, winning the Croix de Guerre and Bronze Star.

Luxembourg

Warned about the imminent invasion of Luxemboug the grand ducal family left for Paris on the night of 9 May 1940. The Nazis invaded Luxembourg the following day. Charlotte, the grand duchess, wrote to Pope Pious XII on 14 May, 'Confiding in the protection of the Patroness of my dear country and in the generous help of the Allied Powers, we unite ourselves in prayer with Your Holiness and hope that my country and my people will soon obtain independence and freedom.'[4] From Paris Charlotte's son and heir, Grand Duke Jean, went to Canada where he studied law and political science before volunteering for the Irish Guards in 1942 and being commissioning the following year. Newly promoted captain, he landed in Normandy on D-Day and took part in the bloody siege and liberation of Caen and the liberation of Brussels before participating in the liberation of Luxembourg. He then moved on to Arnhem and the invasion of Germany. Charlotte herself directed her government from London and was a permanent inspiration to her people in their resistance against their occupiers and in their faith of eventual liberation.

Yugoslavia

King Alexander of Yugoslavia was assassinated in 1934, after which the prime minister introduced an authoritarian regime. Although the regent of the kingdom, Prince Paul, was prepared to join the Axis powers in March 1941, the young 17-year-old King Petar supported by his followers staged a coup against the government and sided with the British against Germany. Hitler was enraged and ordered Operation Punishment to 'destroy Yugoslavia as a state'. Begrade was bombed for three days and nights and the country was invaded by Axis forces, and carved up politically. On 17 April Yugoslavia fell. The king and his government were forced into exile, arriving eventually in Britain where he established his government in exile, attended the University of Cambridge and joined the RAF. Irregular royalist army units fought a resistance movement against the German invaders but fell out with the left-wing republican partisans led by Josip Broz Tito, with whom they came into direct conflict. Seeing the growing effectiveness of the partisans against the Nazis as compared with royalist forces who seemed more intent in defeating their communist compatriots and erstwhile friends, the Allies switched their support. King Petar was deposed in 1945, but it is possible that his stand against the Nazis in 1941 caused Hitler's postponement of Operation Barbarossa until it was too late. Had the Nazis moved sooner Moscow may well have fallen before the onset of the Russian winter. The Soviet Union may have owed its continued existence to the king who was deposed by their representatives after the war was over.

Bulgaria

Boris II of Bulgaria was marginalised in a right-wing coup in May 1934 and political parties abolished. The coup swept away the military dictatorship and replaced it with an authoritarian government. The king then staged a counter-coup and re-established parliamentary representation controlled by a loyal regime. Although Bulgaria remained neutral at the outbreak of the Second World War, powerful factions within the country and outside steered it ever closer within the German orbit. Using territorial inducements and threats, Germany put pressure on Bulgaria to join the Tripartite Pact.[5] *Time* magazine reported that Boris ought to be scared, because his chance of getting aid from Greece, Turkey or Britain to defend his country was not bright. The magazine noted that the Nazis had been using psychological warfare against Bulgaria to undermine its resolve, 'Sending up trial rumours and tentative untruths, paving the way for a Blitzkrieg in the spring [of 1941] just as they did in the Lowlands in 1940 ... "It's a splendid fog," said a happy Berlin spokesman, "and others made it for us."'

Bogdan Filoff voiced the king's attitude when he said that Bulgaria was witnessing one of the 'greatest cataclysms that history has ever known'. He was under no illusion about the situation, which at that time meant German troops massed on the country's borders and called on his countrymen to put Bulgaria first, 'I must warn you that today war and peace do not depend on small nations like Bulgaria. She is so small that she cannot dictate whether there shall be war or peace. We have therefore to be ready for any eventuality.'[6]

As a result of German bribes and threats, a loose alliance was forged between the two countries. Had this not occurred invasion would have been likely as Boris' country lay in the path of Nazi expansion into the Balkans and Greece. In 1943 Germany requested that Bulgaria export its 50,000 Jewish citizens to Poland. This Boris refused to allow. His government even explored the possibility of saving the Jewish population by sending them to Palestine instead. Tsar Boris also refused to declare war on the Soviet Union or send Bulgarian troops to the Eastern Front. Instead a 'symbolic' war was declared on the USA and Britain. Göbbels noted ominously in his diary:

Several reports indicate that anti-German sentiment in certain Bulgarian Government circles is slightly on the increase. Especially Tsar Boris is said to be playing a somewhat double-faced game. He is a sly, crafty fellow, who, obviously impressed by the severity of the defensive battles on the Eastern Front, is looking for some back door by which he might eventually escape. This is a very shortsighted policy, which will, of course, immediately be reversed, once our offensive has started again.

Boris died of apparent heart failure shortly after returning from a meeting with Hitler. Suspicion of foul play quickly followed. The possibility of poison following a stormy meeting with the Führer cannot be ruled out. As a statement of Bulgarian foreign policy Boris said: 'My ministers are pro-German, my wife is pro-Italian, my people are pro-Russian - I am the only neutral in the country.'

Greece

In 1936 General Metaxas became dictator of Greece with the agreement of the king. On 6 April 1941 Germany invaded Yugoslavia and then moved into Greece. Although George II of Greece had announced a policy of no surrender, his prime minister, Alexander Koryzis, advised surrender as the only option. The king refused, but as his country was over-run and the situation became hopeless it was decided that he should not fall into the hands of the enemy who might use him as a puppet. He left with the Crown prince for England, while most of the rest of the royal family left for South Africa.[7] Britain moved to support Greece's independence, but Anglo-Greek resistance was defeated on the mainland and then on Crete, after which the Greek royal family found refuge in the UK. The necessity for Hitler to protect his southern flank against Britain's allies in Greece and Yugoslavia delayed his invasion of Russia (see Yugoslavia). Most of the Greek royal family went into exile with the exception of the equally anti-Nazi Princesses Andrew and Nicholas of Greece.

Princess (Alice) Andrew of Greece and Denmark was the mother of HRH Prince Philip, Duke of Edinburgh and husband of HM Queen Elizabeth II of the UK. She remained in Athens during the war together with her sister-in-law Princess Nicholas of Greece. During the German occupation she worked for the Red Cross, flew to Sweden to obtain medical supplies, and organised soup kitchens for the starving people of Athens. Alice organised and worked in the largest soup kitchen in Athens. Children were fed first after whom the parents were then allowed in to eat.[8] She also established nursing visits for impoverished neighbourhoods and two orphanages. When asked by a German general what he could do for her she placed her hands behind her back to avoid a handshake and answered, 'You can take your troops out of my country.' She sheltered a Jewish widow, Rachel Cohen and two of her children from the Nazis in her residence opposite an SS office, for which she was awarded the title Righteous Among the Nations by Israel. She used her influence in Greece and abroad ceaselessly in the service of her country and the Greek people. Diplomat Jean Charles-Roux observed: 'Princess Alice knew all sorts of people, and she certainly had a very sound and sharp political judgment on people, she had a rather objective view on the tricks of German politics.'[9] When Athens was liberated the princess had eaten nothing except bread and butter for several months. In spite of this she then fearlessly broke curfew to distribute food to children and policemen while the British and communists fought for control of the capital around her. Although Princess Nicholas was deeply religious, Princess Alice founded an order of social-working Orthodox nuns. 'It is all very well for Princess Nicholas forever attending liturgy,' she said, 'but we must be practical.'[10] It was dressed as a nun that she attended the coronation of HM Queen Elizabeth II, her daughter-in-law. The grey of her habit contrasted against the grandeur of visiting royalty and the peers and peeresses in their finery.[11] By the time she died she was penniless, as she had already given all of her possessions away. Her final home was in Buckingham Palace in England.[12]

Romania

Romania's monarch, King Carol II, was unable to influence his country or prevent its membership of the Tripartite Pact. Social unrest and strikes came in the wake of the 1929 economic collapse and as with other central European states in a similar position, extremist parties gained strength particularly the fascist proGerman Iron Guard, which used the murder of its enemies as a political tool. The other parties themselves became increasingly nationalistic. In December 1933 Prime Minister Ion Duca proscribed the Iron Guard and ordered the arrest of its leaders who, in turn, had Duca assassinated. In 1937 King Carol, who was at that time the target of Iron Guard propaganda and threats, had a meeting with Hitler who made plain his desire to see an Iron Guard-led government of Romania. In the ensuing crisis Carol assumed control of the state in 1938 followed by the appointment of a new prime minister and Cabinet. Carol was deposed and his young son Michael was installed as king.

King Carol of Romania returned from exile in 1930 and in 1938 outmanoeuvred Romania's fascists in a royal coup. The Legion of the Archangel Michael was anything but angelic and its paramilitary arm, the Iron Guard, resembled the Nazis in ideology and tactics. Its leader, Codreanu, was arrested in 1931, but in 1933 the Iron Guard became legalised and its electoral success grew election by election, until by 1937 it gained 25 per cent of the vote. The popularity of the movement together with the support of the German government made the Iron Guard a danger to the state. As a consequence, on the 'night of the vampires' its leaders were assassinated. However, Romania, like Bulgaria and Hungary, had little option than to co-operate with Nazi Germany. General Ion Antonescu forced Carol's abdication and formed his own dictatorship while relying on the Iron Guard for support. Teenage King Michael was brought in as a puppet king to legitimise the dictatorship; the young king forged allies and bided his time.

However, in August 1944, King Michael led an alliance of army officers, anti-Nazi politicians and communists in a successful coup against the country's military dictator, Marshal Ion Antonescu, who was arrested by Michael's palace guards. Michel announced a ceasefire of Romanian forces, the acceptance of an armistice and loyalty to the Allied cause. He then declared war on Germany. Unfortunately the Soviet Union did not accept their new ally, invaded, and put the county under military occupation. Around 130,000 Romanian soldiers, the newly sworn enemies of the Nazis, were nevertheless imprisoned in Soviet prison camps. The terms of the armistice imposed by the Russians took little or no account of recent regime change or the likelihood that the coup may have shortened the war by six months.

Although Stalin awarded King Michael the Soviet Order of Victory, 'for the courageous act of the radical change in Romania's politics towards a break-up from Hitler's Germany and an alliance with the United Nations, at the moment when there was no clear sign yet of Germany's 'defeat', he was later forced to abdicate at gunpoint in 1947. Michael was told that thousands would be arrested and the country steeped in blood if he didn't step down. He later recalled the events, 'It was blackmail. They said, "If you don't sign this immediately we are obliged" – why obliged I don't know – "to kill more than 1,000 students" that they had in prison.'

Michael was in close contact with opposition groups and individuals in Romania and secretly became head of the opposition to his own government. He was in communication with the Allies through contacts with Cairo and Turkey and was friendly with the chief rabbi in Bucharest, who visited Michael's mother. In 1942 Michael threatened to abdicate when orders came from Germany to begin the deportation of Romania's Jews to Poland, so saving many lives. Michael planned a coup in conjunction with the opposition parties including communists and socialists. As a culmination to secret talks and schemes between 1942 and 1944, the young king summoned Marshal Antonescu to his palace for a showdown as the Russians violated Romania's eastern border. The dictator of Hungary arrived late and showed little respect to his sovereign. Michael asked him to sign an armistice at once, which he refused to do referring to the king as a child. He resisted because of Romania's pact with Nazi Germany, and asked to be able to contact Berlin before a decision was made. At a given signal Antonescu was arrested by the palace guard and locked up in a room where Michael's father had kept his stamp collection. Directly afterwards Michael and his new government announced an armistice and declared war on Romania's former ally Germany. In the fighting that followed German forces in Romania collapsed and surrendered, and about 50,000 Romanian soldiers died in the liberation of Czechoslovakia. In spite of this, Romania came under Russian occupation. Stalin's envoy Vyshinsky exclaimed to Michael, 'I am Yalta,' referring to the surrender of Romania to Russian influence by the Western powers at the Yalta Conference. Romania was 'double-crossed' and 'let down by all sides' asserts the king on reflection. Although feted by the Soviets for his role in Romania's switch of allegiance and awarded the Soviet Union's Order of Victory, the Russians were not about to leave a monarch in place in their sphere of influence.

King Michael reveals the principles according to which a constitutional monarch ought to live as:

> Listen to the people; always keep in direct contact with them. Remain on good terms with politicians of every party. You can't help being rich because dynasties have often ruled for such a long time. But live simply and never show off except on big official occasions. Lastly, the King is head of state but he is also the first servant of the people. Never forget that. I lived by these rules in the war and when I threw out the Nazis the people knew me, sensed how I was feeling – and they backed me. My philosophy of kingship comes from my great-uncle, King Carol I: 'Nothing without God.'[13]

France

Although claimants to the French throne were not permitted to be members of the French forces both the Orleanist claimant the Count of Paris and Louis Napoléon joined the French Foreign Legion under assumed names. The count, disguised as Swiss citizen Henri Orliac, enlisted as a private in 1940.

On his return to Switzerland Louis Napoléon received an invitation from the Germans to preside over the re-burial of Napoléon II in Paris. He declined, returned to France and decided to join the Free French in England. He was captured trying to cross into Spain and was embarrassingly asked by the Germans to co-operate with Hitler. He again declined, escaped and joined the Resistance where he served for the next two years.[14]

United Kingdom

George VI and his queen, Elizabeth, were exemplary in their behaviour during the Second World War. They refused to go into exile even when there was a threat of invasion and showed themselves to their people as often as possible. Princess Elizabeth, the future queen, joined the services and trained as a mechanic.

Edward VIII and his wife may have been hoodwinked by the Nazis and unfortunate in their choice of friends, but Edward's brother and successor was a quite different man. He wanted to land with his troops on the shores of Normandy on D-Day in 1944. *Time* magazine reported:

> A British monarch had never set foot on American soil until the 1939 state dinner for King George VI. It was held at the height of concern over the belligerent actions taken by Nazi Germany in Europe, and President Franklin D. Roosevelt was well aware of the importance of the US's relationship with Britain. So, as you can imagine, the dinner was meticulously planned. In fact, Roosevelt was reportedly involved in even the most minute details of the visit. But it paid off. The dinner led to closer relations between the two democracies and eventually to one of the world's strongest diplomatic alliances, which endures to this day.[15]

British writer and broadcaster Eric Knight wrote that the American people had gone 'mad and riotously crazy' over the queen. 'In admiration of this one woman, America has somehow blinded herself to Chamberlain, has forgotten Munich, and now sees only the strong British nation once again.' The Roosevelts – and through them the rest of America – were impressed by the royal couple's humanity and the king's down-to-earth humour. Will Smith writes that in the USA King George VI became a 'fully democratic people's king', which did much for Anglo-American relations when it was most needed. Queen Elizabeth forcefully communicated to Roosevelt's representative, Harry Hopkins, the resilience of the British nation, 'The one thing that can counted,' she said, 'was the morale and determination of the great mass of the British people.' Hopkins thought, 'If ever two people realised that Britain is fighting for its life, it is these two.' When Joseph Kennedy suggested to the king that the Balkan countries be sacrificed to the Nazis as they were poor in resources he received a curt letter the next day telling the ambassador that there were important principles at stake, namely the survival of democracy and the right of any nation to exist. The queen wrote of Britain's stand against the Nazis as a 'crusade against slavery and lies'.[16]

The friendship between king and president developed into a warm working relationship once war broke out in Europe and the mutual dependence of their two countries upon one another in the defence of Western civilisation became ever more apparent to them. Early in 1940 George VI wrote to Franklin D. Roosevelt suggesting the setting up of international body to supply food and clothing to refugees in Europe, resources that Britain would need herself all too soon. On 26 June 1940 King George wrote to F.D.R. about Britain's urgent need of some of the USA's 'older destroyers to tide us over next few months'. The king wrote that he knew of the president's difficulties and expressed his confidence that the president would do his best to procure them before it was too late,

'... if we are to carry on our solitary fight for freedom, to a successful conclusion.' In the following September he sent a letter of thanks to the president, 'now a solution to the destroyer question has been happily reached'. He wrote that the friendly action by the USA had brought a warm feeling of gratitude throughout the country and hoped that 'our offer of facilities in the western Atlantic for the defence of North America' would give equal satisfaction, 'I remember so well the talk we had on this particular subject at Hyde Park,' before the outbreak of war.[17] These words tell a great deal about the personal involvement of the king in international affairs and the well-being of his nation before and during the Second World War.

Queen Elizabeth wrote to Eleanor Roosevelt during the Blitz in 1940:

I can honestly say that our hearts have been lightened by the knowledge that friends in America understand what we are fighting for ... It is so terrible to think that all the things we have worked for, these last twenty years are being lost or destroyed in the madness of such a cruel war ... Better housing, education, nursery schools, low cost of living and many others ... But perhaps we have all gone to hard for material benefits, and ignored the Spiritual side of life. I do believe that there is a gradual awakening to the needs of the Spirit, and that, convinced with adversity and sorrow overcome, will lay the seeds of a far better world.[18]

In his letters King George described Winston Churchill as 'indefatigable in his work' and expressed complete confidence in his prime minister, 'He is a great man and has at last come into his own as leader of his country in this fateful time in her history.'[19]

It is clear from the letters between king and president that Roosevelt not only prophesied war in Europe against the prevailing thinking in the USA in 1939, but was more than aware of the need to keep the UK in the war as a vital US interest. On 15 October 1941, F.D.R. wrote to the British king that production was ahead of schedule and that public opinion 'is more strongly with us than the Congress'. The USA's full involvement was to follow soon afterwards. In the same letter he wrote, 'Dicky Mountbatten has been with us for a couple of days and I have learned a lot from him. Get him to tell you of his visit to our fleet in Hawaii. I am a bit worried over the Japanese situation at the moment. The Emperor is for peace I think, but the jingoes are trying to force his hand.'[20]

The Knights of the Garter, award of which was a sign of diplomatic if not military alliance from its inception when applied to foreign heads of state, included Christian X King of Denmark, Luitpold Prince Regent of Bavaria (before the First World War), Emperor Hirohito of Japan, Prince Paul of Yugoslavia, King Gustavus V of Sweden, King Haakon of Norway and, from 1944, Queen Wilhemina of the Netherlands.

Germany

Then there were the German princes. Friedrich Christian of Saxony had constructed a new home (1935–36), Haus Wachwitz, in Dresden that became a gathering place of intellectual dissidents opposed to Hitler including artists, scholars, philosophers, theologians and army officers. In 1943 Prince Georg, a Jesuit priest who had protected Jews from the Nazis, was found drowned. In February 1945 Dresden suffered a 1,000 bomber raid. The 18-year-old Prince Maria Emmanuel wrote a letter to relatives claiming he had heard that Hitler was about to invade Romania, as King Michael had arranged for his country to join the Allies. The letter was intercepted and he was arrested and sentenced to death, but it was not carried out. Philipp von Württemberg, a doctor of law, regarded Hitler with scorn and distaste and helped many refugees during the Second World War.[21]

The Württembergs

Philipp and Albrecht von Württemberg aggravated the Nazis by refusing to associate with the regime. They opted out of Nazi society by refusing to vote in Hitler's 'elections', nor would Philipp fly the Swastika from his castle walls.

Writing in 1946 in the USA the Rev Father Odo Duke Karl Alexander von Württemberg OSB, a Franciscan friar, described in a letter to Queen Mary of Great Britain how his elder brother and his wife and five children were forced to live in two small rooms while the Americans occupied Schloss Lindach, until it was restored to him by General Eisenhower. He further described his family's anti-Nazi sympathies and what their antipathy to the regime meant for them:

> All my relatives had a very hard time during all those years of Hitler's tyranny. They had to suffer a lot from Gestapo persecution. Himmler gave in the last moment the order to shoot my two brethren and my five nephews. God thanks that the Allies moved quicker than the Gestapo agents and so my relations have been saved.[22]

He explained how the brothers' children were kept from being tainted by Nazi ideology or forced (by law) into the Hitler Youth. Therefore they had to be kept from school:

> All these years my two brethren succeeded that their children could stay away from the Hitler Youth. The children were permanently 'sick'. The Nazis have known only too well that they have been fooled by my two brethren. Therefore they gave in the last moment of the war the order to kill them. My eldest

brother [Philipp] was arrested by the Gestapo five days before armistice and put in jail. They bound already his hands to bring him to the firing squad when the French troops moved in and liberated him. My second brother escaped the execution by treating the Gestapo agents with beer in which he mixed a lot of brandy. The fellows got so drunk that they sleeped (sic) until the American troops came and took all these criminals along.[23]

While the Württemberg brothers were avowedly anti-Nazi, not all the family saw the dictator for what he was. Princess Pauline Wied embarrassed the family when she turned up at her father's funeral in 1939 'with an enormous golden swastika cross on her bosom'. Odo commented: 'God thanks that our dear King William had no more to see, how shameful His daughter behaved, whom he loved so much.'[24]

Central European States

The central European states found themselves 'in the way' of the fulfilment of German ambitions and expansion. Most, if not all, wanted to remain neutral but were bullied, blackmailed and bribed (with the return of disputed territory) into alliance. Were there one or more tipping points? When Italy joined the Axis the writing was on the wall for Austria. Munich may well have been the last straw. When states felt isolated and robbed of any guarantee of their neutrality by the far-away Western powers, they were left with little choice but to fight or fall into line. The actions of the central European kings and governments generally reflect their mistrust of Nazism, especially of a possible German-central European hegemony. Hitler had no enthusiastic friends and many bitter enemies.

Western, especially US, protectionist economic policy in the early 1930s had a particularly adverse effect on central European countries whose foreign trade suffered greatly. The Balkans and eastern European states became more authoritarian following the effects of the Depression, and royalty attempted to assert its authority along with traditional parties. David G. Williams comments, 'Yet these authoritarian and essentially conservative regimes in reality blocked the development of genuine Fascist movements by absorbing them into the system so subjecting them to control, or else by outlawing them.'[25] Elsewhere western European monarchs staunchly represented their nations' defiance against Nazi aggression or otherwise put their country's interests before their own.

Notes

1 *Time* magazine, 27 November 1939.
2 Marchione, Margherita, *Pious XII: Architect for Peace* (Religious Teachers Filippini, 2000), p. 129.
3 Stevenson, William, *Spy Mistress, the Life of Vera Atkins*, p. 171.

4 Marchione, Margherita, *Pious XII: Architect for Peace*, p. 129. p. 130.

5 Inducements included southern Dobrudja, which was returned to Bulgaria by Romania under German pressure, and the promise a return of Macedonia.

6 *Time* magazine, 20 January 1941.

7 Vickers, Hugo, *Alice: Princess Andrew of Greece* (St Martins Griffin, 2003) p. 291.

8 Ibid., p. 293.

9 Ibid., p. 306.

10 Ibid., p. 335.

11 Ibid., p. 348.

12 Vickers, Hugo, *Alice: Princess Andrew of Greece*.

13 Montefiore, Simon Segag, 'We reigned in darkness', *The Spectator*, 14 June 1997.

14 Opfell, Olga S., *Royalty who wait: the 21 heads of formerly regnant houses of Europe*, p. 56.

15 *Time* magazine, Wednesday, January 19, 2011.

16 Swift, Will, *Roosevelt and the Royals*.

17 Franklin D. Roosevelt Library Archive, letters George VI to F.D.R. June and September 1940. This letter echoes Churchill's similar pleas to the US president and must be seen as part of a united effort at a time of great peril.

18 Ibid., letter from Queen Elizabeth to Eleanor Roosevelt, 1940.

19 Ibid.

20 Ibid., letter from F.D.R. to George VI, October 1941.

21 Opfell, Olga S., *Royalty Who Wait: the 21 Heads of Formerly Regnant Houses of Europe*, pp. 108, 124.

22 RA/QM/PRIV/CC46/297.

23 RA/QM/PRIV/CC46/303.

24 RA/QM/PRIV/CC46/297.

25 Williamson, David G., *The Age of the Dictators* (Longman, 2007), pp. 372–3.

CONCLUSION

Limited monarchy and not republicanism or dictatorship is the normal framework for human politics. Monarchy, as Metternich would say, is the most
'legitimate' form of Western government. Its overthrow in 1917–18 in central
and Eastern Europe has helped cause the present world instabilities. Its reten-
tion has greatly facilitated peaceful social reform – whether socialist or capitalist
– in the particular monarchies of Scandinavia and England.

Peter Viereck[1]

The apparent cultural malaise that particularly affected (and afflicted) western
Europe between the late 1800s and early 1900s represented an inability to square
social expectations and adapt cultural and national models to industrialisation,
secular philosophy and new scientific theories that could no longer be understood in the context of traditional world views. Responses were several and
included an attempt to adapt apparent chaos into apparent order. The maelstrom
of unbridled change and social dislocation came to be viewed by some as a positive. Industrialisation, secularisation and imperial expansion could be regarded as
progress of national endeavour towards a golden age of science. Physical strength
and beauty, and ordered social cohesion; dominance of race; the triumph of what
seemed to be the natural order – these applied as the law of the jungle. Racial
theory, eugenics, physical exercise to maintain the body beautiful for the benefit of national and Western progress were universally applied in America and
western Europe.

Other responses included searching for an antidote to change by ending it – by
putting a perfect system in place democratically or by means of a culture of one-
off or perpetual revolution – Marxist or (eventually also) fascist. Another was to
make oneself worthy of one's own cultural despair by stripping oneself of belief

and plunging one's expectations, and ultimately society, further into the abyss. All traditional models were regarded as crass, anti-modern, erroneous and an impediment to human scientific progress. Thus the framework of society that had been regarded as the means and vehicle of social improvement was rejected in favour of a religion of modernism still felt today.

If people are deprived of (a belief in) a natural order with which they can identify, an unnatural order can be imposed on them because they will be ready to identify with whatever artificial order is provided for them. The order of the universe was and is still being questioned, undermined and challenged by post-Enlightenment modernist philosophy.

Science manipulates the natural world and tries to fashion it into human desires, but does it answer human need? Politics manipulates people's minds to better rule their bodies, but for whom? People, party or ideology? Who or what guides human endeavour or progress – if one can use that word? Could it perhaps be said that modernism, post-modernism, structuralism and post-structuralism, whether a critique of modern society or a direct influence upon it, are a gift to totalitarianism? Undermine people's beliefs in religion, reality, order, harmony, purpose and they no longer have the will or the vocabulary to resist. In the period between the First World War and the second world conflagration the old order was eroded and its values not only questioned but rejected. Order itself was jettisoned as a worthless impediment to human triumph over the elements and Christian morality was trodden underfoot as the brightest, strongest and fittest (in their arrogant young minds) ran for civilisation's fire exit and plummeted into oblivion.

We should also bear in mind the advances in social welfare and the conflict between scientific rationalism (based on Enlightenment values) and the emotional response of cultures under threat that promoted myth and race over pure science and democracy, which were blameless as regards the very real pressures then affecting Western civilisation. There is more than one view – the writer can do nothing more than explore these (yes) relative positions in order to hopefully glimpse the (undeniably single) wider truth.

All the great social advances of the twentieth century had their roots in the nineteenth century, but with credit rarely being given. Universal suffrage triumphed in a different world to which it had been envisaged, one with very different ideals and expectations. This idealism seduced princes as well as paupers as it promised fairness and prosperity for the commonweal. Indeed, social responsibility and duty were food and drink to those brought up to serve their people even if not all lived up to their calling. Monarchy represented cultural and social continuity and stability in a world where religion was central. It was, therefore, either rejected completely or embraced as the last hope of historical certainty as it started to tumble over the cliff of an uncertain future.

In Germany between the wars, national, social and cultural fears and aspirations were expressed against a background of incredulity and Depression in the face of defeat and the humiliating terms of the Versailles Treaty. There was anger at the dismemberment of the country and the occupation of the Ruhr, and fear of the Slavic peoples of the East and their communistic un-German ideas to which they felt dangerously exposed; similarly Poles and Jews were distrusted as foreign infiltrators of the homeland and spreaders of communism. Germans traditionally saw themselves as evangelical colonisers (whether as Teutonic Knights or Lutheran missionaries) for whom colonisation by outsiders was abhorrent. They were tribally rather than nationally driven and unity of race represented a common destiny across borders, facilitating the unification of the Reich under a single authority. This would have otherwise would have proved impossible without utter defeat and occupation by a Prussian army imposing its will. Germany, in search of a soul, insisted on its exclusivity as a self-chosen people with a destiny identified in some distant mythical past as aimed towards future triumphs over those thought to threaten its rightful position as captain and protector of its race wherever it was to be found.

By the early 1930s Germany was already moving towards a more authoritarian style of government, if only to deny power to extremist groups whose popularity had increased in the wake of the Depression. Although a National Socialist government and/or civil war were not inevitable, they were considered likely if stern measures were not taken to prevent them. It was agreed by both conservative and socialist politicians, however, that the real and only antidote to extreme nationalism was the restoration of the monarchy in some form, most ideally a constitutional monarchy in the British style, but with full presidential powers. Similarly, by 1933, Bavaria was moving towards succession from the Reich under a restored monarchy (to follow a plebiscite) in order to avoid Nazi centralised rule from Berlin. In Austria the government of Dolfuss metamorphed into an authoritarian corporatist model to ensure national independence as a defence against the growth of Nazism and pan-Germanism. Restoration of the monarchy, there also, promised national integrity and moderate government safe from the Nazi menace.

Monarchy (particularly the idea of constitutional monarchy) meant something fundamental in Germany, Austria and Hungary in the 1930s. It meant a potential anchor and moral compass that was 'above the parties'. It meant stability, national unity and the promise of moderate government under its benign non-partisan influence. It presented a final wall of defence against political extremism. It was nationalist but not nationalistic, conservative but not illiberal, representative of supreme authority but without power. It was a glove into which the open hands of socialism and conservatism could fit quite easily, but was no gauntlet for a fascist or communist fist.

The heirs to the great dynasties of Europe were not autocrats in waiting. Prince Louis Ferdinand was an enthusiastic supporter of the republic in his youth and made no attempt to hide his approval of Roosevelt and the Democratic Party in the USA, eventually coming to the conclusion, however, that in his own country a constitutional monarchy would be the best form of government. Crown Prince Rupprecht of Bavaria, although a conservative by nature, shunned any attempt to restore his throne unless it could be achieved peacefully and was the will of his people expressed through a plebiscite called by and with the approval of a freely elected Bavarian government. Prince Hubertus zu Löwenstein was never an heir to a state and so could express his liberal politics openly, which he did in his unswerving support of the German republic. The man Nazis called 'The Red Prince' also went to Spain to support the republicans against the fascists. Dr Otto von Habsburg of Austria-Hungary was never confined by dynastic ambition, he being the perfect European – believing European unity to be the best defence against European war and the dominion of the major powers over the small. Such men are born leaders, brought up to serve their countries and, if denied their destiny, it naturally becomes their perceived duty to serve all humanity. Prince Georg of Saxony was so moved by his duty and his faith that he became a Jesuit priest, saved Jews from the Nazis and was almost certainly assassinated by the Gestapo.

The German resistance movement did not and could not exist in any cohesive form without the unifying element of monarchy represented by the modern, Left-leaning internationalist Prince Louis Ferdinand, who was preferred future head of state following the fall of Hitler and his regime. Monarchy was a potential defence against Hitler before the war became a focus of national unity and identity for exiles and anti-Nazis in Europe during the conflict. Ideas about the post-war geography of Europe that included a Central Europe where monarchy was a central unifying element was seriously entertained by the Allies, particularly Churchill who believed that Hitler could never have come to power if the German and Austrian monarchies had not fallen after the First World War, until Stalin prevented any chance of the fulfilment of royal dreams such as a Danubian Federation – monarchical or not.

The question remains, could monarchy have made a difference in Germany or Austria if it had been restored before 1933–38? If Brüning had successfully restored the monarchy by plebiscite it would have had public endorsement and, as a result, would have been difficult to sway or overthrow by an extremist chancellor like Hitler. Furthermore, it would have had the support of nationalists who would have taken more of a part in politics as a result. Extremist legislation could not have been passed without the monarch's (and the electorate's prior) approval. The army would have remained loyal to their emperor who could not have been deposed easily especially as he would have had the mandate of a referendum behind him. Hitler could not have reversed the will of the people without alienating the electorate and risking civil war with Left and Right aligned against him. Furthermore, these situations would have only occurred if Hitler had been appointed chancellor in the first place, which is most unlikely given the character, youth and modern outlook of Prince Louis Ferdinand as compared with the stiff ever-more senile (and, therefore, easily led) Field Marshall von Hindenburg.[2]

Had Otto von Habsburg come to the throne in Austria the country's sense of national identity and independence would have been assured. There could have been no takeover of Austria without a fight and a real risk of international condemnation and foreign involvement. The Nazis needed an easy walk into Austria. What is more they needed Austria to get to Czechoslovakia and the East. Hitler was so worried about the prospect of a Habsburg restoration that he declared that Germany's forces would march if there were any moves by the Austrian government in that direction.

The power of monarchy, it is said, lies not in the power that it wields but the power it denies to others. Any proselytising politician driven by devotion to an ideology and intent on making his country great or prosperous or free of unruly elements could be tempted by the prospect of being rid of inconvenient opposition and governing by edict. In a modern democratic state monarchy can still represent the unbreakable link between a nation and its faith. It can provide the context for national and cultural identity in a changing world. As a template for duty and as an icon of humanity representing the individual's relationship to the collective – national or global – it remains a valuable alternative to other systems.

When a country becomes ruled by a faction it becomes dangerous. Political parties, if they are not representative of something beyond themselves – of the nation, the land, the wider international interest – cannot be regarded as civilised. Democracy is not automatically representative and what is representative is not always democratic, but sensibly there was general agreement among the princes featured in this book – and there is agreement among their heirs – that democracy should be the principal element of government guided, assisted and defended by other constitutional elements, such as the hereditary principle and the rule of law as enshrined constitutionally. Some might say that better a conscientious and dutiful king who loves his country, than a personally ambitious politician. The clue is in the name; a monarch relates directly to the individual subject one to one, however remote. One might say that ideally the state should serve the individual, not (as with totalitarian regimes such as the Nazis and Bolsheviks) the other way round.

It is often thought that the cultural revolution of the 1960s, including the hippy movement, was a mass movement. But that is not how it originated, 'We have a private revolution going on. A revolution of individuality and diversity that can only be private. Upon becoming a group movement such a revolution ends up being imitators rather than participants,' wrote Bob Stubbs, owner of the Blue Unicorn cafe in Haight Ashbury, San Francisco, in the mid-1960s.[3] If people are treated as 'units of production', psychological types, or at best A, B or C-list celebrities, or any other classification rather than as individuals, they are not being regarded as people at all.

The Enlightenment and Protestantism claimed to represent the freedom of individual, but no one can do that except themselves. Christ, Buddha and other religious teachers have spoken to their followers as individuals inculcating individual responsibility, rather than as collectives, because as it is said the jigsaw needs every single unique little piece in place for the whole picture to be revealed. The idolising of celebrity is the sign of an unhealthy society. C.S. Lewis wrote:

> There, right in the midst of our lives, is that which satisfies the craving for inequality, and acts as a permanent reminder that medicine is not food. Hence a man's reaction to monarchy is a kind of test. Monarchy can easily be 'debunked', but watch the faces, mark the accents of the debunkers. These are the men whose tap-root in Eden has been cut: whom no rumour of the polyphony, the dance, can reach – men to whom pebbles laid in a row are more beautiful than an arch. Yet even if they desire equality, they cannot reach it. Where men are forbidden to honour a king they honour millionaires, athletes or film-stars instead: even famous prostitutes or gangsters. For spiritual nature, like bodily nature, will be served; deny it food and it will gobble poison.

It is questionable whether democracy on its own can fully represent the interests of a country and an entire nation, which is why we have the checks and balances afforded by monarchy and recently in the case of the British House of Lords, a hereditary element to a parliament.

No single ideology should ever govern a party, never mind a country. But is there any nation today that has not had a political system imposed upon it rather than allowing one to grow up organically over a considerable time? Perhaps to work, our political systems need to be more in tune with nature, both the natural world around us and our own (spiritual) natures within. It is for the reader to decide whether monarchy is a good way to protect nations from totalitarianism – or indeed the best.

Princes are the products of, and are and susceptible to, the influences of their age like anyone else, but in some ways their position and upbringing equips them to see over the fence and consider what they are witnessing with a little more clarity, perspective and dispassion than most other people. Anyway, the Princes Otto, Rupprecht, Louis Ferdinand and Hubertus were able to see through National Socialism when others were being taken in and were somewhat apart from social Darwinism, material idealism and other preoccupations of the age. The kind of intellectual and emotional soil in which totalitarianism in general and Hitlerism in particular was able take root could be found the world over and especially in the West. It would be a tragic mistake to assume that we have somehow grown up and would not be taken in again.

The last word I leave to the late Dr Otto von Habsburg. In 1967, in a speech in London, he warned that there was an imminent danger of the rise of political castes in the form of 'the undue influence of political parties, bureaucratic communities and economic power concentrations' replacing the political influence of social classes. As a solution Dr von Habsburg suggested the re-establishing of the authority of the state against undue private influences and to secure individual freedom, 'Which can be achieved,' he said, 'only if institutions are created which are a mixed form of government, that is to say, where the sources of authority are dispersed and permit a more effective system of checks and balances that the one devised by Montesquieu. Here the role of the monarchy, as a factor of community, stability, independence of the State, and as a judicial power in defence of basic rights, assumed a new importance.' In the modern world of globalisation and polyglot political economies the need for the checks and balances provided by extra-democratic systems is even more urgent.

Notes

1 Viereck, Peter, *Shame and Glory of the Intellectuals* (New Brunswick, 2007; first pub. Boston, 1953).

2 When could it have taken place? The earlier the better, but the last best hope was during Chancellor Brüning's administration when restoration would have had the broadest support to counter the increasing possibility of a National Socialist government. Unfortunately, Hindenburg's refusal to make way for any other monarch except Wilhelm II made restoration impossible. It was considered that neither the Western powers nor the German people for that matter would accept a return of the old emperor or his eldest son. A grandson of the kaiser, however, could have ascended the German throne with the aged president acting as regent for life, so providing a stable interim period. When Brüning was dismissed from office the chance was lost. The next chance would have been as a result of a coup against Hitler, but though there were many plots none were successful.

3 From *The Unicorn Philosophy* leaflets by Bob Stubbs.

BIBLIOGRAPHY

Selected Secondary Sources

Adamthwaite, Anthony P., *The Making of the Second World War* (London, Routledge rev. ed., 1979).

Anonymous, *The Persecution of the Catholic Church in the Third Reich* (Pelican, 2008).

Arendt, Hannah, 'Total Domination' in Baehr, Peter (ed.), *The Portable Hannah Arendt* (New York, Penguin, 2000).

Baranowski, Shelly, *Nazi Empire: German Colonisation and Imperialism from Bismarck to Hitler* (Cambridge, Cambridge University Press, 2010).

Beatty, Charles, *Our Admiral* (London, 1980).

Bestenreiner, Erika, *Franz Ferdinand und Sophie von Hohenberg: Verboten Liebe am Kaiserhof* (Zurich, Piper, 2004).

Bonhoeffer, Dietrich in Kelly, Geoffrey B. (ed.) *A Testament of Freedom* (Harper Collins, 1995).

Braun, Chris, Nardin, Terry and Rengger, Nicholas (eds), *International Relations in Political Thought* (Cambridge).

Brook-Shepherd, Gordon, *Uncrowned Emperor: The Life and Times of Otto von Habsburg* (London, 2003).

Ceplair, Larry and England, Steven, *The Inquisition in Hollywood: Politics in the Film Industry, 1930–60* (Ilinois, 2003).

Churchill, Winston S., *The History of the Second World War, vol. I, The Gathering Storm* (Penguin Classics, 2005).

Cooper, Duff, *The Second World War – First Phase* (Charles Scribbner, 1939).

Craig, Gordon A., *Germany 1866–1945* (Oxford, 1981).

Crozier, Andrew J., *The Causes of the Second World War* (Blackwell, 1997).

DeGregori, Thomas R., *Origins of the Organic Agriculture Debate* (Wiley-Blackwell, 2003).

Deutsch Harrold C., *The Conspiracy Against Hitler in the Twilight War* (Minnesota, 1968).

Dippel, John van Houten, *Two Against Hitler: Stealing the Nazi's Best Kept Secrets* (Praeger, Westport, 1992).

Dothie, W.H., *Operation Disembroil: Deception and Escape, Normandy, 1940* (London, Robert Hale, 1985).

Etlin, Richard A., *Art, Culture and Media under the Third Reich* (Chicago, 2002).

Ferdinand of Prussia, Prince Louis *The Rebel Prince: Memoirs of Prince Louis Ferdinand of Prussia* (Chicago, Regnery, 1952).

Fielding, Keith, *The Life of Neville Chamberlain* (London, 1946).

Fritz Richard Stern, *The Politics of Cultural Despair* (California, 1974).

Galandauer, Jan, *Frantisek Ferdinand D'Este* (Pasek, Praha, Litomyšl, 2000).

Gamper, Dr Hans, 'Die Söhne des ermordeten Thronfolgers', *Tiroler Nachrichten*, (13 January 1962).

Garnett, Robert S., *Lion, Eagle and Swastika: Bavarian Monarchism in Weimar Germany, 1918–1933* (New York and London, Garland Publishing Inc., 1991).

Gulick, Charles Adams, *Austria from Habsburg to Hitler* (California, 1948).

Hanfstaengl, Ernst, *Hitler, the Missing Years* (New York, Arcade, reprint, 1994).

Henderson, Sir Neville, *Failure of a Mission* (London, 1940).

Hoffmann, Peter, *History of the German Resistance 1933–1945* (Cambridge, Mass., 1977).

———, *Stauffenberg: A Family History, 1905–1944* (Cambridge, 1995).

Hopkinson, Austin, 'Reflections on Fascism', *The Nineteenth Century* (April 1934).

Howard, M., *The Continental Commitment* (London, Maurice Temple Smith, 1972).

Jung, Carl, *Collected Works*, Vol. 9, 1986 (1936A).

Kelly, Scott, 'The Ghost of Neville Chamberlain: Guilty Men and the 1945 Election', *Conservative History* (Autumn 2005), pp. 18–24.

Klemperer, Klemens von, *German Resistance Against Hitler: The Search For Allies Abroad, 1938–1945* (Oxford, 1994).

Klimczuk, Stephen and Warner, Gerald, *Secret Places, Hidden Sanctuaries: Uncovering Mysterious Sights, Symbols* (Stirling, 2010).

Kruger-Charle, Michael, 'From Reform to Resistance: Carl Goerdeler's 1938 Memorandum' in Clay Large, David (ed.), *Contending with Hitler: Varieties of Resistance in the Third Reich* (Cambridge, 1994).

Lee, Stephen J., *European Dictatorships 1918–1945* (London, Routledge, 2008).

Lenz, John M., *Christ in Dachau* (Roman Catholic Books, 1960).

Lewin, Nicholas Adam, *Jung on War, Politics and Nazi Germany* (Karnac Books, 2009).

Löwenstein, Hubertus zu, *A Catholic in Republican Spain* (London, Gollancz, 1937).

———, *Towards the Further Shore* (Victor Gollancz, 1968).

———, *What was the German Resistance Movement?* (Grafes, Bad Godesburg, 1965).

Marchione, Margherita, *Pious XII: Architect for Peace* (Filippini, Religious Teachers, 2000).

Meinecke, Friedrich, Faye, Sidney B. (trans.), *The German Catastrophe* (Harvard, 1950).

Meysels, Lucian, *Die verhinderte Dynastie: Erzherzog Franz Ferdinand und das Haus Hohenberg* (Molden, 2000).

Melville, Cecil F., *The Russian Face of Germany* (London, 1932).

Metternich, Tatiana, *Tatiana* (London (rev. ed. 2004; first pub. 1976).

Montefiore, Simon Segag, 'We reigned in darkness', *The Spectator* (14 June 1997).

Parrish, Michael E., *Anxious Decades: America in Prosperity and Depression 1920–1941* (New York, Norton, 1994).

Patch, William L., *Heinrich Brüning and the Dissolution of the Weimar Republic* (Cambridge, 2006).

Pearson, Karl, 'National Life from the Standpoint of Science' (lecture, 1900).

Petropoulos, Jonathan, *Royals and the Reich: The Princes von Hessen in Nazi Germany* (Oxford, 2008).

Pois, Robert A., *National Socialism and the Religion of Nature* (Croom Helm Beckenham, 1986).

Proctor, Robert, *Racial Hygine: Medicine Under the Nazis* (Harvard, 1988).

———, *Nazi War on Cancer* (Princeton, 1999).

Robert Rhodes, James, *Memoirs of a Conservative 1910–1937* (London, Weidenfeld and Nicholson, 1969).

Roi, Michael Lawrence, *Alternative to Appeasement, Sir Robert Vansittart and Alliance Diplomacy* (Westport, Praeger, 1997).

Speer, Albert, *Inside the Third Reich* (London, Sphere, 1970).

Vassiltchikov, (Princess) Marie 'Missie', *The Berlin Diaries 1940–1945* (London, 1985).

Vickers, Hugo, *Alice: Princess Andrew of Greece* (St Martins Griffin, 2003).

Vieler, Eric H., 'The Ideological Roots of National Socialism', *McGill European Studies Vol. 2* (New York, Peter Lang, 1999).

Viereck, Peter, *Shame and Glory of the Intellectuals* (New Brunswick, 2007; first pub. Boston, 1953).

Weinberg, Gerhard, *The Foreign Policy of Hitler's Germany Starting World War II* (Chicago, 1980).

Wheeler-Bennett, Sir John, *The Nemesis of Power: the German Army in politics 1918–1945* (London and New York 1953, rev. 1964).

Williamson, David G., *The Age of the Dictators* (Longman, 2007).

Zühlsdorff, Volkmar, *Hitler's Exiles* (New York, Continuum, 2004), pp. 19, 24.

Selected Primary Sources

Archive der KZ-Gedenkstatte Dachau.

Bavaria, HRH Duke Franz of, interview 2 June 2009.

British War Bluebook, The.

Brüning, H., *Die Brüning Papers* in Peter Lang (ed.) (Frankfurt, 1993).

Chartwell Trust, Sir Winston Churchill Archive Trust, CHAR 2/307.

Chartwell Trust, Sir Winston Churchill Archive Trust, CHAR 2/368.

Demmerle, E., *Mein Vater: An Interview with Dr Otto von Habsburg.*

Franklin D. Roosevelt Library Archive, letters George VI to F.D.R., and F.D.R. to George VI, and letters from Queen Elizabeth to Eleanor Roosevelt, 1939–1945.

Habsburg, HR&IH Dr Otto von, correspondence with the office of.

Hansard, Churchill, Winston, speech in the House of Commons, 22 February 1938.

Hansard, Churchill, Winston, speech in the House of Commons, 24 March 1938.

Hansard, Eden, Anthony, speech in the House of Commons in answer to the prime minister's statement, 3 October 1938.

Letter to Prince Louis Ferdinand, Potsdam, Germany, 23 March 1939. Franklin D. Roosevelt Library, PPF 110.

Löwenstein, HSH Princess Konstanza zu, speech, *Der Rote Prinz*, delivered 16 November 2006, Rotes Rathaus Berlin, and further information supplied to the author.

Moeller van den Bruck, Arthur, *Germany's Third Empire*, in Lorimer, E.O. (ed.) (London, George Allen & Unwin, 1934).

New York Times (4 January 1922).

Petrie, C. (ed.), *The Life and Letters of the Rt Hon Sir Austen Chamberlain* (Vol. 2).

Prussia, HRH Prince Georg Friedrich of, interview August 2010.

Political Examiner, The (July 1816).

Poultney Bigelow, radio message, 22 May 1938. Franklin D. Roosevelt Library PPF 110.

Roosevelt, Franklin D., letter to Prince Louis Ferdinand of Prussia, 9 November 1934. Franklin D. Roosevelt Library, PPF 110.

Royal Archives, Windsor Castle; quotes from private letters reproduced by gracious permission of HM Queen Elizabeth II.

Schwanburg, Baron Viktor Kuchina de, from an unpublished book about the von Schwanburg family.

Self, R.C. (ed.), *Austen Chamberlain Diary Letters* (Cambridge, 1995).

Sir Winston Churchill Archive Trust, CHUR 2/140.

Sir Winston Churchill Archive Trust, CHUR 2/140.

Telegram from Prince Louis Ferdinand of Prussia to Franklin D. Roosevelt, 8 November 1934. Franklin D. Roosevelt Library, PPF 110.

The National Archives, TNA FO 371/29929/0016.

The National Archives, TNA FO 371/33219/0011.

Thompson, Vance, *New York Sun* (13 September 1914).

Time magazine (3 April 1939).

Time magazine (20 January 1941).

Time magazine (27 November 1939).

Time magazine (19 January 2011).

Times, The (16 April 1935).

Times, The (19 March 1923).

Times, The (2 January 1937).

Times, The (24 March 1938).

Trevor-Roper, Hugh (ed.), *Hitler's Table Talk* (New York, Enigma, 2000).

Walton, Hon R., Assistant Secretary of State, Washington, memorandum from 23 March 1938, Franklin D. Roosevelt Library, PPF 110.

Washington Post interview of Crown Prince Rupprecht of Bavaria by correspondent Cyril Brown in Munich on 2 January 1922 (appeared on 4 January), p. 2.

Selected Online Sources

http://germanhistorydocs.ghi-dc.org/sub_image.cfm?image_id=426.

http://h-net.org/~german/gtext/kaiserreich/class.html, *Wenn ich der Kaiser wär.* (Accessed December 2009.)

http://oops.uni-oldenburg.de/volltexte/1999/686/, Appelius, Stephan (ed.), *Otto Oertel as a prisoner of the SS* (Library and Information System of the University of Oldenburg, 1990), online document, pp. 125–6. (Accessed 10 January 2010.)

http://ourcivilisation.com/smartboard/shop/festjc/index.htm, Fest, Joachim C., *The Face of the Third Reich*.

http://www.firstworldwar.com/source/germanassembly_ludendorff.htm.

http://www.firstworldwar.com/source/somme_rupprecht.htm, from a report by Crown Prince Rupprecht during the first Battle of the Somme.

http://www.historyofwar.org/articles/people_rupprecht_bavaria.html, Rickard, J., *Crown Prince Rupprecht of Bavaria, 1869–1955* (6 November 2007).

http://www.hungarian-history.hu/lib/montgo/montgo08.htm.

http://www.hungarian-history.hu/lib/montgo/montgo08.htm, Montgomery, John Flournoy, *Hungarian History*, p. 3.

http://www.jewishvirtuallibrary.org/jsource/anti-semitism/Luther_on_Jews.html.

http://www.lib.udel.edu/ud/spec/findaids/html/mss0109.html, George S. Messersmith papers 1907–1955, Special Collections Department of the University of Delaware.

http://www.time.com/time/magazine/article/0,9171,727551-1,00.html, 'Regime of Dictators', *Time* magazine (8 October 1923).

http://www.time.com/time/magazine/article/0,9171,747168-2,00.html#ixzzormXZclnr.

http://www.vaticanbankclaims.com/hapsburg.pdf.

http://www.youtube.com/watch?v=0912bz3DMwE.

INDEX

Abwehr 72–3, 78–9

Adam, Colonel Walter 150

Albert of Belgium, King 25

Alexander, King of Yugoslavia 165

Alice, Princess Andrew of Greece 167–8

Alldeutscher Verband 32

Alpary, Dr Imre 145

American Guild for German Cultural
Freedom 124

Amery, Leo 58

Andics, Hellmut 154

Anglo-German Naval Agreement 50–2,
127

Anschluss 134, 137, 139, 145, 148

anti-Semitism 32, 43, 51, 72, 134, 96

Antonescu, Marshal Ion 169–70

Antrim, Earl of 126

Arbeiter-Zeitung 156

Arco-Valli, Count Antoni 113

Arden Society 126

Arendt, Hannah 38, 44 (n.), 149–50, 158 (n.)

Aretin, Erwein Freiherr, 113

Ariosophy 42–3

Artstetten 155

Astor, David 82 (n.)

Astor, Nancy 51

Astor, Viscount Waldorf 51

Ataturk 27

Atholl, Duchess of 126

Atlantic, Battle of 116

August Wilhelm of Prussia, Prince 8, 13, 14
(n.), 135

Bailey, F.G. 32

Baldwin, Stanley 50

Bamberg Conference 22

Barbarossa, Operation 166

Bar-le-Duc 109

Beatty, Admiral David, Earl 20

Beck, Colonel General Ludwig 74–5, 78, 80,
99–101, 127

Bell, George, Archbishop of Chichester 77

Bellegarde, Countess 117

Bergson, Henri 34

Berlichingen, Götz von 141

Bernhardi, Freidrich von 33, 93

Best, Captain Sigismund Payne 78

Biron, Helen 70

Bismarck, Gottfried von 71–2

Bismarck, Otto von 93

Bismarck, Otto von Jr 71–2

Blavatsky, H.P. 36, 42–3, 84

Blum, Leon 53

Bonham-Carter, Lady Violet 126

Bonhoeffer, Klaus von 98

Bonhoeffer, Pastor Dietrich von 72–3, 77,
98–9, 100

Borenius, Professor Tancred 154

Boris II, Tsar of Bulgaria 166–7

Brauer, Curt 161

Breda, Rudolf 125

Brook-Shepherd, Gordon 136–8

Bruck, Arthur Moeller van den 22, 34, 84

Brüning, Heinrich 12, 20, 24–5, 27, 57, 75,
85, 179, 182 (n.)

Buchenwald 161
Bullitt, William C. 56, 141
Burckel, Josef 141
Burdckhardt, Jakob 93
Bürgerbräukeller 39, 111

Cadogan, Sir Alexander 55, 146
Callejon, Popper de 142
Canaris, Admiral Wilhelm 72, 74, 78–9
Cantwell, Bishop John Joseph 125
Carol II, King of Romania 168
Casablanca Conference 130
Cecile, Crown Princess of Prussia 96
Chamberlain, Austen 17, 55, 123
Chamberlain, Houston Stewart 64, 84
Chamberlain, Neville 51–3, 55, 58–9, 75, 78,
    125, 171
Chaplin, Charles 126
Charlemaigne 41
Charles the Great 152
Chelwood, Viscount Cecil of 123, 126
Chichester, Major 154
Christian X, King of Denmark 162
Churchill, Sir Winston 11, 21, 48, 53–7,
    77–8, 123, 133 (n.), 143–7, 164, 172, 179
Claß, Heinrich, 32–3, 35, 84, 93
Cliveden Set 50–1, 55–6
Cohen, Rachel 168
Concordat (1933) 37, 73, 115
Cooper, Duff 58
Cripps, Sir Stafford 77, 82 (n.)
Cromwell, Oliver 118
Cross, Dr Wilbur L. 124

Dachau 13, 35, 65, 104, 111, 140–1, 148–53,
    155–6, 161
Dagenfeld, Count 142
Dahlman, Freidrich Christoph 32, 84
Dahrendorf, Gustav 80
Daladier, Édouard 53, 56
Damita, Lily 96
Darwin, Charles 60–3, 66, 68 (n.), 84
Darwin, Erasmus 60, 62
Das Dritte Reich 22, 34
Davidson, John 50
Dawes Plan 23, 112
De la Mare, Walter 126
Delbrück, Dr Justus 73, 99
Delbrück, Max 73
Der Stürmer 32
Dietrich, Marlene 126
Dohnanyi, Hans von 71–2, 78, 99, 103

Dollfuss, Engelbert 136,
Donaukonföderation 117
Dothie, William 128
Drang nach Osten 30, 84
Drexler, Anton 33, 43
Duca Ion 168

Eckart, Dietrich 43
Eden, Anthony 55–8, 68, 77, 79, 144
Edinburgh, Princess Victoria Melita of 97
Einstein, Albert 124–5, 132 (n.), 164
Eisernen Ring 135, 137, 148
Eisner, Kurt 107, 137
Elizabeth II, HM the Queen of the United
    Kingdom 167–8, 170–2
Elizabeth, Queen Mother of Belgium 164
Epp, Franz Ritter von 107, 113
Eppstein, John 123
Etlin, Richard A. 40, 46, 183
eugenics 8, 32, 50, 59, 60, 61–3, 65, 68, 85,
    176, 154

Fall Gelb 128
Faulhaber, Cardinal Michael 111, 115
Feder, Gottfried 43, 87
Figl, Leopold 152, 156
Filof, Bogdan 166
Flosssenbürg 13, 155
Franco 52, 126
Franco-Prussian War 18, 78, 93, 104
Frantz, Constantin 93
Franz Ferdinand, Archduke of Austria-
    Hungary 13, 17, 66, 98, 111, 140, 147–9,
    154
Franz, HRH Duke of Bavaria 105, 107, 109,
    112–3, 115, 116–8
Freikorps 33, 107–8
Freud, Sigmund 124
Friedrich (Fritzi), Prince of Prussia 98,
    103 (n.)
Friedrich II (the Great) of Prussia 92, 96
Friedrich Wilhelm IV of Prussia 91–2
Fuchs, Professor 110

Galandaur, Jan 154
Galen, Count 135
Galton, Francis 60–3, 66, 84
Gamper, Dr Hans 152
Garbo, Greta 126
Geer, Dirk Jen de
Georg, HRH Prince of Prussia 97
Geoge II, King of Greece 167

George V, King of the United Kingdom 115, 126

George VI, King of the United Kingdom 170–2

George, Stephan 32

German Academy of Arts and Sciences in Exile 124

Gisevius, Hans Bernd 72

Glauer, Adam Alfred Rudolf (Rudolf von Sebottendorf) 43, 84

Gleichschaltung 34, 81, 86, 113

Gobineau, Joseph-Arthur comte de 64, 84

Goerdeler, Carl Friedrich 70–3, 75, 100–1, 128

Goethe, Johann Wolfgang 42, 93, 141

Göring, Herman 26, 40, 55–6, 97, 136, 138, 141,153

Gort, Lord 128

Gunter, Hans F.K., 84

Gustav, King of Sweden 162–3

Haakon, King of Norway 161–2

Habsburg, Archduke Joseph Ferdinand von 140

Habsburg, Archduke Robert von 143, 146

Habsburg, Archduke Rudolf von 146

Habsburg, Dr Otto von 13, 39, 119, 132, 134–60, 179, 180–1

Habsburg, Emperor Karl von, *see* Karl

Habsburg, Franz Ferdinand, Archduke of Austria-Hungary, *see* Franz Ferdinand

Haeften, Hans Bernd von 73

Haeften, Werner von 73

Haekler, Ernst 84

Hahn, Kurt 81

Halder, General Franz 74–6, 127

Halifax, Lord 51, 55, 59, 75–6, 154

Hamann, Brigitte 42

Hammerstein, Oscar 125

Hammerstein-Equord, Colonel General Kurt von 74, 100

Harnack, Ernst von 73, 99

Harnier, Adolf von 116

Harrer, Karl 43

Harvey, Oliver 144

Hassell, Ulrich von 72

Hawley Smith Tariff 23

Hegel, George Friedrich 31, 35–6, 44 (n.), 84

Heinrich I (der Volger) 44

Heinrici, Colonel General 41

Held, Heinrich 108, 113

Henderson, Sir Neville 49, 55, 76

Herder, Gottfried von 36, 84

Hertha, Pauli 153

Hertling, Georg von 106

Hesse, Philip von, Landgrave of Hesse-Kassell 161

Heydrich, Reynard 154

Hillel the Elder 36

Himmler, Heinrich 42–4, 65, 72, 85–6, 116, 153, 155, 173

Hindenberg, Paul von, President 14 (n.), 20, 24, 26–8, 39, 74, 106, 108, 113, 136, 179, 182

Hirohito, Emperor of Japan 172

Hitler, Adolf 7–8, 11–13, 18, 22–8, 30, 33–52, 55–8, 63–4, 70–87, 89, 93–101, 108, 110–19, 121–43, 145–6, 149, 152, 155, 157, 159, 161–3, 165–70, 173–4, 179–85

Hoffman, Peter 77

Hohenberg, Elizabeth von 153

Hohenberg, Herzog Maximilian 135, 137, 140, 147–9, 151–6

Hohenberg, HH George von 17

Hohenberg, Prince Ernst, 140, 147–9, 151–6

Hohenberg, Princess Sophie 147–8

Hohenberg, Sophie Countess von Nostitz-Rieneck 156

Hohenzollerns 11, 24, 45 (n.), 75, 91–4, 136

Hollywood League Against Nazism 126

Hollywood Now 125

Hooft, Willem Visser't 77

Hopkins, Harry 171

Hopkinson, Austin 30

Horthy, Admiral 138, 145, 163

Hugenberg, Alfred 25

Huizinga, Johan 123

Hume, David 60

Hyde Park (USA) 172

Irminenschaft 44

John, Augustus 126

John, Dr Otto 72, 79, 98, 103 (n.)

Jung, Carl Gustav 11, 23, 35, 86, 176

Juniklub 34

Jus Restistendi of the Golden Bull 122, 145

Kadt, Erich 72

Kahr, Gustav von 110–12

Kaiser, Jakob 73, 80

Kalmar, Dr Rudolf 154

Kant, Immanuel 35, 44 (n.), 84

Kapp Putsch 108

Kapp, Wolfgang 33, 84, 108

Karl (the blessed Charles), Emperor of
    Austria-Hungary 12, 20, 134, 135, 145
Kellogg-Briand Pact 57
Kelly, Scott 55–6
Kelves, Daniel 63
Kennedy, Joseph 171
Keyserlingk, Robert 144
Kira, Grand Duchess (wife of Prince Louis
    Ferdinand) 97
Kirill, Grand Duke of Russia 97
Kleist, Ewald von 101
Klemperer 124
Klop, Lt. Dirk 78
Kluge, Field Marshal von 100
Knight, Eric 171
Knilling, Eugen von 110
Kolnai, Aurel 40
Kordt, Erich 76
Kordt, Theodor 77
Koryzis, Alexander 167
KPD (German Communist Party) 22, 107
Kristallnacht 14 (n.), 36, 86
Kulturkampf 94

Lamarck, Jean-Baptiste 62
Lang, Fritz 125–6
Langbehn, Julius 18, 28 (n.), 34, 84
Lanz, Adolf Josef 36, 42, 84
Lausanne Conference 122
Le Bon, Gustav 23, 34
Lebensraum 30, 44 (n.)
Legarde, Paul de 18, 34, 84
Leipzig, Battle of 37
Lenin, Vladimir 23
Lenz, Fr John M. 149
Leopold III, King of Belgium 164
Leutstetten Castle 118
Levine, Eugen 107–8
Lewin, Nicholas 23
Lewis, C.S. 181
Lippe Biesterfeld, Prince Bernhard von 164
List, Gustav 36
Lloyd George, David 11, 13 (n.), 28 (n.)
Lochner, Louis 76, 97, 99–100, 132 (n.)
Lorraine, Battle of 105
Lossow, Otto von, 110–11
Lothian, Lord 51, 75–6, 157 (n.)
Louis Ferdinand of Prussia, Prince 11, 13, 21,
    27, 29 (n.), 39, 72, 75–77, 91–103, 111, 132,
    158 (n.), 178, 179, 181
Louis II, Prince of Monaco 165
Löwenstein, HSH Fr Rudolf zu 122

Löwenstein, HSH Princess Konstanza zu 9,
    122–4, 131–2
Löwenstein, Prince Hubertus zu 13, 18–19,
    21–2, 26–7, 34, 39, 121–33, 179
Löwenstein, Prince Leopold
Löwenstein, Prince Maximilian zu 123
Löwenstein, Princess Helga zu 122
Lubbe, Marius van der 163
Luce, Clare Booth, 142
Ludendorff, General Erich 19–20, 22, 26, 28
    (n.), 35, 39, 84, 87 (n.), 104, 106, 110–12
Ludwig III of Bavaria, King 12, 105, 107, 109
Luitpold, Prince Regent of Bavaria 172
Luther, Martin 36, 64, 84, 86
Luxembourg, Charlotte Grand Duchess of
    165
Luxembourg, Jean Grand Duke of 165
Luza, Radomír 141

Macht und Geist 93
Mafalda, Princess of Savoy 161
Malthus, Rev Thomas Robert 60, 62–3
Mann, Thomas 124–5
March on Rome, Mussolini's 110
March, Frederick 125
Marx, Karl 31, 41
Mary, Queen of Great Britain 98, 103 (n.),
    118–9, 153–4, 173
Matt, Franz 111
Maximilian IV Fürst von Waldburg zu
    Wolfegg und Waldsee 153
Maximilian, Prince von Baden 20, 81, 106
Mein Kampf 22, 64, 135–6
Meinecke, Friedrich 41, 80, 93
Melville, Cecil F. 52
Menzies, Sir Stewart 79
Messersmith, George S. 134, 149
Metaxas, General 167
Metterninch, Princess Tatiana 40, 60, 70–1,
    128, 149, 151
Meysels, Lucien 149
Michael, King of Romania 168–70
Mill, John Stuart 62
Milner, Alfred Lord 50–1, 56, 59, 76
Mittmeyer, Dr 155
Montgomery, John Flournoy 73, 135
Montgomery, Robert 141
Morgenthau Plan 78
Mosse, George Lachmann 40
Mountbatten, Lord Louis 172
Müller, General Roland 154
Munchener Telegramm 112

Mussolini, Benito 22–3, 27, 39, 84, 86, 95, 97,
    110 135–6, 138, 160

namensweihe (naming ceremonies) 38
Napoleon I 37, 45–6 (n.), 118, 147, 170
Napoleon II 170
Napoléon, Lois 170
Neunzert, Lt. 111
Neutrality Act 23, 141
Newsweek 27
Nicholas, Princess of Greece 167–8
Nietzsche 19, 44, 64
Nodalny, Sten 123
November Criminals 33, 40
November Revolution 34, 95, 110–11

Oberste Heeresleitung 105
Oderplatz 112
Oertel, Hans 151, 155
Ogden-Stewart, Donald 125
Olaf, Crown Prince of Norway 162
Olbricht, General 101
Osborne, D'Arcy 78
Ostara magazine 42
Oster, Hans 71–2, 74–5, 78, 82 (n.)
Ostsiedlung 30

Pacelli, Eugenio, Papal Nuncio and later Pope
    Pious XII 111, 116, 118, 163, 165, 174
Palariet, Michael 149
pan-Germanism 30–2, 34–5, 37, 42, 93, 138,
    140, 178
Papen, Franz von 25–6, 28, 34 (n.), 51, 139,
    149, 153
Pareto, Vilfredo 34
Paris, Count of 170
Parish, Michael E. 23
Parker, Dorothy 125
Paul, Prince of Yugoslavia 165
Pearl Harbor 76, 100, 129
Pearson, Karl 62–3, 84.
Petar, King of Yugoslavia 165–6
Peters, Carl 93
Philby, Kim 60, 79
Philip, Prince, HRH the Duke of
    Edinburgh 167
Picasso, Pablo 126
Pirbright, Lord 123
Planck, Christian 93
Pois, Robert A. 46
Potesta, Princess Sophie von Hohenberg
    de 155

Pressburg, Treaty of 104
Proctor, Robert 64
Prussian-German/North German
    Federation 93, 104

Quisling, Vidkun 161

Ranier, Prince of Monaco 165
Reichsbanner (SRG) (black, red and gold)
    121–3, 132
Reichsbund der Osterreicher 148
Renner, Karl 146
Rhine palatinate 104
Rhodes, Cecil 50, 59
Ribbentrop, Joachim von 56, 97, 128
Robert, Duke of Palma 148
Robespierre, Maximilien 118
Röhm, Ernst 26, 35, 43, 84, 85, 111–12
Roosevelt, Eleanor 76, 172
Roosevelt, President Franklin D. 27, 29,
    76–7, 94, 96–101, 130, 141–6, 171–2, 178
Rosenberg, Alfred 43–4, 84
Rousseau, Jean Jaques 60
Roux, Jean Charles 168
Ruhr 22–3, 34, 78, 108, 110, 112, 178
Rumbold, Sir Horace 25
Rupprecht of Bavaria, Crown Prince 12–13,
    18, 39, 87, 104, 119–44, 149, 158 (n.), 179,
    181

Sachsenhausen 13, 104, 117, 155
Salviati, Dorothea Von 96
Saxony, HRH Maria Emanuele Margrave of
    Meissen 173
Saxony, Prince Fr Georg of 13, 173, 179
Saxony, Prince Friedrich Christian of 173
Sayn-Wittgenstein, Major Heinrich Prinz
    zu 80
Schelling, Friedrich 35, 84
Schleicher, General 24–5
Schönfeld, Hans 77
Schopenhauer, Arthur 44, 84
Schuschnigg, Karl von 137–40
Schuster, Sir Victor 126
Schwanburg, Viktor Kuchina de (von) 47, 145
Seisser 111
Selby, Walford 136
Selznick, David 126
Serving, Professor 135
Sicherheitsdienst (SD) 78
Simon, John 126
sippenhaft 104, 107, 117

Smith, Will 171
social Darwinism 8, 32, 45 (n.), 50, 58–9, 62,
    64–5, 85, 131
Somme, Battle of the 105
Sousa-Mendes, Consul-General Aristide
    de 142
Speer, Albert 14, 41, 44
Spencer, Herbert 62
Spengler, Oswald 29 (n.), 41, 112
St Germain, Treaty of 148
'Stab in the back' legend 21, 33, 80, 106, 110
Stahlhelm 25, 113
Stalin, Joseph 38, 48, 52, 77, 79–80, 118, 128,
    144–5, 169–70, 179
Starhemberg, Prince Ernst Rüdiger 138
Stauffenberg, Claus Graf von 80, 117
Steldt 25
Stevens, Major Richard H. 78
Stimson, US Secretary of War 143
Strasser, Gregor 22, 26, 135
Strasser, Otto 22, 135
Stresa Pact 136
Streseman, Gustav 22–3, 28 (n.), 85, 133 (n.)
Stubbs, Bob 180
Sturm und Drang 84

Teutonic Knights 30, 85, 91, 178
Theosophical Society 36, 42
Thule Society 43–4, 86, 87 (n.)
Tirpitz, Alfred von 33, 45, 72, 93 (n.)
Tito, Josip Broz 165
Tornquist, Carlos 96
Treitschke, Heinrich von 32, 45 (n.), 84, 93
Trevor-Roper, Hugh 79
Tripartite Pact 160, 166, 168
Trotsky, Leon 22
Trott zu Solz, Adam von 72, 75–7, 80,
    82 (n.)

Umbertto, Crown Prince of Italy 160

Valdivia, Luis Ruiz de 95–6
Vansittart, Sir Robert 78
Vassiltchikov, Princess Marie 'Missie' 76, 80,
    185 (n.)
Vaterlandspartie 33
Venlo Incident 78
Versailles, Treaty of 7, 11, 17–18, 21, 25, 30,
    34, 44 (n.), 49–52, 56–7, 85–6, 108–9,
    129, 145, 148, 178

Viereck, Peter 56–7, 176
Villard, Oswald Garrison 124
Vittorio Emanuele, King, and Queen Elena
    116, 160–1
Volksgemeinschaft 33
Vossischen News 123

Wachwitz, Haus 173
Wagner, Adolf 115
Wagner, Richard 64
Wagner, Robert Ferdinand 124
Wall Street Crash 112
Wartburg Castle 36–7, 46
Washington Conference 56–7, 109
Weisner, Baron Friedrich von 137
Weizsäcker, Ernst von 75
Wewelsburg Castle 43–4
Wheeler-Bennett, Sir John 26, 74
Wilhelm II, Kaiser 11–12, 14 (n.), 25, 28
    (n.), 39, 94–5, 99, 163, 182 (n.)
Wilhelm, Crown Prince of Prussia 101
Wilhelmina, Queen of the Netherlands
    163–4
Wiligut, Karl Maria 43–4, 84
Williams, David D. 174
Windecker, General 97
Wingate, General Sir Reginald 126, 129
Winter, Ernst Karl 137
Wirmer, Josef 73, 76, 99
Wittelsbachs 12, 104, 107, 114–15
Witzleben, General Erwin von 74–5
Wood, Captain George Jervis 148, 153
Wood, Maria-Thérèse (Maisie) 153, 156
Wood, Rosa Countess von Lónyay 153
Württemburg, Fr Odo Duke Alexander
    von 173–4
Württemburg, King William of 174
Württemburg, Prince Albrecht Duke of
    173–4
Württemburg, Prince Philip Duke of
    173–4
Württemburg, Princess Pauline Wied 174

X Club 62

Young Plan 23, 112

Zita of Bourbon-Palma, Empress of
    Austria-Hungary 134, 148
Zühlsdorf, Volkmar 122, 125, 131–2, 185